ON WINE

GERALD ASHER

ON WINE

With an Introduction by
Elizabeth David

JILL NORMAN & HOBHOUSE

Jill Norman & Hobhouse Ltd
Gloucester Mansions
Cambridge Circus
London WC2H 8AD

Published in Great Britain by Jill Norman & Hobhouse,
1983

ISBN 0   906908   58   2

Manufactured in the United States of America
Cartography by Anita Karl and James Kemp
Typography and binding design by J. K. Lambert

First Edition

FOR MY SONS
Jeremy and Japhet

CONTENTS

Contents

MAPS

INTRODUCTION

I READ somewhere recently that one of our more unconventional British wine writers once wrote of a wine that it grasped you by the hand and called you by your first name. Well, however unconventional Gerald Asher may be I don't think talking wines are much in his line—the one in question sounds ominously like the Club Buttonholer—but I do think he's a phenomenon equally unexpected. He's such a compelling talker about wine that even the most uninitiated, including myself, is going to listen and be entertained and learn, and as Gerald—to do my own bit of first-name calling—writes exactly like he talks, anyone who reads this book is going to have a lot of entertainment and enlightenment. It is like this. Should Gerald by any chance be saying—he isn't, I'm just supposing—that a wine has a hint of hyacinths he doesn't even wait for the skeptical look to appear on your face. He explains—this time I quote—that "all wines share at least traces of most of the acids, alcohols and esters occurring in everything from bananas to roses." That's something that may be obvious to wine experts and chemists, but until I learned it from Gerald I didn't appreciate the point, so I've always been exasperated by the violets and truffles of wine analysis. I should add that Gerald seldom resorts to that kind of description, preferring to give information more illuminating and exact. Thus we learn that a wine from vineyards halfway down the higher slopes of the Sancerre hills is likely to be one of the best of the district. A particular combination of soil types contributes to this excellence. These fine points once appreciated, we have at least a clue as to why so many bottles of Sancerre don't come up to expectation and why, when one does, it does. I like that. Isn't it what anybody who has just once or twice experienced a bottle of that enchanting wine at its best and is at last about to renounce the search for more of the same will want to know?

The kind of knowledge to be acquired from this book may well of course end in getting a trifle troublesome and expensive. So I should warn potential readers that it's pretty well crammed with tempting invitations to be off on restless quests for this or that rarity. Here's an unexpected sample. One of the most delicious rosés in the world, it turns out, so far from being the overpriced—and overpraised—Tavel of tradition, is German. It comes from the Glottertal, is made from a combination of Spätburgunder and Ruländer grapes, and is to be sought in and around Freiburg. So. And did you ever before hear of a grape from the Neckar valley called the Trollinger, from which is made another rosé which sounds as if it had been named after the poet Schiller? Well, that's a tease, because Schillerwein means that the wine is iridescent, which I take to mean that it has the shimmer of shot silk or taffeta. Still, it's only the wine of the Heidelberg students, and according to Gerald's account it wouldn't be worth going all that way just to drink like a Heidelberg student. We're warned off that one.

Now it would be most wrong of me to give the impression that this book is entirely or even mainly concerned with such unicorns as the faultless Sancerre or with what Gerald himself calls "other wines," and what one of my old friends in the English wine trade used to call funnies, a term he applied to all table wines that didn't come from Bordeaux, Burgundy, Alsace, or the classic vineyards of Germany. But I do have to explain that when I first knew Gerald Asher in London, in the 1950s, it was chiefly for his flair in finding and importing those "other wines" that he had made his firm's name known, in the restaurant world as well as to a very large list of private customers. Joyfully, we discovered that in Asher Storey's cellars there were not only choice rarities like single-vineyard Burgundies and the legendary white Château Grillet from the Rhône, but also rather more approachable treasures in the shape of a quite extraordinary collection of regional wines, some of them encountered perhaps a couple of times on trips to France or Italy but never hitherto on the English side of the Channel because, the wine trade told us, they didn't travel. Under Gerald's auspices, however, unusual wines like the red Saumur-Champigny of Anjou, sweet, mellow Monbazillac, a red Gamay and a fresh dry white Apremont from the Savoie appeared to travel with notable success. (Irrelevant though it is, I can't resist adding here that if Gerald weren't a wine merchant he would probably be the world's best travel agent, tour arranger, courier and guide.)

A beguiling *vin gris* called Cendré de Novembre from the Jura became a London restaurant favorite, and one memorable day an unknown golden dessert wine, bearing on its label the name Muscat de Beaumes-de-Venise, arrived on my doorstep. At the time that delicious wine was the product of just one single vineyard owner, and had rarely traveled further than the boundaries of its native Provence, let alone overseas. Gerald Asher, dauntless as ever, had brought some to London. I fell in love with that wine. Its rapid disappearance from the Asher Storey cellars, partly, I must own, as the result of an article I wrote about it in a small-circulation political weekly, was the occasion of much lamenting among its small band of addicts, myself not least. Beaumes-de-Venise is a familiar name now, and its wine is exported to America as well as to England, but although I still drink it with pleasure it has never again had quite the impact it did on the day Gerald sent it along and left me to discover it for myself.

This small incident I recount because I think discovery of that kind is in many ways the very essence of Gerald's book. He knows that he, as guide, can only take you so far, explain so much, give you the appropriate amount of technical background, communicate his own pleasure—as witness his joyous accounts of trips to the Beaujolais—or, as the case may be, the reverse. Then, expert guide as he is, he will leave you on your own. About wine, as about most things, you must make up your own mind and formulate your own conclusions, and nobody knows that better than Gerald Asher.

In 1981 I visited San Francisco, where Gerald now lives and works, for the very first time in my life. He was my host, and my chief guide around the city and into the country, to restaurants and to food markets, and of course it was he who initially introduced me to the wines of California which are now one of his major interests. It was an enlightening and very happy experience, and although at the time I don't think that this book was even planned, in my mind I connect it with those weeks in California as much as with France and Italy, and the London of Gerald's early days in the wine trade. It all adds up to such a happy, open-hearted, friendly book—nobody has to worry about the author's formidable knowledge and expertise, it is too discreetly concealed to be more than sensed—that it is hard to believe there can be any need for an introduction. But since I was invited to supply one, it has been my privilege to do so.

—*Elizabeth David*
London, April 1982

PREFACE

WHILE STILL a student in London, concerned with Elizabethan
dramatists who had had the misfortune to be contemporaries of
Shakespeare, I took a job from five to seven every evening behind
the counter of a wine shop. It stood in the raffish pedestrian way
between Piccadilly and Curzon Street called Shepherd Market,
though better known, before the Street Offences Act, for its shep-
herdesses. Meat was then still rationed to eight ounces a week, or
something equally measly, and red wine, I was assured, provided
a necessary alternative source of strength. In the early evening, at
least, most sales were half bottles of Beaujolais to solitary ladies.

When I had worked there for less than a week, the manager
told me, as I arrived one afternoon, that we had to meet a delicate
situation. Without warning to allow appropriate preparation, our
Beaujolais supplier had replaced the 1947 vintage. Afraid that the
regular customers would check other stores before accepting the
1949, he instructed me to hand each of those I recognized a free
half bottle. But first he had me taste it against the last of the 1947
so that I could say, with assurance, that the new vintage was every
bit as good, if not better. It was a novel experience, comparing one
wine with another, and though I suppose there are more bizarre
ways of finding a life's vocation, that's when and how I discovered
mine.

I soon migrated from Shepherd Market to Pall Mall, to the
offices of a large London wine shipper, where I checked the identification numbers of wooden crates returned for credit against
records kept in old-fashioned ledgers. It was work tedious beyond
imagining in today's world of disposable cartons and electronic

records. The stock clerk at the next desk had the job I envied. He went down to the cellars once a month to reconcile his books with actual bottles. I would hear him discussing problems over the telephone with the cellar manager and reporting the discrepancies to the managing director. It was his habit to vary pronunciation of the wine names according to circumstances, perhaps to avoid misunderstandings. The Vosne-Romanée of the office, for example, became Vozny-Romany when he spoke to the cellars, Pauillac became Polly-Ack, and Pouilly-Fuissé, inevitably, Pussy-Fussy.

The young men in the office were free to try any wines open in the tasting room. I am sure there wasn't an actual ban on women clerks and secretaries doing the same thing, but it was understood that they didn't. By a process I no longer remember, I was put in charge of the tasting room and was later allowed to be a silent participant at the ritual of checking current stocks, appraising new wines, examining returned bottles. But tasting such a wide range of disconnected wines, both healthy and sick, day after day, was exposure rather than education. A normal working session assembles wines so varied, and for such different purposes, that it is difficult to arrive at the general conclusions necessary to build a framework of tasting reference.

The London wine trade was, and is, close. At that time, at the beginning of the 1950s, prominent companies were still family controlled if not family owned. They clustered on and around Mark Lane and Tower Hill, to be near the docks and the Custom House, and in the Pall Mall and St. James's area, within striking distance of the West End's clubs, restaurants, and hotels. A well-organized system of trade training now takes entrants through a methodically graduated series of lectures, tastings, and practical work, culminating in examinations for the professional diploma of Master of Wine. The trainees of my day, however, sponsored by their respective companies, presented themselves each spring, very self-consciously, at the Upper Thames Street building of the Worshipful Company of Vintners, and in the splendor of a paneled hall where five kings had dined together in 1363, were there introduced to the ancient mysteries of wine. On Thursday mornings, I recall, under the auspices of the Wine Trade Club (which had been founded by André Simon and his contemporaries), distinguished members of the trade imparted to us something of their knowledge and experience, guiding us through tastings for which each of us would bring six tulip-shaped nosing glasses in identical cardboard boxes.

"Wine," we were taught, like an article of the faith, "is the alcoholic beverage obtained from the juice of freshly gathered grapes, the fermentation of which has been carried through in the district of origin and according to local tradition and practice." Winemaking, thirty years ago, lacked the sophistication that has since become universal. Stainless steel, cultured yeasts, temperature-controlled fermentation and clarification by centrifuge were not unknown, but they had not imposed the dominant grapy fragrance that brings out similarities in modern wines rather than the bold differences we knew. Technique has now acquired importance beyond soil and grape variety. We find red Graves, made by carbonic maceration, that taste like tannic Beaujolais, and *trocken* Rheingau wines that can easily be mistaken for merely unsuccessful Alsatians. Recently, in La Mancha, south of Madrid, a wine-maker told me that a well-known brand of Liebfraumilch was his criterion in making and judging his white Valdepeñas. It is all the inevitable result of marketing wine instead of selling it, I suppose. Once we looked for ways to teach the world how to enjoy wine's variety. Now we teach winemakers the ways of the world.

As each spring series ended, we wrote essays that summarized and discussed what we had learned, and depending on their quality we received Certificates of Attendance, Certificates of Merit, or, with luck, bursaries that paid expenses to one of the wine regions where study, and sometimes work, opportunities were arranged. I benefited from these bursaries, and the extended periods I was able to spend in Spain, France, and Germany over three years provided a foundation for my professional training.

Abroad, I saw the physical connection of wines and vineyards, and began to understand the link between wines and those who produce them, especially in the context of the food they ate and the way they lived. My *optique* of wine, as the French would say, was bound up with it as an expression of people, time, and place. I can debate chemical composition of soils with the best of them, but when carried to excess, as they too often are, such preoccupations are a barrier to pleasure, not an enhancement. At the tables of growers and merchants wines were indeed analyzed, pondered, discussed, and compared, sometimes in practical winemaking terms, but always with natural awareness of what we were, after all, talking about, much as a fruit farmer might talk of the cultivation of pears in the course of enjoying one. There was none of the technical one-upmanship, the brittle display, the squandering of pleasure by pointlessly ferreting out and commenting on every fault, real or imagined, that can spell disaster for a convivial evening.

Though I learned a great deal about wine and the wine trade at this time, no one taught me how to make a sales presentation or even how to write an order, because we took for granted that ours was an occupation for gentlemen and that familiarity with wine allied to friendship, rather than salesmanship (a word that would not have been used), was the key to success. So, partly because it was known as the representatives' grave, used both to test the mettle of new men and to dispose of old, but mostly because I was raised there and was presumed to have the qualification of some local acquaintance, I was dispatched to reveal my newly acquired knowledge to the farmers of East Anglia, propelled there in a small, battered Ford, essential transportation nonetheless described by my managing director as a "perk." In providing it, he felt himself relieved of any obligation to increase my salary in keeping with my responsibilities.

Though close to London, East Anglia was still a rural backwater where rook-filled elm trees swayed tall above wide, flat horizons. Except for Ipswich, a city festooned with bus wires and hoardings, I remember nothing ugly about the busy towns and villages of my "territory." But then they included Cambridge and Norwich; Ely, King's Lynn, and Newmarket; Fakenham, Lavenham, and Bury St. Edmunds. Specially satisfying, because I love the pale blur of an East Anglian seashore, were regular visits to Aldeburgh, Southwold, and Cromer. It was a happy time, and within months I had revived for my employers accounts long considered lost, bringing a respectable volume of increased business.

The wine trade was regarded as a convenient refuge for those of good family who were ill equipped for the intellectual challenge of law or medicine, yet insufficiently rich to be placed in private banking in the City. He who had every right to be modest in his expectations was thus kept from the shame of idleness, but, in the process, depressed the expectations of the rest of us. For nearly five years my "salary" had remained unchanged. Proud of my accomplishments, I asked the managing director if he would review it. He was taken aback. "Young man," he said, turning me down, "if I were to grant an increase, it would merely encourage you to ask again another time. There'd be no holding you."

On those conditions there wasn't, and I decided to set up in business on my own. In addition to customers in East Anglia, I had developed a few accounts in London, among them Ivan Storey's Soup Kitchen on Chandos Place adjacent to Charing Cross Hospital, where Ivan was a staff psychiatrist. He had converted an unprepossessing shop front into a student-chic soup, salad, and omelet bar. Blowups of nineteenth-century etchings hung in surreal combinations above tables and benches designed by Terence Conran, then fresh from design school and very much in his post–Festival of Britain bent-wire and plywood period. The venture was hugely successful. Exhilarated, Ivan rented additional premises on Wilton Place near Knightsbridge, where now stands the new Berkeley Hotel, and there he opened an even larger, smarter Soup Kitchen with a consumption of wine, whether by customers, patients, staff, or friends of staff (distinctions were vague) that was prodigious. When he heard what I intended to do, he offered to join me as a partner: hence, Asher Storey & Company.

Except for the bright yellow cover (I was Beardsley-struck at the time), our first list could hardly have been more conventional or dull. I recognized my mistake, and realized that we needed to offer alternatives to other shippers' wines rather than attempt to duplicate them. Their well-established and prestigious labels were too strong for us to compete with directly. I had always been interested in the "lesser" wines of France and went off in search of them. Unlike Bordeaux and Burgundy, meticulously charted and served by brokers and English-speaking shippers who made overseas trade a simple matter, the tributary valleys of the Loire, the far reaches of the southwest, and the slopes of the Jura and Savoie were at that time unsurveyed, and I had only imprecise references by nineteenth-century writers and uninformative pamphlets to go by. Modern books, after dealing adequately with Champagne, Burgundy, and Bordeaux, tended to lump "other French wines" into a few paragraphs that did little more than acknowledge that there were such things. I learned about them as I went,

and having decided for myself what *was* the essential character of
Jurançon, of Irancy, of Jasnières, of Apremont, of whatever, I
had to choose, in each case, the wine that showed that character
best, discover which grower was the most reliable, and arrive myself at definitions of "quality" and "value" in wines isolated from
the mainstream of the trade even within France. (The French are
the most parochial of wine drinkers: few in the Rhône Valley have
tasted Bordeaux; Alsatians do not drink Loire wine; Burgundians
have no curiosity about the wines of Dordogne or Pyrenees.)
Some of the growers had lists of private customers, including a
few in Paris who ordered a case from time to time as a reminder,
perhaps, of a summer vacation or as a sentimental attachment to
their native region. But most sold their wines to local restaurateurs,
and it was through them that I found my most valuable sources.

Just as my later move to California revealed unexpected aspects
of European wines, so my involvement with these "lesser" wines,
set deep in the fabric of rural French life, gave me an uncommon
perspective of the classic wines in which I had been trained. Asher
Storey and its retail side, Wine Vaults, grew, and though we maintained an emphasis on lesser-known French wines (to this day,
from what is said, one might be forgiven for imagining that I
invented them), we needed those classic wines, too. At that period,
Burgundy and Bordeaux were shipped to England mainly through
the established *négoçiants*. There was little estate-bottled Burgundy
imported, surprisingly, and wines of the small, unclassified vineyards of Bordeaux were mostly bottled and sold under the labels
of major shippers. But in my search for the lesser wines I had
formed habits hard to break. In particular, I was used to buying
only in growers' cellars, picking out what I wanted barrel by
barrel. I approached the great regions in the same way, tramping
through *chai* and *cave*, asking the questions I would have asked
in Lot or Languedoc. The growers responded with warmth and
enthusiasm, and our mutual respect became the basis of friend-
ships that have endured.

Since 1967, when we had first received inquiries for our more
esoteric French wines, I had been visiting the United States twice
a year to sell wines for direct shipment from France. Taking the
view that I was selling "British expertise," the British Embassy in
Washington generously sponsored me by providing the chancery
rotunda for the first tasting of our wines. In 1971 I moved to the

United States permanently, leaving a large, old-fashioned house in an overgrown garden near London for a small city apartment high above Manhattan in order to assume responsibility for imported wine sales at Austin, Nichols & Company.

Austin, Nichols were then preeminent in the United States for their unequaled stocks of Bordeaux classified growths. In London, Bordeaux classified growths had played a minor role for me; indeed, my attachment to lesser-known wines had given me somewhat the reputation of an iconoclast. But in New York, to my surprise and amusement, the importance of Austin, Nichols' Bordeaux business was such that I was an instant pillar of the wine establishment.

There were other, less amusing, surprises. If in England the wine trade is a gentlemen's occupation, the "industry" is hardly thought of that way in the United States. I had to supply mug shot, fingerprints, and personal history to the Bureau of Alcohol, Tobacco and Firearms, whose representatives visited friends and acquaintances in the course of their inquiries. It was clear that I was to consider myself henceforth a potential criminal, at very least. Indeed, I was soon to realize that the laws relating to the sale of wine—irrational, demeaning, and absurdly varied from state to state—make certain that everyone involved with the wine and spirit trade of this country will at some time, knowingly or unknowingly, commit an offense. As Bernard Rudofsky, in *Notes and Footnotes on the Lost Art of Living*, comments wryly, "If Jesus Christ should want to visit this country, he certainly would have to mend his ways. A repetition of the multiplication of bread might be greeted with hosannas, but a miracle of changing water into wine would land him in jail in the holier of the states."

State regulations are unbelievably complicated and messy. They add unnecessary costs to the simple distribution of wine, and in many states they seriously restrict the choice of what might reasonably be enjoyed within the bounds of law. For years North Carolina "protected" its residents from fine old Bordeaux because of a state regulation requiring chemical analysis of any wine to be offered for sale. This meant that if we, or any other importer, had a small quantity of, say, Cheval Blanc 1947, none would be offered to the Tarheel State; we were not about to dispatch even one precious bottle to the pipettes and test tubes of a Raleigh laboratory. And the state of Washington still requires chemical analysis of any wine to be sold above the Columbia River.

Winemakers of the world disregard the offensive implication but are cynical about the whole wasteful process. They know that once a wine is "approved," subsequent shipments, even if from later, and therefore different, bottlings, or from later vintages, are not subject to reanalysis. Until quite recently, Michigan subjected all trial bottles to a taste test in the laboratory, as well as chemical analysis. The qualifications a technician might need to fulfill the role of arbiter of what could, and what could not, please the palates of an entire, populous, and sophisticated state would be hard to describe, let alone find, combined, in one mere mortal. The industry suffers this rigmarole quietly as part of the fiscal and emotional cost of doing business, reluctant to disturb relations with state officials, most of whom do their best to make the unworkable workable. Change is unlikely: it can come only through legislation, and the subject is too sensitive for most politicians. They see in it little chance of political advantage to offset the probable political risk.

By representing Austin, Nichols on the Wine Committee (and later on the Champagne Committee) of the National Association of Beverage Importers in New York, I learned a great deal about the structure of the industry and the personalities involved. While absorbing so much that was new, I regretted only that my work as an importer left largely undisturbed my ignorance of American wine.

I had already met California wine under the most propitious of circumstances. In 1967, on my first visit to San Francisco, I had been invited, through a friend's introduction, to a dinner in Pacific Heights where I was served Château Latour 1955 alongside Inglenook Cabernet Sauvignon 1954. Had I nurtured any condescending prejudice, it would have been dispelled. On my return in 1968 I visited the Napa Valley and met Robert Mondavi, then as now overflowing with enthusiasm, and Joe Heitz, calmly matter-of-fact about his wine but as proud as he had a right to be.

Later, when I had moved to New York, I continued to spend a day or two in Napa or Sonoma whenever I visited the West Coast. In a burst of activity, vineyards were spreading in all directions. That included Monterey County, where, early in 1974, a project between Foremost–McKesson, a San Francisco corporation, and a new vineyard and winery was being formed. The purpose of the joint venture was to develop a range of quality wines that would help bring recognition to a new area, and I was invited to California to direct it, a challenge too exciting to refuse. I stayed with it for two years and earned my education in California wine the hard way.

Since then my work has expanded to embrace, once again, European wines as well as our own, and I am sometimes in the odd position of explaining France to California and vice versa. Shuttling from one to the other, I see the mutual influence: wines from California's newer wineries acquiring the grace to accompany food rather than merely the heft to engage in county-fair combat, and French wines becoming less prone to winemaking accidents.

There are days, of course, when I feel twinges of conscience at having deserted my literary muse to follow Dionysus, but if wine is, indeed, "begetter of all arts," I tell myself that perhaps I have served her better this way.

ACKNOWLEDGMENTS

SO MUCH is owed to so many that it becomes impossible to acknowledge every debt. From almost everyone I have met, every book I have read, and every wine I have tasted, I have learned something that I hope to have passed on in these pages. I owe special thanks to Jane Montant of *Gourmet*, who first asked me to write these essays; to Robert Lescher, who encouraged me to assemble this book; and to Ed Hinger, who plied me with wine while I did it.

ON WINE

Guessing Games

I NEVER ASK a guest to identify a wine—it can too easily wreck friendship and cause indignation—though I often leave a wine incognito until everyone has had a chance to form an opinion of it. Some years ago, a guest who knows his stuff started to identify a wine I had just poured for lunch with the words, "Well, it's a Burgundy, that much is clear." Afraid he would pursue this line of discovery and have more words to eat than he might have stomach for, I quickly pointed out that the wine was, in fact, from Bordeaux. Completely unruffled, he put down his glass and said, "Oh. In *that* case, it's La Lagune '61." And, of course, he was right.

Less adroit at a dinner in New York, I tangled with a Pétrus 1964. In the circumstances of the dinner (something one should never be influenced by), I was predisposed to expect a mature California Cabernet, read all the signs the wine gave me as miles instead of kilometers, and managed to get myself hopelessly lost. I connected the smoky bouquet and flavor to the gravelly vineyards of Rutherford in the Napa Valley rather than to the gravelly plateau of Pomerol. When (more accurately) I assessed the wine at roughly fifteen years old, a fellow guest, himself a California winemaker, agreed but asked me who could have been making wine in this style *in Napa* in 1964. A Socratic question that, properly considered, should have put me back on track.

What brought both incidents to mind was the comment of a fellow passenger with whom I was chatting on a recent flight home from Denver. When he heard I was in the wine trade, he modestly disclaimed expertise by telling me he couldn't tell Bordeaux from Burgundy. "In fact," he said, "I sometimes confuse French with California." I suppose he thought I was being tactful when I mumbled, "It can happen to anybody."

Before brewers, computers, and quality-control technicians took it over, the London wine trade made a practice of eating rather indifferent cold lunches in each other's offices relieved only by the quality of the wines, good Stilton, and the ritual of "guessing the Port." (To be a better wine merchant in such circumstances, as Talleyrand knew in another context, required mostly a good cook and a battery of saucepans.) Everyone chipped in half a crown— a taxi fare in those days rather than today's price of a daily newspaper—and if no one got it right, the kitty went to a trade charity. Listening to more experienced colleagues exchanging reasons why the wine might be Cockburn's rather than Taylor's, a 1927 rather than a 1934, taught me more about vintage Port than any number of academic tasting-room sessions. The false starts and spoken thoughts of one would spur on another, and a single remark could illuminate for me and make memorable the style of a shipper, the characteristics of a year, the distinctive contribution of a particular vineyard site. There were no far-fetched analogies in such company: words were few and apt.

Roald Dahl's short story "Taste" exaggerates the sort of language we used (at least, I *hope* it does); but as a baroque exposition of such signpost reading and checking of clues against memory, knowledge, and reason, it is as good an account as any. In it a guest displays a sinister combination of aesthetic scholarship and unscrupulous lust, or perhaps the other way round, by concealing his prior knowledge of what he is drinking so that he might give a convincing performance of identifying a wine and thus win possession of his host's horrified young daughter. To arrive at this conclusion too quickly would arouse suspicion; to do so without showing his reasoning, while gaining his immediate objective, might make an equally disquieting impression. He builds to his conclusion slowly, questioning himself on the significance of each whiff and wink in the glass, rejecting the suggestion of one when it clashes with the certainty of another. (Be reassured, those of you who have not yet read the story: Bacchus will not be mocked. In a masterly ending the girl is saved from a fate worse than a poor vintage.)

My favorite story of wine guessing games, told by Peter Sichel about his cousin Charles, distills the ethos of certain wine-trade encounters. Guests at a luncheon in Paris, they were asked to guess the wine. Almost without pausing, Charles identified it as La Tâche 1929, and their host congratulated him. When they left the house, Peter turned to his cousin and asked why he had made such a ludicrous suggestion, adding, "The wine was no more La Tâche than it was 1929. It wasn't even Burgundy."

"I just wanted to see if D——— is really as excessively polite as everyone says he is," said Charles.

Professionals don't, in fact, spend their lives attaching identities to wines; but the more they taste in the course of their work, the greater their ease in naming what is put before them. Some are more skilled than others, naturally, and for obvious reasons most who specialize have areas of particular competence. Just as an art historian looks for the style associated with a place and period—a characteristic brush technique, a master's assurance—so a taster is taught, or teaches himself, what to expect of wines according to when, where, and how they are made.

Approaching a wine professionally, as opposed to drinking it for pleasure, the taster first gets an overall impression by looking, smelling, and tasting, and then he starts to analyze. Usually he is told what the wine is supposed to be, and he measures it against his expectation of a Pommard, a Graves, a Bernkasteler, or whatever. He must know why individual wines taste as they do, not just in terms of their physical composition—more or less tannin, higher or lower acidity—but in terms of the soil, the climate, and the manner in which the grapes were harvested and fermented. Only then can he judge whether a missing component is an accident of weather, a result of winemaking technique, or an indication of something more seriously amiss. Understanding "what makes a wine taste how" is the basis of identifying an unknown. Each grape variety gives wine distinctive characteristics; the soil in which it is grown and the climate (even the weather of a particular growing season) will influence the style in a predictable way. Picking up the varietal characteristics and "reading" the style is how the taster traces the wine to its origin, including the year it was grown. From first impressions he develops a hypothesis that he tests and modifies against each subsequent clue he finds in smelling and tasting the wine.

On rare occasions, if a wine is very familiar, one can tell by the first look, smell, and taste, but the chances of such instant recognition are remote. In the early 1960s, when Booth's Distilleries in London closed down their wholesale wine department, I bought a few cases of half bottles of Château de Rayne-Vigneau 1923, a Sauternes that was drying slightly but that made a perfect ending to many of our twice-weekly office lunches. Kenneth Bell, who had recently opened his restaurant at Thornbury Castle near Bristol, must have bought some too. When I had consumed so much Rayne-Vigneau so often and for so long that I could have identified it from the smell of an emptied glass, he brought to my table one evening a mysteriously swathed half bottle and promised me a reward of any wine in his cellar (quite a collection at that time) if I could guess the vintage and vineyard of the sweet white wine he poured for me. Identifying sweet white wines, especially older ones, is notoriously difficult. The sugar dominates everything and tends to block out or overwhelm the other clues. Very sweet, late-picked Johannisberg Rieslings from California are almost indistinguishable from German Trockenbeerenauslesen with histories as long and as complicated as that of Alberich's ring for this reason.

Anyway, as luck would have it, Bell had landed on a tiny area of what was, at that time, my particular competence. Unfortunately, I lacked the theatrical talent of the central character of Roald Dahl's story and blurted out the vintage and vineyard so precipitately that Bell's suspicions were aroused. To protect my honor I felt obliged to explain. Worse, I then felt obliged to refuse to despoil him of his best bottle by taking advantage of a coincidence.

Normally, however, the wine reveals itself more slowly. Most tasters try to decide first what grape, or family of grapes, it was made from. Even when the characteristic of a particular grape is low-key, like a Gamay, or possibly neutral, like one of the several white grapes used in the south of France, it is still the dominant factor. If the wine is European, the grape variety points to where the wine was grown. In France, for example, wines made from Pinot Noir, Gamay, and other early-ripening varieties come from the center and the northeast: Beaujolais, Burgundy, Jura, and Champagne. Wines from Cabernet Sauvignon, Cabernet Franc, Merlot, and related varieties are produced down the Atlantic coast and in the valleys that open to the ocean.

When a wine is young, the grape variety gives a very distinctive aroma, but as it ages the influence of soil on bouquet and flavor emerges more clearly and the varietal aroma fades. The effect of soil on vine and wine probably stems more from water-holding properties than from chemical composition, though chalk and iron do affect the style of wine appreciably. Chalk improves color and boosts alcoholic strength; it intensifies varietal aroma and flavor. Compare, for example, a Sauvignon Blanc wine grown on the chalky hillsides of Sancerre with a Sauvignon Blanc grown on the gravel of Bordeaux or on the sandy hills of California. It is chalk, too, that concentrates the Pinot Noir flavor of Côte d'Or Burgundies, and the scantiness of such terrain in California is one possible reason why we do not do as well with Pinot Noir here as we do with Chardonnay.

The significant difference from clay to sand to gravel, however, is the size of the particles and the water space around them. Sand is planted with varieties that are best adapted to light, fast-maturing wines: Gamay grapes, Muscadet, and others that give delicious, fresh young wines with little prospect of long-term maturing. On clay, grape varieties lose much of their personality and give heavy wines—high in tannin, clumsy, and, in France, usually described as having a *goût de terroir*. (In a recent, published interview the buyer for a major British wine group discussed his reasons for choosing a *non-appellation* Gamay wine from the Loire rather than one from Yugoslavia. He preferred the French wine, he said, because it was grown on light, shattered granite, which didn't overwhelm the low-key style of the Gamay. The Yugoslav wine, on the other hand, though "very good," had a "tannic, more aggressive" style, from the heavy clay on which it was grown. Just as one would expect.) Gravel gives the best Bordeaux wines their balance, finesse, and, in mature wines when soil takes over from grape, a special smoky quality that is reminiscent of hot sealing wax, sometimes of charcoal. If we compare a young Pétrus with a young Mission-Haut-Brion, for example, when the grape in each is still dominant, we can see how the preponderance of Cabernet Sauvignon in La Mission-Haut-Brion contrasts with the Merlot of

Pétrus. But in mature vintages of the same two wines, the contrast of grape variety will have diminished and the emerging influence of their common gravel soils brings them closer together.

Tasting wines side by side, in fact, is more instructive and often more enjoyable than tasting each alone. Points of contrast and similarity bring out more clearly their individual styles, and sometimes make identification easier. By way of illustration, here is an extract from my diary entry of a recent dinner:

Two magnums were decanted to accompany the roast lamb and poured blind for discussion and identification. The first had a more dense color, but both showed visual signs of being twenty to thirty years old—confirmed by the "nose" particularly of the second. We were told both were from Bordeaux. Though they seemed to be late 1940s vintages, they had none of the characteristics of 1945 and were obviously of quality above 1946, 1950, and 1951. At first I thought they could be of the same year, perhaps 1948, but from different areas. Then I inclined to 1947 for the second wine because it showed the wear I've noticed in some 1947s recently. I wasn't sure about the first. It seemed to be a 1949 in scale, but P——— didn't find it rich or long enough for a 1949. I agreed, but thought it bigger than the 1948s I remembered. I remained undecided between the two. We were all agreed that it was a Médoc. Nobody felt very sure what the second wine could be. The majority were pro-Graves, but I could detect no Graves characteristic. I had an open mind on the possibility of its being a Pichon-Baron; it had the flat style I associate with the property. J.B. thought a Saint-Emilion. Finally, the vintage of the first wine was confirmed by our host as 1949 and the second 1947. With certainty of the year, J.B. now felt confident in identifying the second wine as Saint-Emilion, and specifically as Château Canon. He was right on both counts. Knowing the first wine to be a 1949 for sure, I felt that its abrupt finish in such a big year placed it as a Saint-Estèphe. I took a guess at Château Montrose because of their tough style. I was right on the *commune* but wrong on the château: it was Cos d'Estournel, and with a little more time in the glass it opened up to reveal the finesse and fruit that one would, indeed, have expected from Cos.

Bordeaux presents an unusual challenge because every vineyard has its own formula of grape varieties: more Cabernet Sauvignon here, less Merlot there, perhaps some Malbec or Cabernet Franc.

And, depending on the vagaries of the vintage, one or another variety might do better. A wine usually recognized for the softness contributed by a higher proportion of Merlot might, in a year when the Merlot failed to "set," produce a wine of unexpectedly hard style. On the other hand, the spring frosts in 1961 caused havoc in the Médoc and reduced the potential crop—when La Lagune, for example, was just coming into production again after years of replanting and restoration. There the proportion of Merlot had been increased, and the frost, by mischance, increased it further. When still quite young, La Lagune 1961 caused a sensation for its full-blown style—quite unlike that of any other young Médoc. Which takes us back, I think, to where we started.

In the Sign
of the Beaujolais

Every man shall eat in safety
Under his own vine what he plants, and sing
The merry songs of peace to all his neighbours.

Shakespeare, *Henry VIII*

JOSEPHINE BAKER, so the legend goes, brought her own heat wave
to Paris back in the 1920s. The one I found there one June was
more than enough for me. As the city became hotter and stick-
ier and my consumption of iced *citrons pressés* reached a stage
where I was in danger of sprouting leaf and branch, the thought
of the cool hills of the Beaujolais became increasingly irresistible.
I longed for a pine-shaded bedroom and the soothing welcome of
garden-aired linen sheets. Finally, one evening when the illuminated sign in the Place de l'Opéra showed a temperature in the
nineties at midnight, I decided to be off the next morning. Before
nine I was on a train to the Beaujolais, to Brouilly, to Château
Thivin, the house of Yvonne Geoffray, my self-appointed god-
mother.

The Beaujolais hills are wide rather than high, the last undulating folds of the Massif Central, softly contoured and generously
draped with vineyards. Houses, barns, and courtyards, built for the
protection and comfort of man and beast, lie scattered about the
hillsides; for this has long been a peaceful region, and there are
few villages of feudal style clustered in fear at the foot of a for-
bidding castle. The men of the Beaujolais built to resist weather
rather than baronial mercenaries. Gabriel Chevalier would still find

the familiar sights and sound of *Clochemerle* everywhere. New washing machines and tractors permit the villagers yet more time to ponder the attractions—real and imagined—of their neighbors' spouses.

The Mont de Brouilly, a great mound of granitic sand that looms at the very center of the Beaujolais, has on its southern slope the finest *appellation* of all. The Côte de Brouilly, a scant 420 acres, is by some standard of *noblesse oblige* the highest *appellation* of the region. French law imposes a higher minimum quality requirement on its small production than on the broader area of Brouilly surrounding it or, for that matter, on any other wine of the Beaujolais, including Juliénas and Moulin-à-Vent. And Thivin's vineyards, older than the house, are at the very heart of this exceptional slope. For three hundred years, until it passed to the local Abbaye de Saint-Augustin in 1446, the vineyard had been the jealously guarded *domaine* of the canons of neighboring Belleville-sur-Saône. It was they who built the earliest part of the house in 1383, leaving a warren of underground passages and cellars. But most of what is visible today, especially the two low, square towers that support the arched entrance to the narrow courtyard, was built in 1828.

It is a sturdy house, solidly buttressed and somnolent with the perpetual cooing of pigeons in their lofts beneath the tiled roof. It is a snug house; on days when snowflakes fall thick as blotting paper, the iron-gray cold outside is only an added quality, increasing our pleasure as we sit in the warm dining room, hung with fading damask, and drink the last of our wine with *chèvretons*, little goat cheeses of the village. And in summer the house is a carefully shuttered refuge from the day's glaring heat, flung open only to the shady cool of evening and the drowsy night fragrance of the creepers and flowers that threaten to smother it.

Lunch had been delayed to allow for my train, but there was still time for a cold apéritif under the canopy of wisteria in the courtyard. Colette, who used to visit the house in the 1940s, described that wisteria in *Le Fanal Bleu* as a "contorted python, rearing up, and lost in its own foliage." The leaves filter the light, and beneath it all is cool and green and secret.

In the dining room, small iced Cavaillon melons were waiting, each moistened with a few drops of Muscat of Beaumes-de-Venise. We followed them with slices of home-cured ham and the bread that Yvonne buys from a village baker far off in the hills.

"He's the only one who still uses wood to fire his oven," she says. She herself still cooks everything on a wood-burning stove— or sometimes over charred vine cuttings in the fireplace of the dining room itself. "Wood gives a softer heat," she often says to me patiently, with the air of one who is embarrassed to have to explain obvious truths.

With the ham we drank a Pouilly-Fuissé 1974, dry but softly, delicately fruity. We were to continue with duckling, but first, in the French manner, we had a dish of *haricots verts*. The beans had been picked in the garden before dawn. "*Haricots* must be picked before the sun is on them," Yvonne says earnestly, "or the flavor is lost." With the duckling, we were able to enjoy the Château Thivin 1974, an elegant Côte de Brouilly with a perfume of sun-warmed strawberries. The salad was dressed with walnut oil that Yvonne buys freshly milled in Beaujeu; then there was farm *fromage blanc*, serene in a flood of thick cream, and a sweet-sharp ice made from raspberries and blackcurrants.

Oh, how richly one eats in the Beaujolais! Not finicky *haute cuisine*, but generous country food that nourishes a man spiritually as well as physically: rabbits and hares, plump pigeons and Limousin steaks; salads from the gardens, mushrooms from the fields, and chickens from Bresse. The rivers and lakes of the Dombes seem to be crammed with crayfish, pike, and perch; and while *chèvreton* cheeses age, suspended in little wicker cages like bewitched songbirds, ropes of piquant sausages hang looped from dark rafters in cellar and kitchen.

No wonder, then, that the wine of the Beaujolais, too, should be as enlivening to the spirit as it is restoring to the senses. It is not a wine to sip, to contemplate or analyze; it is for quaffing, for brightening the eye and loosening the tongue.

The vineyards of the Beaujolais stretch for about forty-five miles from a little south of Mâcon almost to the gates of Lyon. Never more than nine or ten miles wide, the area covers some sixty villages, only a handful of which are ever identified on the label of a bottle. The *crus* of the Beaujolais, those wines entitled to be sold with a village name—Saint-Amour, Juliénas, and Morgon, for example—are clustered in the northern part of the area. They emerge from the broader *appellation* of Beaujolais-Villages, wines from about thirty villages specified by law but not on the label and, again, all in the north. To the south the wine is either just Beaujolais or Beaujolais Supérieur, the latter name applied to plain Beaujolais when the sugar level in the grapes is above a prescribed minimum level and the yield per acre below a prescribed maximum. There is another, more subtle, distinction between the *crus* and Villages on the one hand and the plain wines of Beaujolais—Supérieur or not—on the other. In vineyards producing the latter, the grower may train his vines along wires in what is known universally as the Guyot method of pruning. But in those vineyards planted for the higher *appellations* the vines must be unsupported, pruned by the gobelet method like a stumpy fist of fingers—a natural way to force on the *vigneron* restraint of growth and limited fruiting.

Grape vines are reproduced from cuttings, and by selecting for specific qualities in his vines a grower can gradually change the strain in his vineyard, compared with that of his neighbor. Over many generations—of vines and men—these distinctions can become quite marked and might even appear to be separate varieties. Each strain is called a "clone."

All Beaujolais wines are made from Gamay vines, a variety with a bewildering proliferation of clones. For a start, the clones principally used in the Beaujolais are different from those used to produce the lesser Burgundies of the Côte d'Or. We frequently read and hear exclamations of wonder that the lowly Gamay of the Côte d'Or (where only Pinot Noir is used for fine wines) once translated to the Beaujolais hills miraculously produces better wine. But it is, in fact, a matter of different clones matched to the different conditions of the Beaujolais. Only clones of the Gamay Noir *à jus blanc*, black-skinned but with clear pulp, give quality wine. (The clones with pink pulp, called Gamays *teinturiers*, give coarser wine and are not recommended.) The Gamay Noir *à jus blanc* presents itself in many ways. Sometimes the shoots are stiffly upright, and sometimes they fall in graceful curves; sometimes the bunches are small and sometimes large, even "winged" in the form of a tricorne. Sometimes the bunches are tight and sometimes loose; the individual grape berries are sometimes round, sometimes oval, and sometimes almost oblong. The grape skin will vary in color from deep violet to black and may be thin or thick; and clones vary in their maturity season from early to late. Each grower has his own criteria for selecting among these clones: one might need better flavor, another better color, another better yield. Clones used mainly to increase yield include Gamay Labronde (also called Gamay des Gamays), Gamay Picard, Gamay Malarin (favored because it will put out new shoots if the first are damaged by spring frosts), and Gamay d'Arcenant (very productive but very vulnerable to rot). The three clones used for finest quality—all with relatively low yields—are Gamay Chatillon, Gamay Geoffray (also known as Gamay de Vaux), and Gamay Magny.

To add to the confusion, the clone called Gamay Beaujolais in California is not a Gamay at all and has nothing to do with the Beaujolais. It was introduced here in the nineteenth century, and by constant selection of cuttings toward a desired end the wine produced from it is of Gamay style. The University of California at Davis has recently identified it as a clone of Pinot Noir—not exactly a matter of shame—rather than a clone of Gamay. The plain Gamay introduced to California in the 1930s, and sometimes known as Napa Gamay to distinguish it from the unfortunately misnamed Gamay Beaujolais, is said to be a clone of the true Gamay of the Beaujolais. It is, however, one that has been adapted to our own growing conditions and is, by now, distinct from the clones in France. Professor Galet of the University of Montpellier, a distinguished ampelographer, suggests that even the Napa Gamay is not a true Gamay. Whatever it might be, most California wines labeled Gamay Beaujolais are made from a blend of these two varieties.

In France the choice of Gamay clones for each commune or hillside, whether traditional or personal, probably contributes as much to the style of individual wines as the soil and the particular exposure to the sun. Moulin-à-Vent, Chenas, and Morgon, for example, are known for the heaviness of their wines—a relative term when discussing Beaujolais, I should add. Fleurie and Juliénas are lighter and more flowery, and Brouilly, especially the Côte de Brouilly, is known for its finesse and elegance.

Most Beaujolais wines are made for early drinking, preferably within the twelvemonth of the vintage. But that is neither to say that they *must* be consumed within the twelvemonth nor to deny that some—particularly wines from Morgon and Moulin-à-Vent— often improve with a year or two in bottle. There is little point in holding any Beaujolais for longer than that.

Terms like *nouveau* (new), *primeur* (early), and *de l'année* (of the year) are increasingly bandied about. The date on which new Beaujolais can be released on the market from growers' cellars is controlled in France. Although there has been some pressure to have a "floating" date that could relate to the time of picking, at present the opening date is held rigidly to November 15. On that day the smaller wines that would hardly repay bottling, let alone keeping, were traditionally released in wood to the bistros of nearby Lyon and, in more recent years, to the bistros of Paris. Often this young wine was still working when released, but it was the harbinger of a new crop, and even in its rude qualities there was a link with the mystical cycles of vine and cellar that most Frenchmen crave. *Nouveau* is the undefined, popular way of describing it; *primeur* is the official name for wine released in the first month after the opening date. All *primeur*, then, is *nouveau*; not all *nouveau* (undefined) is *primeur*. Some might think that the practice of releasing Beaujolais *primeur* has been exaggerated of late. Shipping a small cask of still-frothing red wine to Chez Allard in Paris is one thing; stunning it for unsuitable early bottling and shipping it to far-flung continents is another.

De l'année means quite simply wine from the most recent vintage, and it is automatically superseded by the next crop.

Because Beaujolais is now always fruity and is usually drunk quite young, it is best when cool, but not chilled; half an hour or so in the refrigerator is ample time. Fruity red wines can seem excessively so when drunk at room temperature, and young wines, with their greener acidity, need a cooler temperature to keep that acidity in taste balance.

In former days growers would leave the fermenting juice on the skins for a longer period, and they made harder wines as a result. Today they aim for a light, tender style. The wines are also less complex in flavor than they once were. Yvonne Geoffray, with the countrywoman's instinctive response to life around her, complains that the bacteria and yeasts that affect the subtlety of fermentation have changed. "Fifty years ago, the vineyards were tended by horse, hand, and hoe. But now they don't plow so much. The soil is kept clear with herbicides, and that affects the balance of organisms." To be sure that yeasts at Château Thivin remain active, grape-skin residue from the presses is first mixed with earth and then laboriously carted up the hillside to be replaced on the vineyard every year.

In her eight decades, Yvonne Geoffray has seen many changes in the Beaujolais and accepts most of them philosophically. She saw nothing picturesque nor romantic in the old village *lavoir*, fed by an ice-cold hillside spring, where the women once brought their household wash. "They all have washing machines now," she says with evident satisfaction, "and some have dishwashers too."

She regrets television; it ended the neighborliness of her youth. "The winters were so much gayer then. Almost every evening there were *veillées* in different houses—cards, music, and gossip. At least once or twice a year there would be a *méchoui* to roast two or three sheep, and every household would contribute to the cost.

"I loved the village dances," she says, looking down at her hands. "Claude Geoffray"—she refers to her late husband—"first took notice of me at a village dance. Our families were neighbors and had always known each other, but he was older and hadn't paid much attention to me. I was seventeen when he came back from his military service. He asked me to dance.

"Quite soon after, his mother came to see my mother. When I saw she was wearing white gloves I knew her visit was not an ordinary one; it wasn't usual for Madame Geoffray to wear white gloves. She had come to ask if Claude might propose to me." She laughs self-consciously. "He came himself for the answer.

"When we married we had two hectares (about five acres), and eventually we inherited seven or eight more. Good vineyard land is precious, but we had very little money. Over the years we managed to acquire seven or eight more hectares of good, adjacent vineyard land. They were more important to me than bracelets. In those days life was hard for everyone in the Beaujolais. Our wines sold almost exclusively in Lyon, and we were not treated very fairly by the trade there. Claude was the first of the growers to go to Paris to try to get the restaurants there interested in the wines of the Beaujolais. He was always a shy man, and it was not easy for him, but everyone seemed to like him. Theater people and writers started to visit the region, and it was they who really promoted our wines back in the thirties and forties by ordering them in Paris and wherever they went in the world. Now the best Beaujolais goes to Paris, London, even New York. You will find better wines abroad now than in Lyon, even though Lyon is so close."

My visit coincided with an evening reunion of the Confrérie de l'Ordre des Compagnons du Beaujolais. Six hundred of us sat down to dinner in the old *cuverie* at Lacenas, where the Confrérie makes it headquarters. With songs of the Beaujolais on our lips, we attacked jellied roulade of duck stuffed with foie gras, truffles, and pistachio nuts. Before the second dish appeared—a selection of *charcuterie à la mode du Beaujolais* with a vintner's salad—the more energetic guests were already dancing in the aisles, perhaps to make room for the young chickens braised with *morilles*. Cheeses of the area, from goat and cow, were followed by small tarts of strawberries and raspberries. And to make us rejoice, we had, as the menu put it, *"la force de persuasion du vin de Beaujolais."* By French law firemen must be present at every public gathering. Present they were, surveying the scene benignly, hats tipped back, coats unbuttoned, a large glass in hand to sustain each and every one of them. A puff of their breath, I fancied, would do wonders for any fire.

When we left for home in the early hours of the morning, we could hear music drifting across the hills from almost every village we passed. The moon was particularly bright, and we agreed that it was, without doubt, in the seventh house.

Beaune
and the Rest

AN APOCRYPHAL story used to circulate in the London wine
trade of the country wine merchant who, instructing his
staff in the mysteries of Burgundy, would tell them, "There
are two sorts: Beaune, and the rest. We sell Beaune." Substitute
Pommard for Beaune, and the situation in the United States is not
so very different from that of pre–Common Market England. Nor
is it difficult to understand why a wine drinker, faced with the un-
charted tangle of Burgundian labels, might settle on one familiar
and uncomplicated name.

In fact, there is a basic and easily understood pattern to the labels
of Burgundy, even if it is not as neatly apparent as the pyramid of
Bordeaux *appellations* that rises from the broad base of Bordeaux
Rouge to the five-peaked crown of first growths. The difference is
that, where Bordeaux is a hierarchy, Burgundy is a democracy, its
qualities and riches widely dispersed. This is a good time to look at
Burgundy, to refresh the memory of wines long neglected, and to
brush up on less familiar names because prices for well-known
wines like Pommard and Pouilly-Fuissé have soared.

The 1975 vintage in Burgundy was small and, for red wines, disastrous. On the eve of the 1976 vintage, stocks were dangerously
low, down 40 percent from the previous year. In the Beaujolais,

the growers' cellars were depleted. In Chablis the price of a barrel (about sixty U.S. gallons), just 700 francs for the 1975 vintage, rose to 1,200 francs for the 1976—if wine could be found. And in the Côte d'Or the urgent need of the trade to replenish stocks was matched by reluctance on the part of the growers to sell. In the political mood and economic climate of France at the time, a full cellar was preferable to a large bank balance.

Obviously prices were highest where market pressure was greatest. Pommard has one of the largest productions of any Burgundy *commune*, as much as 100,000 cases a year. But in terms of French consumption, let alone the requirements of the rest of the world, the quantity is trifling. So much demand for so little wine pushed the price of even the most ordinary 1976 Pommard to 4,500 francs a barrel. Paradoxically, this affects the prices of Volnay, Beaune, and all the other internationally known *communes*. They consider their wines to be as good, and won't accept prices far behind.

The Côte d'Or—not the *département* of that name but the narrow ribbon of vines that runs from the outskirts of Dijon south to Santenay—is the heart of viticultural Burgundy, which also encompasses Chablis, some eighty miles to the north, the last remnant of a once huge winegrowing area that stretched from Joigny (where there is still one small vineyard on the hill behind the town) to Tonnerre (where the last vineyard was uprooted a bare fifteen years ago). To the south of Santenay, Burgundy also includes the Côte Chalonnaise, long neglected in this country, and the Mâconnais; the Beaujolais, though never a part of Burgundy, is usually considered to be an extension of it viticulturally.

The northern segment of the Côte d'Or, called Côte de Nuits for its commercial hub, Nuits-Saint-Georges, produces red wines of deep color, great force, and taut flavor. The Côte de Beaune, to its south, produces some of the finest white wines in France and reds that are softer than those of the Côte de Nuits, their flavors and aroma subtly blurred. I have always thought of these two halves of the Côte d'Or as the Rembrandt and Rubens of the wine world, one darkly spiritual, the other light and sensuous.

Reading a wine label from the Côte d'Or is easier if one remembers that Burgundy uses both *commune* (village) and *climat* (vineyard site) names. Over the centuries every parcel of vines has been delimited and identified with a name that distinguishes its *climat*,

a word that shows an early, perhaps unconscious, understanding of the effect of microclimate at each turn and undulation of the hill on the style and quality of the wine produced.

Sometimes a *climat* is quite large and extends beyond a *commune* border. Les Marconnets, for instance, a *climat* mostly in Beaune, extends into neighboring Savigny. It is possible to find a wine labeled Beaune–Les Marconnets as well as wine labeled Savigny–Les Marconnets. Sometimes the *climat* is so renowned that it is used without reference to the *commune* that contains it. Richebourg, for example, does not usually have any mention of the Vosne-Romanée *commune* on the label.

Climats, though delimited and named, are not the Burgundian equivalents of Bordeaux châteaux. Few are under single ownership. Clos Vougeot, the best known and largest *climat*, though not much more than a hundred acres, is divided among more than sixty proprietors, each of whom makes wine from his own vines in accordance with his own way of thinking. Given the idiosyncrasies of man and nature, *appellation contrôlée* regulations, in such circumstances, can go only so far in imposing conditions for potential quality; they cannot guarantee it, and variations occur even among wines that one might expect to be the same.

Over the years, some simple gradings have developed for the *climats*, and these have been acknowledged and incorporated into the *appellation contrôlée* laws. The finest *climats*, those of such reputation that their names stand alone on the label without reference to *commune*, are designated *grand cru*. Chambertin, Clos Saint-Denis, Musigny, Romanée, and Corton are examples of *grands crus* that have had their names annexed by the respective *communes* within whose borders they lie. This practice reserves, perhaps questionably, some of the glory from the finest vineyard for the wines of the *commune* as a whole. It is the first and most basic trap for Burgundy buyers. By adding Chambertin to its name, the *commune* of Gevrey, in particular, risks a confusion of its communal wine with those of other *grands crus* associated with the Chambertin *climat*. Gevrey-Chambertin is merely the *commune* wine; Charmes-Chambertin, Latricière-Chambertin, Mazis-Chambertin, and others are *grands crus* encircling Chambertin. Morey-Saint-Denis, Chambolle-Musigny, Vosne-Romanée, and Aloxe-Corton are further examples of *commune* names that incorporate reference to a famous *grand cru*. Montrachet, a *grand cru* that lies astraddle the neighboring *communes* of Puligny and Chassagne, has been coopted into both village names.

Behind the *grands crus* in rank, but usually alongside them in the center section, halfway up the slope, where all the finest wines of the Côte d'Or are grown, are the *premiers crus* of each *commune*. On labels their names are always in conjunction with the *commune* name, and the law requires that both names be of equal size; for example, Beaune-Grèves or Volnay-Santenots. Sometimes a wine is blended from two *premiers crus* in the same *commune* and is then labeled, for instance, Volnay Premier Cru without specifying which.

All other unclassified *climat* names may be used or not at the discretion of the grower or bottler. When they are used, the type size may not be larger than half that of the *commune* name; for example, Meursault-Perrières denotes a *premier cru* of Meursault; Pommard, Les Perrières, denotes a wine from an unclassified *climat* of Pommard. One of the first places to look for good value, if not bargains, is among these unclassified *climats*. Most of the owners of sections of the *grands crus* and *premiers crus* have a following, and their wines are inevitably in short supply. The wines of the un-classified *climats*, on the other hand, are generally sold for blending as *commune* wines bottled under shippers' brands. If such a wine is held back, there is probably good reason, and because there is little commercial advantage in using an unknown *climat* name, the mention of it often is the sign of a small grower proud of his un-unblended wine. You might find his pride unjustified, of course, but such a wine can occasionally be as good as a more prestigious *premier cru* at a considerably lower price. A grower's name, incidentally, is identified in Burgundy by the term *propriétaire-recoltant*, as opposed to *négoçiant*, which denotes a merchant-shipper.

The second place to look for good value is among the wines of the less fashionable communes of the Côte d'Or. Without the demand enjoyed by the popular names, they have less pressure to produce every possible drop from their vines. The quality of their *commune* wines is often as good as those of any other of the Côte d'Or and at appreciably lower prices, and their *premier crus* can be surprisingly distinguished and delicious. If one likes the wines of Côte de Beaune, a Santenay or Monthélie is a good alternative to Volnay; a red Chassagne-Montrachet (usually a good buy) can

be a substitute for Pommard. Savigny-les-Beaune, which has suffered from the shadow of its neighbor, has wine that is described
in the lintel stone of an old gateway in the town as *"nourrisant,
théologique, et morbifuge."* Be on the lookout, too, for red and
white wines from Saint-Romain, nearby. Though light and not
recommended for keeping, they are good value.

Shippers' blends from these lesser *communes* are often better
balanced than the wines of individual growers, so watch for both.
There are fewer overlooked *communes* in the Côte de Nuits, but
the wines of Fixin (the *x* in names like Fixin, Aloxe, and Auxey is
pronounced like a double *s*) are always undervalued.

Some of the best value in Burgundy is away from the Côte d'Or,
however, in the Côte Chalonnaise. The *communes* of Mercurey,
Rully, Givry, and Montagny produce wines whose quality has
long been acknowledged among French wine merchants. Montagny
produces white wines only; Rully, both red and white; the other
two, mostly red. Mercurey has the largest production and probably
the best red Burgundies outside the Côte d'Or. They are not difficult to find.

From the Mâconnais there is such an abundance of good, reasonably priced white wine that it isn't necessary to pay the present
high prices for Pouilly-Fuissé, the best known of them. Most are
labeled simply as Mâcon or as Mâcon-Villages, and occasionally a
village name is used. Saint-Veran, an *appellation* created in 1971,
has not yet achieved the popularity expected for it. It is crisply dry,
fresh, and has a fuller flavor than most Pouilly-Fuissé wines. In
tasting through these byways of Burgundy, one often wonders
what stroke of fortune left some delicious find in the shadow of a
more famous neighbor. Obviously not all Burgundies are great or
even fine wines, but there are far more than might be expected.

A word on vintages. White wines of the Mâconnais and of the
communes mentioned on the Côte Chalonnaise are not for long
keeping. Since recent years have been reasonably good for white
wines, the youngest being offered is generally the one to buy. If
one of these wines is more than three or four years old, however,
buy it with caution, trying a bottle before risking a case.

One is unlikely to find red wines of the disastrous 1975 vintage
from Burgundy. Both 1969 and 1971 produced well-balanced
wines that have kept well and are certainly ready for drinking. The
wines of 1970 are lighter and might have faded by now, so caution

is urged. The vintage of 1972 in Burgundy suffered from the poor reputation of the 1972 crop in Bordeaux; but, in fact, most of the red wines were good and some magnificent. They were expensive at the time, and few are likely to turn up now as bargains. If they do, don't be put off by the vintage. As the result of an enormous crop, 1973 wines were modestly priced and can be good values. Like the 1970s they are light and are not for long keeping; most 1974s have better color and more stamina. The best vintage since then was 1979, a year that gave dense, tannic red wines and impeccably balanced whites.

Les Trois Glorieuses

NICOLAS ROLIN founded the Hospices de Beaune in 1443 and endowed this charity hospital with some fine vineyards. Through the years other pious Burgundians have also bequeathed vineyards to the Hospices, which kept the choicest ones and sold the rest. Today the *domaines* of the Hospices extend over more than a hundred acres of the best grape-growing land in the Côte de Beaune, more than half of it in Beaune itself. (Since 1977 there has been added a small lot from Mazis-Chambertin in the Côte de Nuits.)

The wines from these vineyards are traditionally put up into distinctive *cuvées*, or vats, mostly named for benefactors of the Hospices: Nicolas Rolin (usually the finest), Guigone de Salins, Dames Hospitalières, Brunet, Clos des Avaux, Hugues & Louis Betault, Rousseau-Deslandes, and Maurice Drouhin. With the exception of Clos des Avaux, only village appellations are shown on the label, but all the Beaune wines are from *premier cru* vineyards. Nicolas Rolin usually composed of wines from Les Grèves, Les Cent-Vignes, and En Genêt; Guigone de Salins, from Bressandes, Les Seurey, and Les Champs-Pimont; and Dames Hospitalières, from Les Bressandes, Les Teurons, Les Grèves, and La Mignotte. For the rest, the connection between a *cuvée* and specific vineyards is not constant. Only the village names and the *cuvée* names remain in permanent relationship. In any scale of quality, the wines of the Hospices de Beaune stand high, but it is open to question whether they really represent the Côte de Beaune at its best. The Pommard of Monsieur Parent and that of Madame de Courcel, for example, are decidedly better than anything the Hospices has to offer; and there are several artisan growers at Savigny who produce wines that are consistently better than the Forneret *cuvée* of the Hospices.

This is not to decry the Hospices, but to put the *cuvées* in proper perspective with other wines from a consumer's point of view. In good years—as was the case in 1966 and 1969—the best *cuvées* of the Hospices are big wines, but they rarely have the finesse and delicacy of flavor one has a right to expect from such august origins. The reason for this seems to lie in the nature and timing of the annual auction at which the wines are sold, always on the third Sunday of November.

It takes influence to obtain a seat in the market hall of Beaune, draped for the occasion with the splendid Flemish tapestries of the Hospices, and there is always a crush of people in the gallery and in a roped-off section at the back. As each lot is offered, a tiny taper is lit, then a second, and bidding continues until both tapers have burned out. Bidding is accomplished more quickly than one might think—perhaps in two or three minutes for each lot. All the *cuvées* are available for tasting in the cellars under the Hospices on the day before the sale, for a charge of a few francs.

But there is pressure on the cellar staff to have wines ready for buyers to taste in this way in November, when sometimes the grapes are picked barely six weeks before. It calls for rapid initial fermentation, with no chance to take the wines straight into a secondary, malolactic fermentation to reduce acidity, now almost universal practice in Burgundy. There are those who believe that long-term development of the wines is sacrificed to short-term presentability.

Furthermore, because the sale and the tasting are the first public viewing of any new vintage of Burgundy, subject to intense publicity, the world is given a less-than-just first impression of the Burgundy vintage as a whole. Psychologically the auction fits in well with postvintage festivities: the three traditional banquets that accompany the sale, Les Trois Glorieuses, have the air of stupendous Thanksgiving dinners. Nevertheless, quality of the wines would improve if the sale were held in January, perhaps to coincide with the Saint Vincent celebrations (Saint Vincent is the patron saint of winegrowers). By that time the wines would have finished the malolactic fermentation and would be tasted in full harmony.

Raising the standard of wines bearing the name of the Hospices would give greater satisfaction and therefore better value, and the prestige would be more appropriate, if some way could be devised to care for the wines and bottle them under the supervision of the Hospices. At present, the wine, once sold, is moved to the cellars of any number of *negociants*, each with his own idea of "raising" the wine until ready for bottling. Thus there is no consistency in a *cuvée* from a single year purchased by different bottlers, and there can be little confidence in the name of the Hospices as a hallmark. If bottled by the Hospices itself, or at least centrally under its direction, these wines could constitute the most important collection of *domaine*-bottled wines in Burgundy. The Hospices funds—still used to support one of the best hospitals in France—would benefit, and so would the wine lover.

Not that I would want to suggest that prices paid at the Hospices auction are depressed; in fact, the contrary is true. Motives of public standing and ostentation, quite apart from charity, combine to exaggerate prices. The amounts paid, when compared with those of earlier years, provide a weathervane for the vintage as a whole. In recent years prices have tended to mount steadily, reflecting not only quality but also increased world demand for Burgundy. The total sale value of the 1972 vintage reached an all-time record of more than 7.5 million francs (about 1.5 million dollars at the rate of exchange at the time), and even 1981, a small crop following a series of weather disasters, yielded more than 6.5 million.

Hospices de Beaune wines are usually sold and distributed through normal trade channels at normal profit margins. But there are exceptions. For instance, a well-known Burgundy shipper, who makes it a point of honor to make the highest bid for a lot, usually returns the wine to the auctioneer for resale so that the Hospices will benefit twice over, and the highest prices paid for outstanding *cuvées* are rarely passed on to the consumer. The top price paid at the 1981 sale, for example, was 46,000 francs a hogshead for the Corton-Charlemagne *cuvée* François de Salins. With normal bottling and shipping costs and standard margins, the wine would have to sell to the consumer in New York at over $100 a bottle. We can be sure that it won't. In this respect, the wine trade of the world makes a gesture to the Hospices de Beaune, following a tradition set by centuries of Burgundians.

The monetary value of the sale at the Hospices is only a part of the benefit. The auction and the associated feasts are the grandest events of the year in the wine world and spread a warmth and luster far beyond the town of Beaune and the borders of France.

Beaune is protected in its entirety by the French state: every steeple, every gateway, and every crooked roof tile is a *monument historique*. On the Sunday of the Hospices sale, Beaune becomes a fairground as well. All day, crowds of small winegrowers from the surrounding villages visit the stands of agricultural machinery and household goods, view the sideshows, and eat *saucissons chauds*. In the chaste elegance of the seventeenth-century Hôtel de Ville, there are booths at which wines from any number of independent growers can be tasted, to be compared with the *cuvées* of the Hospices and to give a broader impression of the vintage.

Yet above all else, this third weekend in November is devoted to Les Trois Glorieuses, each offering a different face of the region. First, on the Saturday evening before the auction, there is a banquet organized by the Confrérie des Chevaliers du Tastevin at Clos de Vougeot. The most "grand" of the three feasts, it is intended to show the international face of Burgundy. The guests are largely ambassadors, ministers, and other distinguished foreign visitors from outside the world of wine.

On Sunday evening, after the auction, a candlelit dinner is held in the huge cellars under the old bastion towers of the town. Several hundred sit down together—mostly wine merchants of Beaune, vineyard owners, and guests.

Chatter reverberates on stone, so the silence when everyone is at last seated and the lights are extinguished is all the more dramatic. Suddenly, from a small doorway, dozens of young men who are to wait on table file into the vast cellars, each carrying a lighted candle. It is simple but effective. Courses and wines are presented with impeccable flourish and well-rehearsed precision, but there is no inappropriate solemnity. Despite numbers, there is a great family feeling, and everyone joins in the singing of the *ban bourguignon* between courses. Perhaps the tradition of boisterously waving hands in the air to the beat of the music was to show a medieval assembly that fingers could be trusted in the sauce?

The food is superb and abundant. My menu from the 1967 dinner shows that we started with a *consommé Celestine* and then drank Beaune Blanc 1964 with a partridge tart, followed by a *suprême de saumon à la norvégienne* with Puligny-Montrachet Clos du Cailleret 1964. Diners regained their breath on a *salmis* of wild duck with a Pommard *cuvée* Dames de la Charité 1964 of the Hospices de Beaune. Then there was a *côte de charolais* accompanied by 1962 Corton in magnums, which we continued to drink with a selection of cheeses. A Champagne Brut 1961 was served with an enormous frosted cake (I can never understand why the French, logical in all else, drink dry Champagne with sweet dishes), and we toyed with petits fours, coffee, and *prunelle de Bourgogne* —the white brandy distilled from the little Burgundy plums—into the small hours. As well as the wines officially accompanying each course, the menu listed twenty-six others, which were presented by growers and merchants and were available, on request, as extra or alternative choices.

Monday morning comes too soon if the Dîner aux Chandelles has been preceded by the Chevaliers du Tastevin banquet at Clos de Vougeot. But gastronomically undaunted, we set off to Meursault for La Paulée. No one knows the origin of the Rabelaisian luncheon that concludes Les Trois Glorieuses. Essentially it is a vineyard workers' banquet, presenting the third and most basic of the three faces of Burgundy. Each guest brings his own bottle, which is to say that each brings several, and there is a great deal of sipping and sampling of one another's wines in an atmosphere of *fête champêtre*. Most of the participants are from the town of Meursault and the surrounding area.

In 1967 I was the guest of Berthe Morey, and we drank Meursault and Volnay from her vineyards. A *jambon persillé*, specialty of the region, was followed by *pâté en croûte* and a glorious *pochouse verdunoise*, a stew of delicate river fish in white wine, savory with garlic. We witnessed the ceremony of marrying *pochouse*—from the other side of the river Saône—with the white wine of Meursault. "*Je vous annonce gastronomiquement mariés*," sang out the mayor of Meursault to the fish cauldron and the bottle, and we all agreed. At least, no one could think of any reason why the two should not be joined in gastronomic matrimony. Then a huge boar was carried round the hall in triumph, head and bristles replaced for decoration. (I was provoked to rather ungastronomic thought, I must confess.)

After La Paulée, the growers throw open their cellars and expect their neighbors to come and taste. Nobody feels very much like eating supper that night.

Champagne: The Brilliant Image

W HEN SIR EDWARD BARRY of the Royal College of Physicians in London published his *Observations, Historical, Critical and Medical on the Wines of the Ancients and the Analogy Between them and Modern Wines* in 1775, England was reeling from the excessive indulgence in Port wine that had resulted from the 1703 Methuen treaty with Portugal. "High politics and high tariff," as H. Warner Allen has put it, "had almost extinguished the importation of French wines." Few of those still entering the country were worthy of attention, according to Sir Edward, but he excepted wines from Champagne. By "Champagne," however, he expected his reader to understand the still wine of that region, not the upstart "sparkling, frothy Champagne," which he dismissed as a "depraved taste" passing out of fashion.

Known as *vin d'Ay*, an allusion to the small town of Ay in the valley of the Marne, east of Paris, where some of the finest Champagne vineyards are still to be found, Champagne was originally a still, light red wine, well reputed even before the Middle Ages, and consumed at the sixteenth-century court of Henri IV of France, along with others that were of easy access to the capital. However, the King's Chancellor at the time, Nicholas de Brulart, was himself proprietor of immense vineyards at Sillery-en-Champagne, just northeast of Ay on what is now known as the Montagne de Reims (though hardly a mountain). It would be unworldly to be surprised that Brulart might want the satisfaction of seeing the court enjoy wine from his estates. Such was his influence that its most discreet exercise (with suspiciously partisan endorsement from the court physicians) was enough to ensure social (and therefore commercial) success. Though a distinction had previously been maintained between the wines of Ay from the valley of the Marne and wines from the Montagne de Reims, at about that time, in deference to Brulart's Sillery-en-Champagne, *all* wines from the region became known as Champagne, thereby gently and profitably engaging the ancient reputation of the wines of Ay to the interests of the Brulart family.

Brulart knew, as we would say, his market. Determined to satisfy the taste of an aristocratic clientele, he encouraged his growers to preserve refinement and freshness of flavor above all else. Growers were urged, for example, to pick no later than ten o'clock in the morning so that grapes might be brought cool to the cellars for crushing. Winemakers were commended to separate juice from the black grape skins as quickly as possible, not in order to avoid color (though eventually wine of palest color became most prized) but to attain the most delicate style possible. As a result, Champagne destined for court palates ceased to be light red; by the late seventeenth century, it had barely a tint of straw-pink and was known as *vin gris*.

To preserve its elusive, fresh flavor, the wine was dispatched in barrels as soon as winter cold had helped it fall bright of sediment, and, on arrival, was promptly drawn off into tightly sealed glass flagons. Northern wines, especially when harvested late before an early winter, were characteristically fizzy when young; for although the connection between grape sugar and alcohol was recognized, there was no real understanding of fermentation before Pasteur, and there were then no means of gauging that all sugar had been converted. Invariably, fermentations that stuck as temperatures fell would start again only in warm spring weather, and since, in those days, most wine was drunk within a year of the vintage, a bubble or two remaining from revived fermentation, "winking at the brim," must have been taken for granted. No doubt that was why the usual closure of bottle or crock was not a tight-fitting cork, as today, but a piece of cloth or a film of olive oil that would allow gas to escape.

The gas formed in the tightly sealed flagons of Champagne, however, foamed and sparkled when released, enchanting the French court. Refined sugar to assist continued fermentation in the bottle was widely available by this period, but, without control of the actual bottling, the growers could not be certain if a barrel of wine, once shipped, would froth or not. In 1724 they appealed to the government for the right to ship their *vin gris de Champagne* in bottles instead of barrels, the better to ensure and control the sparkle. With permission finally given in 1728, and the development of the St. Gobain glassworks to provide the vast numbers of bottles that would be required, real sparkling Champagne, if not quite as we know it today, was born.

Its success was absolute. Voltaire, in 1756, referred to it as "the brilliant image of France," though by modern standards it was still an unpredictable, rather primitive, cloudy wine. It was not until the early nineteenth century (perhaps just in time to avoid that fall from grace predicted by Sir Edward Barry) that experiment led to discovery of the precise pressure of carbonic acid gas generated through fermentation of a given measure of sugar, and Madame Clicquot (founder, with her departed husband, of the Champagne house that still bears her name) devised a way to remove the *débris* of fermentation from the bottle without the pent-up sparkle escaping. Inverted in holes set in a sloping table, the bottles of wine were shaken and gradually twisted from an oblique to an upright position, coaxing the sediment to settle on the cork itself. Then, with one deft movement removing the restraining wire, both cork and *débris* were thrust together from the bottle by the pressure of gas, and a new cork inserted and secured so swiftly that almost no wine or sparkle was lost. (Since then this method, called "riddling" in English, has been improved further by passing the tips of the bottles through a freezing mixture before the disgorging so that the sediment now flies out within a small pellet of ice, the space left in the bottle to be filled with wine carefully adjusted for sweetness to restore balance.) Later, the discoveries of Pasteur on the nature of yeast activity gave Champagne makers all they needed to perfect their technique of controlled, induced, secondary fermentation in the bottle, the essential element of what we call the *méthode champenoise* of making sparkling wines, a *méthode* that would have astounded Dom Perignon, who is credited with having invented it more than a century before.

Dom Perignon, the extraordinarily capable and gifted cellar master of the Abbey at Hautvillers in the valley of the Marne from 1668 to 1715, is properly credited, however, with the idea of blending grapes of disparate origin to arrive at a balance of qualities superior to any that could be found naturally. A worthy successor to those who had developed Champagne's characteristic delicacy of style, he checked all grapes on arrival at the Abbey press house to find the right combinations for his blends *before* fermentation. So sensitive was he to the possibilities of each of the Abbey's vineyards, reported his contemporaries, that to taste a single grape was enough for him to say which vineyard the basket came from, and to decide for which vat it should be reserved. He had not the advantage of the master blenders of today, who can test-blend small quantities of the year's newly fermented wines in the tasting room before assembling their *cuvée*. For him, there was no induced "secondary fermentation" as today, just a continuation of the first into bottle.

At first Champagne was made from black grapes only, but the addition of white grapes revealed both delicacy and sparkle improved, so that in the eighteenth century Pinot Blanc and Chardonnay vines began to appear among the Pinot Noir and Meunier (a distant, humble cousin of the Pinot Noir whose role in making Champagne is rarely acknowledged, although contributing greatly to the soft quality of certain blends). Gradually they found their way along the valley of the Marne and onto the Montagne de Reims, while entire vineyards of them spread over the hillsides south of the river, earning the region the name Côte des Blancs, by which it is still known.

For all this time, of course, and, indeed, until the highly controversial changes of the 1860s and 1870s, Champagne was always a sweet wine, hence the tradition in France of serving Champagne with desserts. The problem is that the wine is now more often dry than not, and dry sparkling wine is hardly the most appropriate accompaniment for a rich St.-Honoré. But, as long as there are French birthdays to celebrate, no doubt they will continue to appear in tandem.

The move to dry Champagne started with a shipment of the

Champagne
and Sancerre

FRANCE

Area of map

N

CHAMPAGNE

Reims
Sillery
MONTAGNE
DE REIMS
Hautvillers
VALLEY OF Ay
THE MARNE Epernay
CÔTE DES BLANCS

PARIS

© 1982 A. Karl/J. Kemp

Marne R.

Seine R.

Miles
0   30
Kms.
0   30

Serein R.
Chablis

Loire R.

See
inset
Sancerre
Pouilly-sur-Loire
La Charité-
sur-Loire
Quincy
Bourges

Sury-en-Vaux
Verdigny
Chavignol
Saint-Thibault
Amigny
SANCERRE
Saint-
Andelain
Bué
les Loges
POUILLY-SUR-LOIRE

1846 vintage of Perrier-Jouët to London, an experiment, urged by
the firm's British representative, that failed dismally. In 1860, however, several houses, including Clicquot, sent to London Champagnes of the 1857 vintage that were drier—and more mature—
than usual. The extra maturing, crucial to the balance of the wines,
was of great economic consequence to the Champagne houses.
Patrick Forbes explains in his book *Champagne: The Wine, the
Land and the People* that the sweetness added to the disgorged
bottles just before shipping "masked the tartness of a young Champagne and enabled the makers to sell the majority of their wines
two years, sometimes one year, after they were made; a 'dry'
Champagne would need to age for at least three years in the cellars
before its rough edges were rounded off, and this would involve
an increase not only in the size of the cellars but in overhead and
locked-up capital as well." This time the market responded en-
thusiastically, and although some houses (especially Roederer, who
announced that "there would be no bowing to the dry Baal" in
their cellars) held out until the 1874 vintage—the first that was
almost universally shipped dry to England—the change was
rapid and opposition faded when the Champagne producers saw
the expansion that followed. By 1865, within five years of that
first introduction of a dry style, sales of Champagne abroad had
more than doubled to 10 million bottles a year, and by the close
of the century that number had more than doubled again. Champagne, no longer a dessert wine, competing for attention with
Sauternes, Port, Madeira, and the rich, mahogany-colored sherries
beloved of the period, had created an unassailable niche of its own.
Saintsbury, grudgingly accepting the change in his *Notes on a
Cellar Book*, nevertheless commented that dry Champagnes were
apt to lose their flavor, and regretted the passing of "the rich and
full-flavored variety as an alternative."

But by then Champagne had become something beyond wine
itself, and even the *sound* of a cork popping would provoke ani-
mated gaiety and cosmic expectation at almost all social levels.
Sometimes, of course, the gaiety could be extravagantly misplaced.
Maurice Healy describes, in *Stay Me With Flagons*, the visit of a
small opera company to his Irish hometown of Cork some eighty
years ago, for whom the Lord Mayor of the city, in private life a
wine merchant, decided to give a Champagne reception by way of
a civic welcome. Secure in his seat, waiting for the opening per-

formance of *La Traviata* to begin, Healy could hear that the Lord Mayor's hospitality, started some hours earlier, had been transferred onto the stage.

A creditable performance of the overture took place, and the curtain rose upon the revel of the first act. The cast was dressed in eighteenth century costumes, but [the Lord Mayor's] waiters lent a modern note, and continued to uncork Champagne with an assiduity and a hospitality that filled me with direful presages. Never was the drinking song rendered with greater gusto; the chorus splashed Champagne in every direction, and the principals sang with the chorus. Mr. G. Hilton St. Just, no mean tenor, was in excellent voice; and I felt that for once, if I was not getting exactly what Verdi had intended, I was undoubtedly enjoying the authentic atmosphere which Dumas had meant to create. The volatile wine carried the company through the first act with tremendous *élan*; but when the curtain rose for the second it soon became evident that there was something rotten in the state of Denmark. When Alfredo's father came to reason with his son, the latter sat down at a table and buried his face in his hands; at the end of each line of the *Di provenza* he lifted it, glared at his father, and buried it again; occasionally a sob of emotion (which looked uncommonly like a hiccup) shook his body. Meantime his father, who enjoyed a powerful bass-baritone, kept alternating between hissed pianissimi and thundered fortissimi. By this time there was no restraining the gallery. "Tis great stuff Gussie's been giving 'em," cried one voice, and fifty others joined in a chorus of not unfriendly chaff, which did not affect the performers in the slightest. The opera finished triumphantly, Mr. St. Just's final "O, Violetta!" being a magnificent degeneration from a musical note into a hysterical sobbing.

Undoubtedly, the popularity of dry Champagne made the producers exceedingly rich, but, more important, it restored a taste for delicacy, the origin of Champagne's success too often lost, subsequently, in a froth of sweet bubbles. Without a mask of sugar, style and quality were again plainly evident, and as luck would have it there followed a series of Champagne vintages of unparalleled splendor. Charles Walter Berry, of Berry Bros. and Rudd, the London wine merchants, described a dinner with the head of Perrier-Jouët in 1934 when the 1892, one of the greatest of them all, was served. "It was so wonderful," he recorded in his diary, "that the horrid commercial instinct was difficult to quieten. I wondered if there were any for sale, I dared not ask, being a guest at the table . . . also I felt there could only be a very small quantity remaining in Monsieur Budin's private cellar for use on special occasions."

But eventually he found a way to draw out his host, and was surprised to learn that what remained of the wine did not belong to Monsieur Budin but to his brother-in-law, who, lying at that very moment dangerously ill, would perhaps "never drink the sixty bottles that remain to him." Berry kept discreet silence, but on parting, he plucked up courage and whispered, while tenderly pressing Budin's hand, "Wouldn't it be a charitable thing if I offered to buy that 1892 Perrier-Jouët . . . and thus put a temptation out of the way of your invalid brother-in-law?" We shall never know whether Monsieur Budin's acquiescence came in a surge of gratitude for such generous concern or in a paralyzing shock of disbelief, but we do know that Berry took the remaining stock of 1892 away with him. A few years ago, in San Francisco, I had an unexpected opportunity to taste it. Alas, I held in my glass only the brown ghost of former magnificence.

Most vintage Champagnes, and it was probably as true then as it is today, are at their best from six to ten years from the vintage date, though exceptional wines can age superbly for fifty years or more, losing sparkle but not vivacity. On the evening when we mourned the 1892 Perrier-Jouët we were lucky enough to have a bottle of 1926 Roederer to console us. Its color was clear gold, and though greatly diminished, it offered a bouquet and flavor of toasted almonds that we were catching just this side of being maderized. But the oldest Champagnes that I have drunk for other than intellectual pleasure have been the 1929s. Even in the past year or two, I have found 1929 Bollinger (in magnum) full flavored and fresh. Recently, a bottle of 1929 Roederer, though darkened in color, was equally fresh on the palate, with an unusual bouquet of vanilla biscuits.

If old Champagne is an acquired taste, pink Champagne need not be. It is a pity that the color carries with it suggestions of frivolity, because a well-made pink Champagne is not just Champagne of a different hue. Some houses make their pink *cuvée* by adding to the blend a little Bouzy (there are growers on this south-facing slope who still make their Pinot Noir into a red wine in favorable years). But others trouble to make a specifically pink wine—leaving juice and skins together just long enough for the pink color to take before separating them and then putting the resultant wine through the usual blending and secondary fermentation process. Along with the color the wine absorbs flavor from the skins, which gives a different balance and style to the wine. The rosé of the growers' cooperative at Mailly has the added interest (and distinctive characteristic) of being made entirely from Mailly *commune* grapes, but it is difficult to find in the United States. Charles Heidsieck offers one that confirms their full-bodied, deeply flavored house style; and Ruinart, the oldest Champagne house, founded by Dom Perignon's assistant, makes a pink vintage Champagne that develops richly complex character in bottle.

The great Champagne houses, of course, take pains with all their vintage wines to ensure such development. (It is assumed that nonvintage wines, by and large, will be consumed soon after release, as they should be.) The mature style that each house aims for has evolved over the years, and though sometimes a result of geographic happenstance (houses with larger vineyard holdings on the Côte des Blancs, in particular, are likely to use their position to make lighter, more elegant wines), usually it is the result of a past personal preference, refined and established by succeeding generations. Pol Roger, for example, blending for a dry, elegant style, uses 60 percent Pinot Noir and 40 percent Chardonnay, thereby increasing slightly the amount of white grapes over the standard blend in Champagne of two-thirds red and one-third white. Roederer, blending for a more complex, fuller style, uses a third Pinot Noir from the Montagne de Reims and a third from vineyards in the valley of the Marne; the other third is made up of white Chardonnay grapes. Piper-Heidsieck does not aim for such a full-bodied style as Roederer.

Mumm looks for "character," taking red grapes from the valley and from the Montagne de Reims in the manner of Roederer. But Mumm introduces some Meunier with the Pinot Noir and uses a slightly higher proportion of white grapes to tone down and lighten their blend. Taittinger blends for a light, delicate style in the tradition of early Champagnes, and has made a specialty of Blanc de Blancs, made, of course, from 100 percent white grapes.

Krug is one of the few firms that still ferment their wines in oak casks. Others use stainless steel for the first fermentation, though Bollinger ferments two thirds in old barrels (new barrels are used first to ferment second pressings, which are then sold to others in bulk) and one third in stainless steel. Fermentation in wood plus a high proportion of Pinot Noir (mostly from the firm's own vineyards on the Montagne de Reims) combine to give Bollinger vintage wines their characteristic body. The best of them are reserved for Bollinger's RD (recently disgorged) Champagne that is allowed to remain with its bottled sediment for eight to ten years. The richness of flavor that results is extraordinarily delicious. In fact, the length of time that wine and sediment remain together before disgorging plays at least as great a role in the development of flavor as the choice of grapes and the method of fermentation.

Recently, Krug has decided to concentrate on production of its Grande Cuvée, which will eventually represent at least three quarters of the firm's total output. Using a blend that will vary from year to year, and which will incorporate wines from several vintages for consistency of style, the wine will be based on roughly half white grapes and half red, of which about half will be Meunier for "charm and fruitiness," as Rémi Krug put it to me. Since it will be aged on the sediment over a six-year cycle, Grande Cuvée should need little sweetening.

Moët et Chandon, by far the largest of the Grande Marque Champagne producers, follows a blend for its California wine that is not too dissimilar from the proportions the firm uses in France. Edmond Maudière, responsible for the *cuvées* in both places, uses 60 percent Pinot Noir, 25 percent Chardonnay, and 15 percent Pinot Blanc at Domaine Chandon. In California, where the problem is one of maintaining the acidity rather than modifying it, there is no need for Meunier. On the other hand, picking of California Pinot Noir and Chardonnay for the Champagne vats must start two or more weeks before the general harvest to obtain the crisp acidity essential for the *prise de mousse*.

Most Champagnes today are fermented to give a pressure of sparkle equivalent to about six atmospheres. *Crémant* Champagne, increasingly rare, is fermented to only four atmospheres, however, and therefore seems softer to the palate even when quite dry. Most Blanc de Blancs, even when not described as *crémant*, are usually made with less pressure, too, to enhance the soft elegance of their style.

A vintage Champagne is best appreciated as a preamble to a fine dinner: by stimulating both palate and mind, it helps focus on wines to follow. As accompaniment to the toasts and good wishes that accompany our triumphs, great and small, and mark the passage of our lives, it has no equal, despite Hemingway's perplexity that "anyone would want to mix emotions with a wine like that." But above all, and who knows by what magic, a fine vintage Champagne makes any one of us feel younger, better looking, and wittier. And whatever Sir Edward Barry thought, I'm all for such depravity.

Rustic Pleasures

I**N THE EARLY** seventies, a special committee of the French *Institut National des Appellations d'Origine*, working with the blessing of the French government and the support of Food and Wine from France, an agency promoting French agricultural products and responsible somewhere along the line to the French Minister of Agriculture, conducted a campaign in various states—New York, California, and Florida, in particular—to popularize the country wines of France.

The term "country wines" is vague. As used before the campaign, the term *did* mean, if it meant anything, the wines one quaffed in the country as opposed to those one sipped in town. Corbières was, and is, a country wine; Champagne was, and is, not. Country wines, above all, are made for the satisfaction of those who produce them and for local consumers rather than with an eye to an international market, so they usually share a rustic simplicity, and that is not for everyone.

With the exceptions only of Brittany and Normandy, where there is too much cloud for ripening grapes, every region of France produces wine. Over the centuries, such local wines have developed to suit local conditions, local food, and—though not often considered, but just as important—local temperament.

The special committee wanted to draw attention to this plethora, to get away from the high-gloss image of the great wines of Bordeaux, Burgundy, and Champagne. They recognized that these wines give prestige, but they felt that this served no purpose if the average American had little chance to taste French wines as a whole.

Putting the idea into effect was not easy. Few of the country-wine districts were organized to export their wines; nor had they all wines of sufficient quality to make that worthwhile. One visits Nancy in Lorraine to see the exquisite wrought iron of the Place Stanislas, not to taste the pinched little local rosé from the Côtes de Toul. On the other hand, there is barely enough of the delicate and delicious wines of Savoie to satisfy demand in the local ski resorts, let alone the rest of France and markets overseas. But the rural southwest and the valleys of the Loire and the Rhône, on the other hand, offer an abundance of good wine; Alsace produces three times as much good wine as the Médoc; and Provence has more to show than the elaborately packaged rosés of the Riviera would lead one to believe.

It was a condition of participation that regional committees of growers contribute to the funding of the project. Financial participation, it was felt, would ensure proper support for the aims of the campaign and for its commercial effort, without which the whole exercise was pointless. Areas large enough to afford a contribution and realistic enough to make it, however, were the very ones that had already made some move toward international markets. Muscadet, Anjou Rosé, Côtes du Rhône, and Alsace wines are not exactly unknown, and Bordeaux Rouge and Mâcon Blanc have ebbed and flowed in popular acceptance for many years. Where were Cahors, Costières du Gard, the light white wines of Saint-Pourçain, and flowery Montlouis—poor man's Vouvray, if you like, but just as good as most Vouvray that one is likely to come across?

Even if the list of wines included in the initial campaign missed some of the excitement that it might have had, it encouraged us to look afresh at French wines and even to see familiar names in a different light. Bordeaux Rouge, for example, was re-presented to us as a simple rustic wine that should be accepted and enjoyed on its own terms, rather than as a lowly cousin of the *grands seigneurs* of the Médoc. So, however conventional the choice of unconventional wines, the committee succeeded, at very least, in shaking us from rigid attitudes.

Though anyone might be daunted by the fear of appearing Thurberishly pretentious in offering "an amusing little wine from Clermont-Ferrand," or some such, to drink wine and ignore these lesser pleasures is like traveling without ever leaving the grand hotel circuit. The country wines of France are in fact so varied that through them anyone can continually rediscover the surprise and delight of his first glass of wine. Yet no matter how varied, they are easy to place and to understand, because French wines fall into three broad groups.

The wide sweep of vineyards between the Massif Central and the Atlantic, from the Loire in the north to the Pyrenees in the south, encompasses wines from all the river valleys that open to the ocean: Loire, Dordogne, Lot, Garonne, Tarn and Gave de Pau. In all of them the red wines are made from grapes that have a certain resistance to Atlantic humidity, especially Cabernet Sauvignon, Cabernet Franc, and varieties that share their basic characteristics. As a result, all the red wines from this western zone, great and small, town or country, have a noticeable zest of tannin. They have a tendency to be tough, even harsh, when young. This is as true of red Loire wines such as Chinon and Bourgueil as it is of red wines of the Médoc. Red wines from these valleys need a little age, and even when they don't, they are likely to be brisk.

White wines produced in this zone can be either sweet or dry. In the Loire, Muscadet is always dry, but wines made from Chenin Blanc grapes—Vouvray, Coteaux du Layon, Montlouis, Savennières—vary on a sweet-dry scale according to the warmth and stability of the growing season. Years that rank high in Bordeaux are likely to give sweet, even luscious, wines in the Loire valley. Years that are less successful in Bordeaux are likely to produce dry white wines in the Loire, even from Chenin grapes. But sweet Chenin wines—Bonnezeaux from the Coteaux du Layon, for example, or fine Vouvray—never cloy; there is always a balance of sweetness and acidity supported by flavor that deepens with age. Served with fresh fruit at the close of a meal, such wines, when mature, are incomparable and easily convert those who claim not to appreciate sweet wines.

In northeastern France winters are colder, but farther from the ocean summers are brighter and warmer, grape skins thinner and more aromatic. Burgundy is in this region; so are the Jura, Champagne, Beaujolais, and lesser known areas of the upper Loire, such as Saint-Pourçain and the Côtes de Forez. It is a region of soft red wines made from Pinot and Gamay grapes, and whites, from Chardonnay, Pinot Blanc, and Aligoté, that are always dry but rarely tart.

The Mediterranean belt of France, from the Spanish to the Italian borders, the third broad region, produces a bewildering variety of wines, mostly red and rosé, with a few, not very distinguished, white. The grapes on a vine in heat stress easily lose acidity, and give dull wine. Red and rosé wines of the south—Corbières, Minervois, Fitou—are therefore made either from varieties with good natural acidity or from a combination of varieties calculated to ensure balance at the time of picking. These wines are quick to mature and rarely too young to drink. There are exceptions—Châteauneuf-du-Pape, for example, and red Bandol, which share the plump, straightforward, easy-to-drink characteristics of the south, but do repay keeping. The rosés, particularly those from the hills of Provence (the best come from the villages of Cuers and Pierrefeu), are also made from a mixture of grape varieties, each one of which brings a particular quality and flavor to the wine.

Any French wine, whether met here or in the course of traveling through France, will belong to one or other of these broad groups, and once it has been placed in relation to the Massif Central—west, northeast, or south—one has some idea of what to expect. Remembering well-known key wines in each group helps recall the basic overall styles—a brisk Bordeaux being typical of the west, an elegantly soft Beaune being typical of the northeast, and a big, plump Châteauneuf-du-Pape being typical of the south. Most country wines, in brief, are variations in style and in quality on such classic types. Since country wine in France is usually enjoyed under the most obvious and natural circumstances, there is rarely a problem in matching it to appropriate food. In a village near Toulon recently I was served local Provençal dishes with wines produced within a few miles: white Côtes de Provence with seafood hors d'oeuvre, Bandol rosé to accompany a Marseille dish of tripe and trotters, and magnums of red Domaine Tempier 1967 with leaf-wrapped Banon cheeses. Today, when there is less formality in the composition of a menu and more originality in the

dishes, an unpretentious country wine may be more appropriate
with what we choose to eat than something grander and better
known from Burgundy or Bordeaux would be. With cassoulet, for
example, what more natural than Fitou or Corbières? A pork
dish is better for a white or rosé wine from the Loire: the richness
of the meat is well matched by the fullness of any white Chenin
wine, and even by an Anjou rosé with a slight hint of sweetness.
Cahors, from the valley of the Lot, has the right persistence to
accompany hare, pigeon, or anything gamy; and a white Jura wine,
soft and slightly nutty, is delicious with trout and other freshwater
fish. Hot sausage (preferably cooked in a court bouillon made
with a little red or white wine) and boiled potatoes is a country
dish that brings out the best in any simple robust wine, and there
seems to be natural harmony between the cheese of any part of
France and the local wine.

I am not suggesting still more which-wine-with-which-dish rules.
On the contrary, because all country wines and foods have developed naturally as ordinary people have sought constantly to
improve what was basically available to them, there is an easy relationship between them all, and they are easy to enjoy. Complicated
dishes created by skilled chefs to enliven jaded palates and wines
carefully oriented toward sophisticated city markets can be exquisite: sweetbreads financière and a bottle of mature Montrachet
are not to be eschewed. But when I sit down to a plain daube of
lamb and a bottle of Côtes du Rhône, I know that God's in his
heaven, and all's right with the world.

Venerable Hermitage

T HE CLOSET I use as a wine cellar has only the sketchiest sem-
blance of order, a state of affairs I promise to correct whenever I search in exasperation for a bottle that I *know* to be
there somewhere. Too much is crammed into too small a space,
of course (a common complaint), and I make matters worse by
lazily separating bottles from newly delivered cases to fill gaps
here and there instead of taking the trouble to rearrange the bins.
But in the resulting chaos I sometimes come across a wine that I
thought finished long since and then feel the same joy as finding a
favorite book, assumed lost, caught behind the stack or meeting in
a faraway place a long-missed friend in circumstances that allow
time for a drink and a gossip.

A few weeks ago, rummaging in the corner reserved for uncertain wines discreetly brought out for family drinking only, I came
across a bottle of 1962 Hermitage that had been bottled in our
company's former cellars in London. I didn't remember having
brought any of it to San Francisco, and had I known it to be there
I would have drunk it long ago. There was beef stew on the stove,
the 1962 had been a good wine, and it seemed to be as appropriate
a choice as any. I looked forward to seeing what had happened
since I had last tasted it, at least five years before.

Expecting some deposit, I decanted the wine. There was very little sediment, but down one side of the bottle a light crust had formed. The color was deeper than I had expected, with hardly a hint of browning; the bouquet and taste showed vigor rather than complexity. Though considerably mellowed, the wine had taken seventeen years in its stride.

The crust recalled my earliest memory of drinking old Hermitage in London, during the late fifties. With some braised pigeons (an unfortunate choice for the evening, as I remember clearly; much of that morning had been spent coping with an obstinate pigeon stuck in our chimney), a friend had shared with me his last bottle of the great 1923. The wine had thrown a crust every bit as heavy and as firm as any Port would have done. To my bewilderment it had contradicted my bible of the time, P. Morton Shands' engagingly opinionated book on French wines. First qualifying his ever-dogmatic view with a mischievous "when not pasteurised," Shand says that Hermitage "throws a heavy deposit, like a violet mud, which is apt to precipitate itself to the bottom rather than adhere to the sides in the form of a hard crust . . ." But deposit or not, that wine, too, had amazed me by its unexpectedly vigorous color and lively quality after thirty years in bottle.

Perhaps it was an obvious promise of such long life that caused Hermitage, of all French wines, to be the first to be set aside for aging in bottle. Dr. Middleton, that eighteenth-century master of lucid English, theological controversy, and companionable drinking, gave Hermitage as one of the three wines that "did not compare," because of its capacity to "grow to an extreme old age." (The other two, oddly, were "port" and "hock," rather vague and all-embracing categories, one might have thought, to be put on such elevated pedestals.) Professor Saintsbury's much quoted description of Hermitage as the "manliest of wines" referred in fact to a specific 1846, drunk forty years after the vintage, and was probably an allusion to this same remarkable vigor-in-age. On the other hand, having once described an 1874 Hermitage in language so sensational that I hesitate to quote it directly, H. Warner Allen later regretted his early excess, saying that he had since drunk many bottles of Hermitage and of other wines and that "today I should be less extravagant in my eulogy." None of which is surprising, for though we look for subtleties and complex harmonies in most aged red wines as recompense for our patience in keeping them, my experience has been that the longevity of Hermitage is itself the chief attraction; the gradual but persistent ripening, on a sustained even note, is the aesthetic reward.

Like Falernian and Malmsey, Hermitage is a literary wine, one of legend and myth. With its southern exposure, rare in the Rhône Valley, the hill was first planted as a vineyard by the Greeks who traded along the valley from their settlement at Marseilles. By the time the Romans had made Vienne an important administrative post, the hill was already bearing the Syrah grapes still cultivated there, fanciful stories of this variety arriving from Persia in the knapsack of some errant medieval knight notwithstanding. The legend that the vines were planted (or replanted) by Saint Patrick himself is hardly credible; but Gaspard de Stérimberg's retirement there in 1224 to a hermitage that eventually gave the hill its name, is adequately documented, though the popular image of an ascetic soldier piously beating sword into plowshare to make wine flow from what was barren rock to the greater glory of God is at very least poetic exaggeration.

For a man seeking a life of self-denial and penitence, petitioning to possess the hill of Saint Christopher (as it was then called), which was already covered with vineyards that for over a thousand years had been reputed to produce the finest wines in France, was an unusual beginning. There must have been mutual, tacit understanding that he was, in fact, asking his due for services rendered the French crown in the barbaric crusade against the Albigensians, a barely disguised military destruction of the Languedoc to geld the powerful counts of Toulouse.

We can imagine how impressive Hermitage, then known as *vin de Tournon*, must have seemed at the time. Even during those centuries when most other red wines, made to be drunk within months of the vintage, were closer to our idea of a rosé, it is impossible that a wine made from Syrah grapes could have been anything other than solid and deep-colored. Louis XIV thought so highly of it that he included it in a gift to Charles II of England as evidence both of his affection and of the prestige of French wines; and other references show that, rare and expensive, it was regarded as the optimal wine in seventeenth-century Paris.

But it was the opening of the Canal du Midi in 1681, linking the Mediterranean and Bordeaux, that finally brought Hermitage to the tables of northern Europe. Before the end of the century, at least one grower had started to ship his wines by that route; and, doubtless in the same way, Lord Townsend, British ambassador to The Hague, brought a quantity to the cellar of his embassy, the first recorded purchase of Hermitage by an Englishman. The Earl of Bristol, an ardent collector of French wines, followed Townsend's example in 1714 (but then he had long been an admirer of Rhône wines, having purchased "Avignon" wine—possibly what today we would call Châteauneuf-du-Pape—as early as 1704). A 1760 Hermitage stole the show at the Paris Exhibition of 1862, and at the Vienna Exhibition of 1875 Henry Vizetelly said that Châteauneuf-du-Pape was hardly to be noticed, such was the dominance of Hermitage as far as Rhône wines were concerned.

But these days Hermitage is a wine more often talked about than tasted. Production is small, and the speed with which modern wine merchants travel usually takes them straight from the *negoçiants* of Burgundy to the cooperatives of the lower Rhône, with hardly a pause at Tain-l'Hermitage. Though almost as far from Orange, the commercial wine center of the southern Rhône, as from Beaune, Hermitage, with its handful of associated *appellations* in the forty-mile stretch from Vienne to Valence, is too often seen as merely an adjunct to the lower Rhône. But apart from differences of scale (the eight *appellations* together rarely give more than 2 percent of the total output of wine of the Rhône Valley), the grapes used, method of cultivation, soil, and climate are quite different from those farther downstream. The wines have almost nothing in common.

Hermitage and Crozes-Hermitage adjacent to it seem to be exceptions to a rule that all the fine wines of what the French call the *Rhône septentrional* are produced on the granitic bluffs of the west bank. They start with the red wines of Côte Rôtie, opposite Vienne, continue through the white wines of Condrieu and Château Grillet, include red and white wines under the *appellation* St. Joseph, and end, opposite Valence, with the interlocking *appellations* of Cornas for red wines and Saint-Péray for white. Actually, Hermitage is less an exception to this rule than at first appears. A gigantic lump of granite, the hill of Hermitage must have been separated from its original formation through some primordial cataclysm. Geologically it, too, belongs to the west bank. Crozes, on the other hand, mostly clay, is exactly where it should be, possibly explaining why the red and white wines of Saint-Joseph more closely resemble in style and quality the red and white wines of Hermitage, though separated by the breadth of the river, than do those of the neighboring vineyards of Crozes-Hermitage.

Saint-Joseph is grown on terraced vineyards that meander through the little river port of Tournon, with its old *château fort* facing Tain-l'Hermitage, and neighboring *communes*. The wines were always sold as *vin de Mauves*, the name of one of the communes, in the nineteenth century and enjoyed a high reputation. But that name was rejected when the communes had to agree on a joint *appellation* in 1956. Perhaps Glun and Lemps, two of the villages with names obviously bereft of sales appeal, resented the idea of continuing to play second fiddle to their exotically named neighbor. Whatever the reason for the choice, the unfamiliarity of the name Saint-Joseph has since been a commercial obstacle. Crozes-Hermitage, with the advantage of the suffix and its proximity to Hermitage, commands as high a price as a good Saint-Joseph, though rarely is it as distinguished. Red Crozes doesn't age well and is inclined to be clumsy when young.

All three *appellations* are based on the Syrah grape for their red wines, though the statutes tolerate a slight admission of the permitted white grapes, Roussanne and Marsanne. The Syrah is a low-yielding, fragile vine that grows supported by stakes fixed in tripods, the better to resist the fierce winds that roar down the Rhône Valley. The wine it gives, deeply colored and vigorously tannic, has an unmistakable aroma of violets when made from fully ripened grapes; but this becomes less intense in time, and the style and bouquet of the wine then vary according to origin. French growers distinguish between *petite* Syrah and *grosse* Syrah, the latter having the advantage of yield rather than quality. Neither is related to what is called the Petite Sirah in California. That vine is thought to have been most likely developed from a variety propagated in France by a Dr. Duriff and named for him in the 1880s. Related or not, there are powerful examples of the California Petite Sirah that share certain sturdy characteristics of northern Rhône wines (the Robert Mondavi Petite Sirah 1973 is one), giving hope for better things to come. One or two California growers, however, notably Joseph Phelps on the Silverado Trail in Napa, have a few acres of true Syrah that are beginning to bear. It remains to be seen what this grape will give in California: early examples of the wine are still too raw to judge.

Saint-Joseph, without quite the intensity or weight of Hermitage, comes close and shares its capacity for aging. Shortly before I enjoyed my unexpected 1962 Hermitage I had shared a bottle of 1962 Saint-Joseph, which, had I been able to taste it alongside the Hermitage, would have lost little in the comparison. Both are very direct wines that need to be matched to substantial dishes, and other wines served with them at the same meal should be equally uncomplicated.

Hermitage, Saint-Joseph, and even Crozes-Hermitage are more robust than the red wines from the other two *appellations* of this mini-region: Côte Rôtie and Cornas. Côte Rôtie is still tempered by a proportion of white Viognier grapes (the variety used on its own to make Condrieu and Château Grillet), but the practice is diminishing. In those two wines, Viognier gives a distinctive smell of hawthorn blossom, and in Côte Rôtie—as I noticed again recently when by lucky chance I found a bottle of *cru* La Garde 1973 on a restaurant list in a suburb of San Francisco—Viognier brings an aromatic strain as well as softening the style of the Syrah. The wine made a perfect match for a *suprême* of pheasant, where an Hermitage or even a Saint-Joseph might have been overpowering.

Cornas, which I used to drink often at the Beau Rivage at Condrieu, is made from Syrah grapes alone, but much of the territory of the *appellation* extends over pebbly terrain that was once the bed of a torrent draining the Vivarais hills into the Rhône. Whether for this reason or for some other, Cornas wines have always seemed to me to have briskness in youth, rather than the sometimes brutal harshness of a young Hermitage, and in age less denseness, softening almost to a point of sweetness. The last time I was at the Beau Rivage I had just such a 1966 Cornas, elegant though still rather out of scale for the *volaille au poivre vert* that I had mistakenly elected to eat with it. But I had already chalked up a perfect match of *rouget en papillote*, the Mediterranean red mullet that was an obsession with wealthy Romans in the early years of the Empire (obviously for good reason), and a 1976 Condrieu.

Condrieu and its appendix, Château Grillet (the only single *domaine* in France, and a handkerchief-size one at that, to have an *appellation* of its own), are white wines that stand apart. I have already mentioned their distinctive aroma of hawthorn flower; with a year or two in bottle it seems to intensify as the wine fills out—not that I recommend long aging for these wines. In London we imported Château Grillet regularly, and it was quite disappointing after a few years in bottle.

Though often dismissed as unimportant, and admittedly unpredictable in quality, the white wines of Hermitage and Crozes-Hermitage have given me much pleasure. The first bottle of wine I paid for with my own earned money was a 1947 Hermitage Blanc. I bought it in 1950 from the wine shop that stood on the corner of Old Compton Street in London, an adjunct to Kettner's restaurant. Perhaps that has prejudiced me in its favor. Sadly, there has been a deterioration in recent years caused by the persistent replacement of Roussanne vines, their small yield giving grapes with zest and flavor, by more prolific but milder Marsanne. Both varieties are permitted, and ideally each would contribute to a perfect balance. But if your favorite Hermitage Blanc now has less assertive flavor than once it did, and ages more rapidly than it should, you can be sure that the vineyard has converted largely to Marsanne. A fine Hermitage Blanc, with a year or two in bottle, should develop a bouquet that I liken to macadamia nuts and honey.

White Crozes-Hermitage, grown on heavier soil, is not just a secondary Hermitage but a different style of wine. It needs, in particular, a chance to aerate. What might at first seem a dumb, tired wine often opens miraculously after a few minutes in the glass and a slight raising of the temperature (white Rhône wines are usually served too cold: they should be chilled, not iced). A Crozes-Hermitage Les Meysonniers 1976 that I had in a restaurant near Chicago last fall, for example, after a very disappointing start opened up with an astonishing bouquet redolent of almonds and glazed fruits.

At Saint-Péray the Roussanne and Marsanne grapes give wine of much less character, most of it made to sparkle by fermentation in the bottle, the *méthode champenoise*. Wagner was fond of it and was said to be drinking it copiously while composing *Parsifal*. It cannot be relied upon to have the same effect on others.

Southern Rhône, Wine Cellar of France

MANY WINE BOOKS and restaurant lists present the wines of the Rhône Valley as a unity, and, if I once had difficulty in understanding, let alone appreciating, Hermitage and Châteauneuf-du-Pape, my problem stemmed, I am sure, from my confused attempts to taste a connection between the two. Eventually I realized that the northern Rhône has as much to do with the southern Rhône as either of them has with the unexceptional wines of Bugey in the elbow of the Rhône above Lyon or with the wines of the Valais—that stretch of the Rhône above Lake Geneva where vineyards on an arid mountainside are watered by melting snows through an intricate system of wooden conduits.

Some see the difference as just a matter of scale, because the small production of Hermitage, Côte Rôtie, and the rest of the northerly vineyards between Vienne and Valence bears no comparison with the massive output of the southern Rhône. Others dismiss the whole thing as a mere divergence of style, like the Côte de Beaune and Côte de Nuits in Burgundy or the Médoc and Saint-Emilion in Bordeaux. The difference is in fact much more stark.

Except for a traditional supplement of white Viognier grapes at Côte Rôtie, all the northern Rhône red wines are made from the

Syrah alone, a black grape well adapted to unstable weather and difficult terrain. It has been the principal, if not the sole, red wine grape in the northern Rhône since the fourth century and probably was brought there even earlier by Greeks trading pots for metals. Vigorously harsh when young, superb when aged, its wines require a measured investment of patience, a final effort of concentration, to be fully enjoyed. In short, they are wines for laying down; and that implies time, money, and a certain way of thinking about wine.

In the south, the bulk of the production is ordinary red Côtes du Rhône, though that should not obscure the considerable quantity of distinguished red wines, especially those of Gigondas and Châteauneuf-du-Pape. They are all wines that can be appreciated sooner than those of the north and are more easily approached, even when more alcoholic, as they frequently are. Softer, rounder, fruitier, these southern wines are made, unlike those of the north, from a cornucopia of grape varieties that are shared, often under other names, with neighboring regions and neighboring countries. Indeed, they could be more accurately described as wines of Provence, of the Mediterranean. When Keats called for a "beaker full of the warm South . . . With beaded bubbles winking at the brim," he was probably hoping for a glass of young Côtes du Rhône, still purple, drawn from the wood.

A matter of words—but a matter of perception and use, too. In the south the enjoyment of wine is direct. There is no long view or distant expectation, no time lost analyzing or discussing a wine that has failed in its immediate essential—to satisfy. Despite highways, tractors, and power presses, the Rhône delta is an antique world where a bottle of wine is, after all, a bottle of wine. This unpretentiously serious local attitude led first to respect for a wine's natural origin, and from that the phenomenon of controlled geographic *appellations* developed in France. It was Baron Le Roy of Châteauneuf-du-Pape who initiated both the idea and the apparatus for putting it into effect. Ironically, the same down-to-earth view that wine is, well, wine, within two years extended the region's principal controlled *appellation*, Côtes du Rhône (which in 1935 defined the hill vineyards where wines had a distinction that was worth recognizing and preserving), to the plain between Orange and Avignon, land from which the wine is certainly drinkable but not the sort, if I might paraphrase Dr. Johnson, that one would *ask* a man to. It is this dilemma of reconciling the huge volume of sound, everyday wines—an achievement, I agree, that must contribute more to the total sum of human pleasure than does the sublime but minute quantity of, say, Richebourg—with the limited production of quality wines that causes problems for both growers and consumers. In fact, the lower Rhône, as the smug and simplistic phrase of our time would have it, has an identity problem.

The region I refer to starts in the *département* of the Drôme, extends south over most of the Vaucluse and then westward across the Rhône into the Gard. From above Bollène (though at that point there is hardly a vine to be seen from the *autoroute*) to below Avignon vineyards stretch east and west. To the east, they cover the alluvial plain, interspersed with orchards and market gardens, fill valleys, and spread over hills. They climb the slope of Mont Ventoux itself, a mountain dominating the area, as near perfect in its symmetry as Fuji. To the west of the Rhône, the vineyards reach the limits of the *garrigue*, the first tormented abutments of the Massif Central, where they merge with even vaster plantings of hybrids used for the nameless table wines of French grocery stores. In both directions the landscape has been molded by millennia of waters flowing from the pre-Alps on one side and the Cévennes on the other. Their deposits of pebble and rock, sand and clay have left a terrain so variable that uniformity of soil, even within one vineyard, is impossible to find.

In his classic ampelography, *Cépages et Vignobles de France*, Professor Galet of the University of Montpellier rationally breaks down the Vaucluse into seven principal areas and numerous subdivisions, let alone the extensions of the region into the Drôme and the Gard. For those whose interest is more general, the lower Rhône can be imagined as a lopsided, very irregular saucer with a slight rise in the center. To the northeast, vineyards cover the last spurs of the pre-Alps, descending to the river Aigues at Sérignan and Sainte Cécile-les-Vignes; to the east, beyond the Ouvèze river, a chalky bench extends from Mont Ventoux and the heights of Montmirail to support the sometimes gravelly, sometimes sandy, vineyards of Gigondas, Vacqueyras, Séguret, and Sablet.

Extending further east beyond Gigondas and Vacqueyras, the vineyards of Mont Ventoux could be said to start at Beaumes-de-Venise, a *commune* producing delicious Muscat dessert wine as well as robust reds. Soon after, they start to climb, hectare after hectare,

to surround Puyméras, Mormoiron, and a score of other old villages, all of pale gray stones and faded stucco under worn, terra-
cotta tiles. Their grapes are used to produce rosy-red wines,
the mainstay of French cafés. Traditionally juice and skins are left
to ferment together only overnight to make a soft, fruity, light red
wine called, appropriately enough, *vin d'une nuit*. At Flassan, on
the mountain, there is an inn where the wine can be drunk by the
liter with locally cured ham and sausage. There might also be some
grisets de Ventoux (wild mushrooms sautéed with garlic and oil),
the thyme-scented thrush pâté of the region, and, if the proprietor
has been lucky, a *civet de lièvre*.

To the southeast are the hills of Gardagne, producing red wines
that were equated more than a century ago with the wines of
Châteauneuf, and behind them the Lubéron, where some indifferent
white wine is made; to the west across the Rhône, the cliff of
Roquemaure at the end of the bridge appears to defend the vineyard slopes of Tavel and Lirac; and to the northwest are the series
of slopes that make up the vineyards of Saint Gervais, Chusclan,
and Laudun. In the middle is the plain of the Comtat Venaissin,
papal land until the eighteenth century. It spreads from Orange
and Avignon east to the plane tree–shaded villages of Travaillan,
Violès, and Jonquières and reaches into the lower valleys of the
Aigues and Ouvèze.

Châteauneuf-du-Pape is set on a rise in the center, and its vineyards are often referred to as covering a series of hills. In fact, the
terrain is more like an undulating plateau, thickly covered with
characteristic stones, round as pebbles and large and smooth as
ostrich eggs.

The average vineyard holding in the lower Rhône is twenty-five
acres, but thousands of growers, certainly the majority, have fewer
than five. Because ordinary red Côtes du Rhône sells at prices that
barely cover the rudimentary costs of cultivation, such small growers work at other crops and other jobs in addition to tending their
vines. It would make little sense for them to be equipped for winemaking when their production is so small, and more than 70 percent
of the grapes are taken to communal wineries.

The banding of small vineyard proprietors into cooperatives has
been the strength and the bane of the region since it was resurrected
after the phylloxera devastation of the late nineteenth century.
Most have efficient, modern installations, professionally trained per-

sonnel, and the capacity to allow wine of consistent quality to be offered to large distributors. Some cooperatives, depending on the force of personality of the director as much as anything else, work with their members much as do California wineries with contracted growers, imposing vineyard and cropping standards, dictating the when and what of treatments, and deciding picking dates. They often use a system of bonus payments to encourage the planting of varieties that will improve the cooperative product.

Yet other cooperatives seem unable or unwilling to combat the apathy of their growers, who, removed from the personal ritual of making their own wine, find no satisfaction in the tens of thousands of hectoliters that issue from a winery to which each might have delivered his scant twenty tons of grapes. In such circumstances there can be no engagement of pride to inhibit pushing grape yields as far as the law will allow. This heavy cropping, especially when it occurs in the plain, almost inevitably lowers quality and swells supply. As a result, though sales of Rhône wines increase steadily, residual stocks have increased even faster. Despite inflation in France, winery bulk prices for Côtes du Rhône, the kind that is sold by the tankload to merchant-bottlers, slipped again in 1980 by as much as 10 percent compared with the previous year.

The tragedy (from the conscientious growers' point of view) is that all Côtes du Rhône prices are held down by the pressure of the quantity of ordinary wine. The market makes little price distinction between the unimpressive product of some cooperatives and the quality wines produced by others, not to mention the many private estates. That is why Côtes du Rhône wines tend to be underpriced and exceptional value can be found if discrimination is used.

The best are still those from areas that were first accorded the Côtes du Rhône *appellation* in 1935. In an attempt to restore something of the distinction recognized at that time, those wines are now entitled to use the superior *appellation* Côtes du Rhône Villages or to link their basic Côtes du Rhône *appellation* with village names such as Côtes du Rhône Vacqueyras or Côtes du Rhône Beaumes-de-Venise. (The village name Beaumes-de-Venise used alone, incidentally, is the *appellation* of the Muscat dessert wine produced there, not to be confused with its red table wine.) The *communes* concerned agree to stricter controls of vine varieties used, yields permitted, and minimum alcohol levels in the wines, a rough-and-ready indicator of grape maturity and quality at time of picking. Some *communes*, in addition to Châteauneuf-du-Pape, which had it from the beginning, have earned separate controlled *appellation* status: Gigondas, Lirac, and Tavel, the last for its rosés.

In this part of France, stricter control of vine varieties usually means eliminating or severely restricting the Carignan grape, a variety about which there is much ambivalence. Most basic Côtes du Rhône is made from a combination of Grenache and Carignan. To see these two vines together is to sense right away the contrasting wine that each will produce. The Grenache is luxuriant. Its smoothly shaped leaves, barely indented, protect large, floppy bunches of grapes. The rough, jagged leaves of the Carignan, on the other hand, are sharply indented, and its grapes are small and tightly compact. As one might expect, Grenache wine is structurally loose: high in alcohol, low in flavor, and dangerously quick to age. Carignan wine is hard, sometimes sharp, even bitter; it brings a tough, coarse element to blends even while adding stamina to an otherwise flabby Grenache. For this reason the Côtes du Rhône and the Côtes du Rhône Villages *appellation* statutes limit the quantities of Carignan that may legally be used. At Lirac and Tavel, it is allowed but discouraged; at Gigondas and Châteauneuf-du-Pape, it is not permitted at all.

That is all very well, but Grenache, if used alone, would be short of flavor and acidity as a young wine and lack backbone for aging. Apart from Carignan, however, there are eleven allowable varieties, some of which, in combination, can provide the necessary balance. Certain varieties are even compulsory now, though most are only acknowledged or merely tolerated. The two most widely encouraged, to give balance to local red wines, are Cinsault for its young, fresh bite and perfumed aroma, and Syrah, the grape of the northern Rhône, for its depth of flavor and its aging potential; most of the other grapes dutifully listed in all the texts—the Bourboulenc, Picpoul, Picardan, Vacarèse, and so on—have probably caused more ink to flow than wine. Their use is less than might be supposed, though every grower will claim that this or that nuance in his wine is due to a row or two of some obscure variety. Châteauneuf-du-Pape and Gigondas rely on ancillary varieties (especially Mourvèdre) more than do most other *communes*, and a firmer, richer, headier style is the result.

Growers at Châteauneuf-du-Pape experimented for a while in

the 1960s with fermentation techniques that made their wine more supple and faster maturing. But the characteristic force of a classic Châteauneuf-du-Pape was exactly what most enthusiasts wanted, and there has since been a complete return to the full-bodied style introduced by the Marquis de la Nerthe in the early 1800s, after centuries during which Châteauneuf-du-Pape had been neglected. De la Nerthe was notorious (and envied) for an erotic life that continued to an unprecedented and unseemly age. He claimed that the wine produced at his vineyard at Châteauneuf-du-Pape was "an elixir for prolonging youth and even life itself." His widespread reputation probably contributed in a small way to the revival of Châteauneuf-du-Pape's popularity during the last century, but his is not a claim that should be relied on in all circumstances.

Wherever red Côtes du Rhône is made, some rosé wine will be found, but the best is grown on the west bank. Using a high proportion of the elegant Cinsault with their heady Grenache, the growers of Tavel, for example, have succeeded in developing a rosé that has for long been a benchmark. It combines warmth and finesse to a rare degree and at its best has a sustained flavor that lifts it almost to the level of the great classics. Lirac, an *appellation* that covers four *communes*, produces a rosé that is almost indistinguishable from Tavel, but in the last ten years the growers have veered increasingly toward the production of red. Due to the emphasis on Cinsault in their grape proportions, however, even the red wines of Lirac are unusually aromatic when young and are elegantly structured. Chusclan, too, produces a good rosé, though heavier and less subtle than that of either Tavel or Lirac. Perhaps the grape mix is different. (The cooperative at Chusclan is one of the most efficient in the region.) At Laudun, one of the four *communes* first to be given the superior Côtes du Rhône Villages *appellation* in 1953, there is little rosé but some of the freshest and cleanest of the limited white wine production of the lower Rhône. Most other white wines of the region, I am sorry to say, are neutral at best and age too quickly to make them of interest for shipment overseas.

Though some years are especially memorable for their quality (in the last decade this is particularly true of 1971, despite a difficult flowering, and of 1978), the lower Rhône has less dramatic variation from year to year than does, say, Burgundy. In 1980, for example, a problematic year for much of France, the lower Rhône was conspicuously successful, and one of the finest bottles of

Châteauneuf-du-Pape that I have enjoyed recently was a 1977 (as difficult a year in the Rhône as it was in the rest of France) from the Clos de l'Oratoire des Papes. I drank it from a half bottle, in fact, when lunching alone at a restaurant in Châteauneuf-du-Pape itself. There was a bitterly cold mistral outside, and with my *boeuf carmargais*, nothing could have been more restoring. The wine was richly colored and wonderfully full on nose and palate, smoothly balanced, imposing but neither heavy nor overbearing. Rhône wines, in fact, seem to me always to have just such a rich, autumnal quality appropriate to the "season of mists and mellow fruitfulness." So I wouldn't complain exactly if I were to find a forgotten case of that Clos de l'Oratoire in my cellar when the days start to shorten.

Graceful Wines
of Alsace

ITH A PILGRIMAGE to the Auberge de l'Ill at Illhaeusern almost mandatory these days, one might have thought that exposure to the refinement of the Haeberlin's kitchen and cellar would have converted more Americans to the wines of Alsace. If it has, the effect is hardly noticeable.

Although shipments of Alsace wines to the United States in 1977 and 1978 rose to almost 60,000 cases a year from a mere 40,000 cases in 1976, they have slumped back again in 1981—a consequence, I suppose, of the currently fashionable view that French wines are expensive. If it puzzles me that a frost or a storm in Bordeaux can lead some to assume the vintage ruined all over France, I am even more bewildered by those who allow the price of Pouilly-Fuissé to deprive them of moderately priced Rieslings and aromatic Gewürztraminers.

Those French wines that reach dizzy prices do so because they have a low production combined with an exaggeratedly high profile. In an abundant year, Pouilly-Fuissé produces 300,000 cases at best: not much to satisfy a thirsty world. But even in 1978, one of the smallest crops of the decade, Alsace produced 7 *million* cases of dry, fragrant, reasonably priced wine. It is difficult to understand why they don't do better here. To start with, the bulk of production—almost 100 percent of it—is white, at a time when there seems never to be enough white wine to go around; the labeling is probably the simplest to understand and re-member among all French wines, based as it is on grape variety rather than on a complicated hierarchy of classified vineyards; the wines themselves—light, fruity, and dry—are very much to the taste of most Americans today; and the Comité Interprofessionnel du Vin d'Alsace (Committee of Growers and Shippers) has worked persistently over the years to show and explain its wines to the retailers of America.

The switchback history of Alsace during the past hundred years—from France to Germany to France to Germany and, finally, to France again—made it difficult for the region to enjoy the expanding reputation of other French wines during that period. The prestige it had in the sixteenth century, when its wines were the most prized in northern Europe (even Shakespeare had nice things to say about them), was lost in the appalling destruction of the Thirty Years' War, which culminated in Alsace being absorbed into the French kingdom of Louis XIV. Since 1918, and especially since 1945, the growers have followed a policy of improving and controlling quality that has been more rigorously self-enforced than that of any other wine region of France. Alsatians have had to work harder than those who could fall back on long familiar names of local classed growths or use the reflected glamour of a handful of aristocratic estates.

Although popularly associated with the Rhine (and for that reason often confused with the wine regions of Germany), the vineyards of Alsace are some twenty miles distant. Thirty thousand acres of them stretch for more than sixty miles from Marlenheim, near Strasbourg, in the north to Thann in the south, mostly on the lower slopes of the Vosges and more intimately connected with, and dependent on, the climate and terrain of the mountains than that of the riverbank. The Rhine, where it borders Alsace, is wide and shallow and was barely navigable until the Germans deepened and embanked it in the late nineteenth century. Frequent flooding had deterred settlement, and, except for the rare bridgehead (such as Strasbourg), towns and villages grew up at a safe distance from the water, usually on higher ground.

To the east beyond the Rhine, the massive Black Forest protects the towns and vineyards of Alsace from bleak east winds; and to the west the Vosges themselves, though seeming little more than a decorative crest when approached across the long, gentle tilt of the Lorraine plateau, provide a barrier to the Atlantic storms that sweep across northern France. Rainfall in Alsace is barely a quarter of what it is on the western side of the Vosges: Colmar is the driest town in France.

The long strip of vineyards mostly faces east, catching the morning sun, but growers take advantage of every thrusting knoll that might give a southeasterly or even a southern exposure to the vines. A complicated geological history has given them a variety of soils, unusual in such a compact zone. At Turckheim and Wintzenheim, for example, there are granitic terraces side by side with calcareous strips; sandstone and schist lie next to limestone and marl at Riquewihr; and throughout there are scattered layers of loess, the yellowish-gray loam for which the Rhine Valley is known. These chaotic soil patterns and the microclimates of the mountain folds have taught growers to match carefully each vine variety to a parcel of land best suited to it. In summer, when the vines are uniformly green, the subtle complications of this patchwork are difficult to discern, but in the fall, when each variety of vine changes color at its own pace and to its own autumnal shade, the slopes become a vast and brilliant tapestry.

An Alsace wine is identified by the grape variety from which it is made. Sylvaner is the grape most widely planted (more than a quarter of all bearing vineyards). Though not the most robust of vines, it produces regular and reasonably abundant crops that ripen late, an advantage in a region where dry and sunny autumns permit a late harvest. Sylvaner wines are mild, with freshness (and therefore youth) their chief quality; nevertheless, the grapes grown on the slope rather than on the plain can display a firm character more usually associated with Riesling wines.

The Riesling, most distinguished of the Alsace varieties, ripens latest of all. It continues to mature even in poor weather, which is why it lends itself to late harvest pickings wherever it is grown. With consistent yield, when grown on favored sites it will give wines of unmatched elegance and depth of flavor.

The variety most closely associated with Alsace, however, is the Gewürztraminer, an early-ripening grape descended from the old Traminer Rosé, first introduced about a century ago and now one of the most popular varieties. When picked at the precise moment of maturity, Gewürztraminer grapes give a wine of intense aroma and full flavor, more reminiscent of an old-fashioned damask rose than of spice. After these three classic varieties, the Pinot Blanc is presently spreading in Alsace because extensions to the vineyard are on the plain rather than the slope, and there Pinot Blanc is preferred. In cold soils it ripens more easily than either Riesling or Gewürztraminer and yet gives wines of more substance than Sylvaner.

The Chasselas of Alsace, one important for carafe wines, is disappearing. In the past ten years the acreage has dwindled to less than half. Pinot Gris, giving wine once more commonly (and confusingly) labeled Tokay d'Alsace, is grown only on a small scale in Alsace. The grapes ripen early and give wine that combines the characteristic intense fruitiness of Alsace with the body and softness of a Côte d'Or Burgundy. Though usually dry, in some years, contrary to normal practice in Alsace, it can retain a little residual sugar. I remember a Pinot Gris of the 1967 vintage (one of the great years of Alsace) with a slightly sweet finish that went perfectly with the roast veal and glazed carrots a grower served me for lunch a few years back. (On that same day, again contrary to what one is told about Alsace wines always being fermented dry, the grower served me a Special Reserve 1967 Gewürztraminer with 13.5 percent alcohol and 4.9 percent residual sugar. We drank it with an apple tart warm from the oven. I was in heaven.) A small amount of Pinot Noir is grown for the production of rosé.

Of all varieties, however, the most surprising to those unfamiliar with Alsace is Muscat d'Alsace. Whether made from the early-ripening Muscat d'Ottonel or the more intense Muscat à Petits Grains, a very late ripener, the wine is always dry and light, unexpected after such a beguiling aroma. Muscat d'Alsace makes an excellent apéritif.

Zwicker, or Edelzwicker, describes wine made from a blend of grape varieties. There was once a distinction between the two words based on the fact that Chasselas could be admitted into the blend of a Zwicker but not into an Edelzwicker. That distinction has now been dropped, and the shorter version will probably disappear.

Those who visit Alsace will find a carefully signposted Route du Vin passing through all the wine villages. It runs along the lower slope past the vineyards so that one can see close at hand the high training of the vines—to six feet or more—and the pitch of the vineyards, some so steep that cultivation must be done by hand or by winch rather than with tractor and plow. Though repeatedly battered by wars (there was not a doorpost standing in Bennwihr after a particularly fierce engagement between American and German troops in 1944), most towns and villages retain at least a few old houses, a church with stork nest on the steeple, or medieval fortifications. Dambach, with picturesque gateways and gabled houses; Barr, with its Renaissance mansions; and Riquewihr, with a mixture of Baroque and high Middle Ages, are enchanting places to visit. Less obvious, and maybe for that reason even more captivating, is the walled town of Turckheim, where one can walk round the old ramparts.

These towns and villages exude domestic order, well-being, and abundance. Gardens overflow with flowers, trees are heavy with fruit, and the dogs are sleepy. From kitchen windows the smell of cooking is rich and succulent: goose fat and cabbage, chicken poaching in Riesling, quetsch tarts. Alsatians like to eat well.

They like to drink well, too, their wines always cool but not too cool for fear of stunning the "fruit." They use the word in a special way. To others, "fruit" might mean the general redolence of fruit in the developed bouquet and flavor of a mature wine. But to Alsatians it means the aroma and flavor of a particular variety: they expect to find it again in the wine, transmuted and intensified, perhaps, but clearly identifiable. The better to enjoy it, they serve their wines in careful sequence, leading from light, discreet Sylvaners to assertive Rieslings before heady Gewürztraminers. The wines are versatile and adapt well, but each is matched to an appropriate dish. Sylvaner, young and fragrant, perfect with a savory quiche or an onion tart, mild ham or boiled sausage. Pinot Blanc, with more body, is good with *charcuterie*; but the richer texture of a pâté, especially foie gras, needs the full flavor of a Tokay d'Alsace or even a Gewürztraminer. Riesling is a natural partner for fish, especially from river or lake. Choose a *réserve* Riesling, or one from a big year like 1976, when the wine must balance a creamy sauce, yet notice how even a modest Riesling will bring out the hazelnut flavor of a freshly caught trout.

The style of Alsace wine is unlikely to change, but we might soon see unfamiliar words on the label. The spread of vineyards onto the plain has met resistance from those who feel that quality could be threatened, and there is talk of a compromise that will give a separate *appellation* to such lesser wines. At the other extreme, the words *grand cru*, used in the past to denote an exceptional wine, will soon be reserved for wines from specific, designated vineyard sites, rather like the *crus* of Burgundy. The Schlossberg near Kientzheim, for example, and the Rebgarten at Bennwihr are expected to be among the first. This new direction is not supported unanimously by the committee of growers and shippers. Some members argue that simplicity of *appellation* has been their strength. But others glance covetously at the complicated panoply of classifications in Bordeaux and Burgundy and reflect that, at least as far as the United States market is concerned, simplicity hasn't got them very far.

Bandol: A Personal Preference

THERE IS a point on Route Nationale 7 between Avignon and Aix-en-Provence where a slight rise leads through a cutting. Especially on a summer evening, it is here that a traveler on the road from Paris first breathes the air of the Mediterranean. I drive through that gap with a sense of release, of entering a world more languid yet more ardent, more elegant yet more sensuous, more intelligent yet more frivolous, with priorities ranged in good-humored perspective.

Along with the scent of thyme and pine, memories flow through the open car windows: familiar hilltop villages, buffeted by wind and bleached by sun, fade into visions of herb and lemon stalls in the Toulon street markets; images of fishermen at Sanary-sur-Mer, unloading their catch for early-morning sale under the manicured palms that surround, at a respectful distance, the very proper town bandstand, merge with remembrances of lazy afternoons on the beach at Les Lecques, shared, of course, with half the population of Marseilles, and memories of fresh-caught sardines grilled on the embers of vine cuttings at the kitchen door of the Peyrauds' house. Yes, above all, I think Mediterranean means to me the Peyrauds' house, the most loving and serene of ships, comfortably adrift in a sea of vines. Plain and gray, like many another Provençal *mas*, it speaks contentment, less in its signs of mellow calm—the patina of crumbled stucco and faded window shutters—than in the message of a child's worn swing that hangs from a lopsided cherry tree, in the umbrella pine that doubles as an outdoor family *salon*, protecting an old millstone table and a clutter of dusty wooden chairs from the late afternoon sun, in the ancient vine that curls over the west front of the house and covers an uneven brick terrace with a shady green canopy, and in the wide front door with its fist-size key.

One evening in early summer, a few years back, I took the familiar turn off the highway at Le Canet, through the hills of Le Beausset, and then followed the narrow, high-banked road that leads to Le Plan-du-Castellet, to the Peyrauds'. The drive from Paris is long, and it was almost nine o'clock when the noise of the engine and the barking of the dogs brought the family out to greet me. There were Lucie and Lucien Peyraud (it is strange that two such names should come together, like the shepherd and shepherdess in an early Mozart opera); their sons, François and Jean-Marie; their sons' wives, Catherine and Paule; Veronique, the last daughter to remain at home; and in the background, shyly, some sleepy grandchildren. With a glass of Champagne we crossed the year that had elapsed since we had last seen each other, and by the time we went into the dining room it was as if I had left them only yesterday.

Lucie Tempier Peyraud is known to everyone as Lulu. Descended from a line of Marseilles merchants, she inherited this country *mas*, the Domaine Tempier, originally built for her great-great-grandmother. The vineyards around it, mostly spilling down narrow, terraced ledges that the labor of centuries created, were destroyed by phylloxera about a hundred years ago, and their replanting and regeneration has been an act of faith and courage. Lucien Peyraud's devotion to the Tempier vineyards is almost mystical, as if in marrying Lulu he had also married these few scattered acres that remain attached to their steep hillsides only through the will of God and backbreaking work on the supporting terrace walls. Some of the ledges, rarely more than thirty or forty yards long, are so narrow that they can hold only a row or two of vines each, and most of the cultivation must be done by hand. His face and hands roughened by sun and wind, Lucien Peyraud is a down-to-earth man if ever there was one, yet he is as proud and tender in his regard for his vines as any father for his child. No other vineyard I know is nourished by passion to equal his.

The wine region of Bandol is one of the oldest is France. We can be certain that the Greeks, whose settlements led to the founding of the cities of Marseilles and Nice, brought vines and planted them where they seemed most likely to flourish. They undoubtedly saw, as we still can see today, that the hills above the bay of Bandol, quite close to Marseilles, form an arena protected by the mountains behind them. Here, vine-covered slopes face south and benefit from the clear sunlight reflected off the sea, as well as from the tempering effect of the water.

There is evidence of trading in Bandol wines as far back as Roman times. Wine jars, or fragments of them, continually turn up in the nets of local fishermen, and in a geography of Provence, published in 1787, the region was lauded for its red wines "of first quality . . . mostly highly prized. They sum up quite simply the real virtues of the Provençal soil and its products: honesty, finesse and ardour." By the mid-nineteenth century wines from all the villages that surround the port were being shipped to markets as far away as Brazil and India. Just as Bordeaux—on a much grander scale, of course—gave its name to the whole region that shipped from its quays, so Bandol gave its name to the wines of La Cadière-d'Azur, Le Plan-du-Castellet, Le Castellet, Le Beausset, Saint-Cyr-sur-Mer, Sanary-sur-Mer, Ollioules, Le Brulat and Sainte-Anne-d'Evenos. It is impossible to say whether the million gallons of wine exported each year by the close of the Second Empire were all Bandol in the sense that the *appellation* is defined today, but the region, if fully planted, is capable of producing that much wine. In 1941, when a decree officially granted Bandol growers their own *appellation contrôlée*, annual production of wine from the entire area had dropped to barely 30,000 cases. Production in 1981 was about 300,000 cases of red, rosé, and white wines, from the vineyards of some two hundred small growers—a fragmented, but very personal, wine region.

There was, and is, very little white wine. In that climate it is difficult to produce the crispness that one would most want. Clairette and Ugni Blanc grapes are used, primarily for wines to be consumed by the grower's family. Oddly enough, the fishing village of Cassis, only a few miles away, manages to produce a quite passable white wine from the same grapes; but then the deep *calanques* that bring cool sea air well into the hillsides there probably help. The best white wine of Bandol that I remember was from Château Milhière, near Sanary, a vineyard now threatened with extinction by the spread of grotesque little villas. Monsieur Roethlisberger, a Swiss winegrower, had brought a light touch with white wines from his native Alpine vineyards and until his death produced wines of delicacy and flavor.

The rosés, found in every good restaurant from Marseilles to Nice, have more character than most others and are superior to the general run of Provence rosés. Over the years that I shipped them regularly to London—where they met with some success— I found that, though delicious when young, they aged well, developing an aroma of ripe pears. Ranging from the heavy, tannic wines of Château Pradeaux at Saint-Cyr to the racy, elegant wines of Lucien Peyraud at the Domaine Tempier, the reds are obviously in a class with wines from far more distinguished regions. They repay keeping.

Grenache vines are common throughout the south, and are as important in Bandol as they are at nearby Châteauneuf-du-Pape and Gigondas. Important, too, is the Cinsault vine, thought, because of its country name of *le romain*, to have been brought to the region by some wandering centurion. These two varieties are the basis of the rosé wines of Bandol, but small patches of the uncommon Tibouren or the local Pécoui-Touar are to be found here and there, adding a more subtle strain of flavor.

The special quality of the reds is due entirely to the Mourvèdre and its adaptation to the particular conditions of Bandol. It is a variety of vine that spread through southern France from the Mediterranean coast of Spain during the Middle Ages. In most areas its popularity was short-lived. Though vigorous in growth, it is low in yield; and the wine, deep-colored and tannic, has an intense personality that needs careful aging to give of its best. There are Mourvèdre vines at Châteauneuf-du-Pape and even as far away as Cognac in the Charentes (where it has the inexplicable name of Balzac Noir), but it seems to have found its natural home in the band of chalk and silica that runs through the Bandol hills. In most cases I have found that the quality of any red wine of Bandol can be directly related to the proportion of Mourvèdre in the vineyard. The *appellation* law has established that, of the vine varieties permitted, a minimum of 10 percent must be Mourvèdre;

and although a wine made entirely from Mourvèdre grapes might be overwhelming in scale even when mature, I am certain that the basis of Lucien Peyraud's quality is the sacrifice he makes to maintain such a high proportion of these vines, difficult and ungenerous though he knows them to be.

Altitude also affects the quality of the wine, but whether this is a result of the greater exposure to sunlight, the cooling effect of the breezes, or the more arid spare soils one finds on the hilltops, I wouldn't like to say. Perhaps it is a combination of all three. Lucien ferments separately the grapes from each small lot of vines, eventually blending them to produce a uniform wine for each vintage. Checking the young wines with him, noting the differences of character and style that mark each one, is an exciting experience. At a tasting the morning after my arrival, a colleague traveling with me, a man whose training and experience had been in the wider acres of California, was astounded at the family's care to preserve every nuance of their wines and at their familiarity with the shading of taste that each small terrace brings.

Before dinner that night we drank a neighbor's white wine because Lucien doesn't produce one. With it we ate the typical hors d'oeuvre of Provence: cold spinach omelet, purée of eggplant, *tapenade* of olive and anchovy. They were followed by a superb *mérou*, a Mediterranean fish related to the grouper, gently poached and served simply with lemon and a fruity olive oil as sauce. Lucien produced a rosé in an unfamiliar bottle. It was from Bellet, a village above Nice possessing one of the few other *appellations contrôlées* in the south of France. It was at least fifteen years since I had last tasted one, on a visit to that very village, to the personal vineyard of a prosperous Nice wine merchant. Standing at the roadside near his house, I had seen how the suburbs of Nice were poised to engulf his vines. The wine, as I remember it, artfully packaged in a dumpy bottle with gold thread around it, was among the less distinguished wines that I have tasted; and, though it might seem uncharitable, I was able to contemplate its possible end without feeling much distress.

But here was a wine from Bellet from a grower I hadn't known of, a wine that showed why this tiny enclave of vines had been recognized with an *appellation* of its own in the first place. It was delicately fruity, crisply dry, and with a fresh, lingering aftertaste. It was lighter than most of the Bandol rosés, which, though not particularly alcoholic, seem to have a richness of glycerin that gives them a muscular, full-bodied style.

Lucien followed the rosé with both the 1969 and 1970 reds of the Domaine Tempier, while Lulu produced a leg of lamb, fragrant with garlic and pungent herbs of the *garrigue*, to accompany them. The 1969, with which I was already familiar thanks to a small stock at home in San Francisco, was one of Lucien's most elegant wines—dark, with a bouquet that I found, perhaps fancifully, to have an echo of the thyme and pine perfume of those hills. Well balanced, it was soft enough to enjoy and zesty enough to promise pleasure for quite some time. The 1970, which I had previously tasted only in wood, was a bigger wine, heavier than the 1969, less revealing in bouquet and flavor, its youthful tannin still quite bold. We preferred first the pleasure of one, then the promise of the other, and then weren't sure, and went on tasting and talking and nibbling at fresh little Banon cheeses that had appeared on the table. Nobody noticed how late it was getting to be.

Wine of Holy Satyrs: Sancerre

I N THE EARLY 1950s in London, no serious merchant would have
considered buying a wine until it had completed its first year in
wood and could be evaluated calmly. Bordeaux might have to
make up its mind sooner, but London rarely made a commitment
to a vintage until the following autumn.

The frosts of 1956 changed all that. Shortages became so acute
(or we thought they were so acute) that London importers were
persuaded to buy their wines on the vine, contracting for quantities mostly, but not only, of the classed growths before the grapes
were visible, let alone transformed into wine.

Though it reduced a skilled trade to the level of dealing in
pork-belly futures, the growers, impoverished by the war years
and the low prices paid in the period after them, were compelled
to do business as best they could while they financed the replanting
of their devastated vineyards. Smaller crops and reduced income
deprived them of the means to carry a crop on the field, let alone
two vintages in wood in the *chais*. Needless to say, with pounds
sterling maturing on Cabernet vines in the Médoc, the weather
in southwestern France became a subject of passionate interest in
London; even members of the British wine trade on Scottish moors
in September were less perturbed by the thought of a storm inter-

fering with a day's shooting than they were by news of a light shower a thousand miles away in Bordeaux.

Once the growers had overcome their need for an accelerated cash flow, the practice of such early buying largely disappeared. But there was never a return to the slower, more patient ways in which the trade had taken a year to reach its conclusion about a vintage. In those earlier days, I should add, wines that *had* to be judged sooner—especially some of the lighter whites that often needed drinking within the year, let alone assessing—were largely ignored as unimportant, or dismissed with that catchall phrase, "Won't travel, old boy."

Now, whether the wine is for early shipping or for long keeping, international merchants make their buying decisions at the first round of tastings, once the initial rackings from the murk of heavy lees just make possible a notion of quality and future style. In January and February—and sometimes even before Christmas—the side roads of France are filled with merchants, scurrying under leafless trees to be the first at the best barrel. Young red wines, rude with tannin, and whites that have lost their grapiness and have not yet recomposed themselves are hardly prescribed drinking on a frosty morning: there is much of absorbing interest but little of sybaritic delight in these wintry jaunts.

What a relief it is, then, to arrive at Sancerre, where, no matter how young, the wines seem always to be tender and delightful. Even a cold cellar on a raw February day cannot spoil the pleasure of these young Sauvignon Blanc wines. They shimmer with aroma and flavor, recalling first a ripe white peach, then perhaps a whiff of caraway or a smoky hint of gunpowder. Sancerre is so close to Paris—hardly more than a hundred miles—that I usually make it the last stop on a long trip round the wine regions, a reward for all that has gone before.

Isolated on a low hill that nevertheless dominates the Loire at this point, the town is some distance from the folds of hills surrounding it. Those hills were covered with vines before the Romans arrived in the wake of Julius Caesar, and over the centuries references to Sancerre wines have been frequent enough to show that their delicacy is no new phenomenon.

The Sauvignon Blanc grape is thought to have originated there in the Middle Ages and later to have spread to Bordeaux rather than the other way around. Monks of the neighboring Abbey of

Saint-Satur, active in viticultural experiments almost a thousand years ago, probably made the selection of cuttings that led to the varietal grape as we know it today. (The name Saint-Satur, incidentally, is linked to the Roman name for Sancerre itself, *castrum sancti satyri*, "fort of the holy satyrs," an appropriately Dionysiac reference in a region noted for its vines and its goats, but one that it might be tactless to examine too closely.)

For those who like comfort and rather grand food, the elegant Auberge des Templiers at Les Bézards, about thirty miles north of Sancerre, will offer every luxury, including the opportunity to taste Sancerre wines from some of the best producers. But I prefer a modest inn in Saint-Thibault, the village by the Loire at the foot of the Sancerre hill, where the rooms are small if pleasant, and where there is a particular pleasure in coming downstairs to home-made jams and fresh croissants in the cozy bar *cum* parlor.

As is so often the case in France, the *appellation* Sancerre doesn't belong just to the town of that name. Wines grown in some parts of at least a dozen adjoining *communes* are entitled to it, too, but vineyards are important in only seven of them. Overall, there are about 3,000 acres planted with vines and entitled to the *appellation*, compared with barely 1,000 twenty-five years ago. And where there was, perhaps, an annual production of 100,000 cases in the 1950s, Sancerre now produces 400,000 to 500,000 cases of wine every year. It seems a lot, but such is the demand in Paris alone that there is never enough, and scarcity is aggravated by the scale of the growers' holdings—an average of two acres of vines each, and that usually split into at least ten tiny parcels scattered over a hillside and, on occasion, over two or three neighboring hamlets. It is instructive as well as delightful to stand at the top of one of the hills and look down at the patchwork of vineyards surrounding the villages. In recent years there has been some attempt to rationalize by exchanging land, but growers here are traditional and tenacious. Does one need to explain that a small patch of land is infinitely more precious than a huge estate? Besides, with good reason, many growers believe that their scattered holdings are an insurance against frost or hail damage; and then, depending on where his parcels of land are, each man's wine is often improved by its diverse origin.

Essentially chalky, the hills of Sancerre range from the compact chalk of the low hills and of the bases of the higher ones—known as *caillotes*—to marl on the upper parts of the higher slopes. The plateaus above the slopes are clay and are not used for vineyards. *Caillotes* give wines of great finesse with exuberant aroma, wines that are best bottled young and consumed as soon after the vintage as possible. These are the wines, especially, that brighten those chilly morning tastings. The Clos du Chêne Marchand at Bué is entirely on *caillotes*; so are Les Cous de Brault at Chavignol, Le Paradis at Sancerre, and L'Epée at Amigny.

Marl vineyards, on the other hand, known as *terres blanches*, give wines that are bigger, less aromatic, with more definite character and yet more suppleness. And although Sancerre should never be thought of as a wine for long keeping, wines from the *terres blanches* do keep and develop better than those from the *caillotes*. A combination of the two, however, gives wine that is better than either, so that a grower whose parcels include some of each is unwilling to give up one or the other. The best vineyards, in fact, for reasons that are easily understood, are halfway down slopes where the terrain is something of a mixture of the two soil types. To make the connection between soil and style clear, Sancerre growers are never content to explain their wines on the sole basis of what they themselves produce. One is led to taste in a neighbor's cellar, the better to understand some fine point of *caillote* or exposure, and each is as proud of his neighbor's wine as he is of his own.

In addition to Sauvignon Blanc, there have always been some patches of Pinot Noir, much of it in Sury-en-Vaux, north of Sancerre, but more has been planted in recent years. Until 1959 the red wine made from it was sold as nameless *vin rouge*, but in that year the Sancerre *appellation* was extended to cover red wine as well as white. There is an annual production of red Sancerre close to 100,000 cases, as much as there was of the white twenty-five years ago, though in poor years a large portion of it is vinified as rosé. Despite this considerable quantity, it is hard to find, even in France, and I am not sure where it all goes. In style not unlike a light red Burgundy, it has sometimes a more intense Pinot Noir character than do wines of the Côte d'Or but rarely as much weight or depth of flavor.

I remember well how much I enjoyed my first taste of the 1959, the first vintage of Pinot Noir that could be called Sancerre. I drank it with a local grower who invited me to share his lunch of a hare that had foolishly strayed across his path. Roasted and served with baked celeriac (a vegetable that until then, I must confess, I thought was compulsorily served in strips drenched in *sauce rémoulade*—what a revelation), the hare was as perfect as the wine. Inevitably, we followed it with mature *crottins* of Chavignol, the tiny goat cheeses of Sancerre, just at that point when the outer surface is mottled delicately blue-gray and the cheese crumbles without being dry. My memory fails me, but I shouldn't be surprised if we didn't drink a second bottle with them.

Fresh *crottins*, chalk-white and creamy textured, are served with bread still warm from the oven for cellar tastings, and although the admonition of those who taught me always rings in my head ("Buy on bread, sell on cheese"), a day that starts with fresh *crottins*, a warm crust, and a cold glass of Sancerre is moving in the right direction. *Crottins* were once made mostly by the growers' wives. Ten years ago every household still had half a dozen goats. Haltered with triangles of sticks round their necks to deter them from penetrating too far into the vines, they were allowed to eat what they could find. An assortment of grasses and herbs enriched the milk and improved its flavor, and if one of the goats chose to rummage in a neighbor's flower patch or nibble some tender vine shoots from his vineyard, one could always pretend not to see.

Money from the cheeses kept the family going from one vintage to the next and provided a means to survive if there was a total loss of the crop. The growers still live modestly, but, because there is less economic need for the goats, few families have more than one or two to provide for their own consumption of cheese. *Crottins* on sale in the stores are now produced from commercial flocks, and the Sancerrois are convinced that they don't have quite the same flavor.

Some of the best *crottins* of the growers' kitchens find their way to the Espérance restaurant across the river at Pouilly-sur-Loire; but there, of course, one will accompany them with a Pouilly-Fumé rather than a Sancerre. There is no hostility, nor even rivalry, between the two banks, but it just wouldn't occur to anyone to drink wine from the other side. Though the past twenty-five years have seen changes at Pouilly, too, there has not been an expansion of the vineyards as there has at Sancerre. Vineyards in Pouilly itself and in the neighboring *communes* of Saint-Andelain and

Tracy, close to the river, have been extended, and vineyards have been switched from the humble Chasselas to Sauvignon Blanc. But in other *communes* with the right to the Pouilly *appellation* vineyards have been abandoned, especially those that slope to the east and the southeast, where repeated spring frosts have demoralized the growers. In 1977, for example, when the growers of Sancerre scraped by with partial loss from the frosts in April, many growers at Pouilly lost all but a quarter of their crop—and on such tiny holdings that means penury.

The Chasselas is not used to produce Pouilly-Fumé, but only the rather undistinguished wine known simply as Pouilly-sur-Loire. Sauvignon Blanc is the only grape allowed for Pouilly-Fumé (or Blanc Fumé de Pouilly, as the wine is also called, Blanc Fumé being a local name for the grape). Even in a normal year there is only half as much Pouilly-Fumé as there is Sancerre. What distinguishes one from the other is the absence of *caillotes* on the Pouilly side of the river. The slopes of Pouilly, though less high than those of Sancerre and less sharply inclined, are mostly marl mixed with chalk and quartz. Thus the wines have less of the bright, early aroma of certain Sancerre wines and more of the slow-developing qualities that one finds, for example, in Sancerre of Les Monts Damnés and other *terres blanches* vineyards. For this reason, Pouilly-Fumé, unlike Sancerre, is almost always at its best a year from the vintage; and, although it would be foolish to suggest that it ages well, Pouilly-Fumé from a big year—like 1976— can be astonishing with a year or two in bottle.

Sauvignon Blanc vines are also grown at Quincy, some thirty-five miles southwest of Sancerre, on a plateau that slopes gently to the banks of the river Cher. The river once flowed over the land, leaving a thick bed of gravel and quartz that assures the wine an unusual combination of body and delicacy; it is more muscular than Sancerre, and with that wine's intensely fruity aroma much subdued. In France it is considered the perfect wine for oysters, and I have always found it the ideal white to precede red wines that are classically made but suffer from what we would call, these days, nonassertiveness.

A few miles farther southwest is another small *appellation* based on Sauvignon Blanc, but the white wines of Reuilly are rare to the point of having almost disappeared except in the village where they grow. With apologies for my own insensitivity in the matter, I must say that the few examples I have met do not inspire me with much concern for a revival. On the other hand, recent plantings there of Pinot Gris, vinified as a golden-pink rosé, have been successful and are now recognized with an *appellation contrôlée* of their own.

Sauvignon Blanc vines have long been planted in California, but until recently the wines made from them were usually sold as "sauterne," without a final *s* and, unlike French Sauternes, usually dry. They were dull, heavy wines; and, whatever success they might have had in the past, they were not the most sought-after in recent years.

Then Robert Mondavi, a few years ago, brought out a Sauvignon Blanc wine that he labeled Fumé Blanc, using an inversion of the alternative French name for the grape. He did it to get away from the name "sauterne" (he has always followed a laudable policy of avoiding French geographic names) and also to draw attention to the way in which his wine differed from what was usually expected of Sauvignon Blanc in California. Our soils are nothing like those of Pouilly and Sancerre, but with low-temperature fermentation (something the Sancerrois had always had naturally, thanks to the chill of their underground cellars) he was able to produce a wine with more grace and more aroma than before. It was bigger and rounder than the Sauvignon Blancs of the Loire, but the experiment has been a success, and others have followed suit. It is significant that whereas there were only some 600 acres of Sauvignon Blanc vineyards in California in 1970, the popularity of Fumé Blanc has caused expansion to more than 7,000 acres within a decade. There are now at least half a dozen California wineries producing varied Fumé Blancs; in addition to the wine of Robert Mondavi, now settled down to its rather plump style, the crisply perfumed Fumé Blanc of Château St. Jean in Sonoma County is a favorite of mine. None duplicates a Pouilly-Fumé or a Sancerre, but there is no reason to expect that. The diversity of wine adds to our pleasure.

Bordeaux: 1980

DECEMBER IS NOT a good time to visit Bordeaux. The new wine, still in lingering phases of fermentation and usually reeking of the tanks, is impossible to taste, let alone judge; wine of the previous vintage, though always interesting to reconsider, has rarely evolved to an extent that will show a difference from the past spring's tasting sufficient to *vaut le voyage*, as the Michelin guide puts it; and wines of the year before are usually just in bottle or in course of preparation for bottling and, in either case, mostly unavailable. And then, even when the new crop has brought general satisfaction, or the low angle of a late autumn sun softens the landscape and adds charm to the usually charmless country houses of the Médoc, there is always something melancholy in the vistas of denuded brown vines at this time of year. There is also a contagious weariness from growers recently exhausted by the effort and anxiety of picking and a withdrawn atmosphere fostered by the *negoçiants'* need to research, reflect, and consult among themselves before making those opening moves toward the growers or in the overseas markets that will set the reputation of the vintage and the commercial mood for the ensuing year. December 1980 was no exception: reports of the vintage were ambiguous at best, the market was confused, and the freezing air that swept down from Norway to make my post-Thanksgiving weekend in Paris one long struggle to keep warm had spread to Bordeaux (and, from what I heard, even beyond the Pyrenees).

I had come to Bordeaux to settle some unfinished business, but, tastable or not, the 1980 vintage was on my mind, and I hoped to learn at least enough to form an idea of what to expect from it. A visit in May had been particularly hurried, and I needed to look again at the 1979s and to revise my perspective, given two subsequent vintages, of the 1978 classed growths, just in bottle and ready to leave.

The 1980 vintage shared with 1979 and 1978 both a cold spring and a late, October picking. But, though the year was neither very much colder nor very much wetter than average, it suffered a summer that lacked sunshine. Fine weather in September, at last, continued into October but ended with Atlantic rainstorms that rolled through the vineyards just as picking, three weeks late, got under way. The rain was followed by low temperatures that brought further problems in the fermenting vats of those vineyards not equipped with heating installations. Though the measure of sugar in grapes—and, therefore, the scale of wine made from them—is a result primarily of sunshine, lack of sunshine does not necessarily arrest the cycle of the vine, nor does it prevent grapes from attaining "maturity," though grapes so "matured" usually fall short of ideal for winemaking purposes. From all that I heard, 1980 Bordeaux was distinguished from 1977 in that the grapes, despite lower sugars, did at least "mature," and the raw, green quality that marred so many 1977 red wines was avoided.

Nevertheless, many 1980 red Bordeaux will be light-bodied, even though color in the new wine was deep and associated tannins presented an early spurious robustness. Before I cause 1980 to be summarily dismissed by vintage chart addicts, however, let me add that years like this, when as well balanced as 1980 will be, are often more suited to our needs in the United States than the "big" years we get so excited about. We have only to look at city restaurant lists to see how many of the great Bordeaux vintages are drunk long before they can possibly reveal the qualities for which we pay so dearly. Except for those whose thrill comes from the *idea* of what they are drinking rather than from the experience itself, it makes more sense to be drinking, say, a 1973 or a 1974, humble vintages on the scale of potential but delicious when drunk at the right time, rather than to confront a 1975, bred, no doubt, for great things in the future, when it is still undeveloped unresponsive, and barely agreeable. The difficulty we have in finding classed growths ripe for drinking on a list indicates how rarely most of us can experience the mature reality of a great Bordeaux vintage despite the enormous quantities shipped to the United States. Under the circumstances, vintages like 1980, light but balanced, are well suited to the time span in which we consume most of our wines, especially in restaurants. We would receive better value and more pleasure if we paid more attention to them.

Because red Bordeaux wines are released and consumed over a period of years, quantity and quality fluctuations from harvest to harvest affect the market less abruptly than one might imagine. Until recently, the same was true for white Bordeaux wines, though for a different reason. The truth is that, with the possible exception of classed-growth Sauternes (and for a long period even they were not excepted), there was little interest anywhere in white Bordeaux. The *appellation* Bordeaux Blanc had so far lost its value that the market price hardly differed from that of basic white *vin ordinaire*. Indeed, many growers found it expedient not to claim their right to the *appellation*, thus freeing themselves to increase their yields per acre at least and make up in quantity their costs of cultivation. Others progressively pulled up white grape vines, converting vineyards to red or letting them lie fallow.

The recent revival of interest in dry white Bordeaux, especially in wines fermented at low temperatures from Sauvignon Blanc grapes, has taken everyone by surprise because the effect of increased demand was first hidden by the profusion of the 1979 crop. The ready market, immediate consumption (hence no problem with high interest rates), and greater ease in producing a marketable product even in adverse weather conditions have suddenly made white-wine production popular again in Bordeaux. The strength of demand (and the temporary imbalance of supply) was clear from a newspaper article, on the morning of my arrival, that announced prices for basic white Bordeaux wines rising briskly from the depressed level at which they had been roughly parallel with bulk blending wines of the California Central Valley. Fortunately, most of the 1980 dry whites were picked before the rains began in earnest on October 11 and are not very different from the light, fresh 1979s. In Sauternes the rain did nothing

Bordeaux

N

Atlantic
Ocean

Gironde R.

Miles
0   20
0   Kms.   20

St. Estèphe

M
É
D
O
C

Pauillac

St. Julien

Blaye
CÔTES DE
BOURG
Bourg

Margaux

Dordogne R.

Pomerol

Fronsac   Libourne
           St. Emilion

BORDEAUX

ENTRE-
DEUX-MERS

GRAVES

Garonne R.

SAUTERNES

Sauternes

Giron R.

FRANCE

Area of
map

© 1982 A. Karl/J. Kemp

worse than ensure the spread of the botrytis that growers always hope for, much to everyone's astonishment. In quantity, too, the combined harvest declarations of Sauternes and Barsac came close to 90 percent of those of 1979 declarations.

However disappointed Bordeaux growers might have been by the effect of the October rains on the quality of their red wines (without those storms 1980 would have ranked with 1967 and 1976), they could hardly have been too upset at the smaller size of the 1980 crop, given the enormous quantities of the 1979 red wines that they had in hand, all of them attractive and likely to be ready for drinking sooner than the 1978s. Their soft, easy style reminds us that in abundant years—1962, 1970, and 1973 are other recent examples—Bordeaux wines always have a higher proportion of Merlot grapes. Because Merlot is very susceptible to *coulure* (failure to set fruit), far more Merlot will fail to set than will Cabernet, even in a calm flowering season. An abundant year requires a good fruit-set, and in Bordeaux that means the Merlot must have done well. A small vintage, on the other hand—1961, 1971, and 1978 are examples—is usually the result of a poor fruit-set, and because Merlot is more fragile in this respect than is Cabernet, small vintages are almost always "Cabernet" years in the sense that Médoc growths that rely on a proportion of both varieties will then usually lack the grace and inner softness of their full proportion of Merlot.

Such conditions have a different effect in Pomerol and Saint-Emilion, of course, where Merlot is usually the principal rather than the supporting variety. Those growths—Pétrus being the most important—that rely almost entirely on Merlot will simply yield a reduced crop and in so doing are likely to produce one of outstanding quality if conditions are right. That was certainly the case in 1961 and 1971 and explains the success of Pétrus in those years. It is likely to have been the case in 1978, too, even though lack of rain for weeks prior to the vintage blocked activity in the vines and held back full potential. Other growths, especially in Saint-Emilion, have their proportions of Cabernet Sauvignon and Cabernet Franc thrown into greater relief in years when the Merlot fails to set, and, no matter how perfect the summer may subsequently be, they will then seem untypically severe in style. Such is true of many 1978 Saint-Emilion wines, a vintage that is frequently ranked behind 1976 and 1979 in the *appellation* for this reason.

Our early attitude toward the 1979s was cautious, even skeptical. At best we perceived them as lesser 1978s, rather as we accepted, with greater justification, the 1976s as lesser 1975s. But 1979s throughout Bordeaux, rich in Merlot and ripened in weather conditions particularly conducive to a balance of qualities, echo the charm of the 1970s, even of the 1953s, at this same stage. I fear that we might underestimate them in the same way and for the same reasons that the 1953s were underestimated. Seen at the time against the austerely classic 1952s, 1953 wines seemed too easily approachable to be serious. And, in any case, the 1952s had already monopolized all possible praise, following as they did the neglected 1950s and the disastrous 1951s.

The 1978s, as we shall see from the shipments just arriving on merchants' shelves, follow the same austerely classic style as the 1952s, though they are not as sturdy. Often ranked with 1975s, they differ in a way that was brought home to me tactfully but brilliantly by Jean Delmas, *régisseur* of Château Haut-Brion, at a dinner at his house on one of the evenings of my visit. He served me two pairs of Haut-Brion wines: 1978 and 1975 followed by 1961 and 1959. There was no suggestion that one pair directly resembled the other, but Delmas helped me to see that 1978 stood in relationship to 1975 much as the austere 1961 had stood in relation to the rounder, fuller 1959. I wondered how the 1961, delicious but still less accessible than the 1959, would have measured against Haut-Brion 1953, one of my favorite wines. As luck would have it, on my last evening in Bordeaux I was invited to dinner by the Bories at Grand-Puy-Lacoste. With a *civet de marcassin* we drank Grand-Puy-Lacoste 1961 and 1953, pairing the classic Bordeaux "Cabernet" vintage with a softer, more approachable "Merlot" year, one that provides, I believe, a model of what we might expect for the 1979s. The 1961 again seemed young for its age, but mainly in the sense that it was restrained and rather tight. The 1953, on the other hand, though still equally youthful, was attractively balanced, open, easy to enjoy. My hopes for the 1979s became increasingly positive. I even began to change my ideas about Bordeaux in December.

Bordeaux: 1970

I REMEMBER hearing of a practical joker in a private club who put on twelve bottles of Château Kirwan 1964, all twelve drawn from a single case, for a blind comparative tasting. The connection was clear, but differences from bottle to bottle were startlingly real, so the joke was on him. The story came back to me not long ago, when I noticed that two bottles of Mouton Rothschild 1962, each bearing the name of a different shipper and served together at a dinner, revealed differences so plain that it was hard to accept their common origin. Such differences are certainly not there when wine is first bottled, of course. But a trace more air in a bottle allows a different development of bouquet and flavor; and storage somewhere just a fraction of a degree warmer, over many years, matures wine at a faster rate. Once under the cork, in fact, every bottle of wine develops in its own way, and although I have never encountered two bottles of the same wine so different that one was superb and the other abysmally poor (I speak of intrinsic quality, of course, not of accidents that can wreck a single bottle), I know never to take a wine for granted. Drawing a cork is like attendance at a concert or at a play that one knows well, when there is all the uncertainty of no two performances ever being quite the same. That is why the French say, "There are no good wines, only good bottles."

Such inconsistency adds to the pleasure of wine but should impose a measure of caution when we start to praise or condemn a *wine* on the evidence of a *bottle*. In fact, I am awed by the temerity of those who, not content with sharing their impressions of wines, print lists of them graded to fine decimal points of a percentage, all on chance reactions to haphazard bottles. Leaving out of consideration the casual damage done to serious wineries, they should know (or at least we should) that above a certain quality level such ratings are of questionable value. If a group of twenty listed in order of personal preference the six basic colors of the spectrum, and blue were the most preferred, would we be learning something about blue or something about the group? Only the passage of time allows impressions and exchanged opinions of a wine to condense so that they reflect, eventually, its real worth.

There was little passage of time in establishing the reputation of the 1970 vintage of Bordeaux. 1967 had brought an abundance of moderate wine with uncertain prospects for long-term development, and 1969 had been received with an acclaim soon seen to have been unreasonably exaggerated. As a result, its collective credibility damaged, the Bordeaux trade hesitated at first to say that the 1970 vintage was indisputably the best since 1966, probably the best since 1961, and just possibly the best since World War II. But for some time interest in fine wine had been spreading on both sides of the Atlantic, and reports of a successful vintage in Bordeaux fell on newly sensitized ears. Excitement and impatience unprecedented inside the trade, let alone outside it, built an early pressure of demand. Before winter was out, when still at a stage when professionals could make no more than a broad assessment, magnums of the purple, barely fermented wines were flown to New York for public tasting. Seduced by rich grapy aromas and flavor, consumers ordered against shipments not expected for another two or three years, and wine merchants were swept into feverish activity.

The classified châteaux of Bordeaux release their crop in a series of lots, each called a *tranche*, or slice. As each *tranche* was released, it was bought up without hesitation, swiftly resold, and sometimes resold again three or four times in a matter of weeks, with prices jumping at a pace that startled the staid Bordeaux trade. (The wine, all this while, remained quietly in barrel in the château, of course.) The temporary collapse of 1973 and 1974 was inevitable.

The size of the 1970 vintage had been predetermined by the maturity of the vinewood in 1969. The stage had been set then for vigorous shoots and a copious harvest, at very least, to follow. But spring was late—in early May there was still hardly a leaf on a tree in my London garden—and in Bordeaux the vines were fully three weeks behind their normal growth pattern when exceptionally fine, stable weather in June brought on the flowering under perfect conditions. The calm, warm days continued on and on through July, August, and September. Eventually, the same lack of rain that turned English lawns brown slowed down circulation of sap and restrained the level of sugar in the Cabernet Sauvignon grapes as they ripened. But Merlot ripens earlier, so it was hardly affected. And as an abundant year in Bordeaux is always a "Merlot" year, 1970 showed every indication of particular success for wines with high proportions of Merlot: Pomerols and Saint-Emilions, obviously, but also Médoc châteaux like La Lagune, Pichon-Lalande, Palmer, and Lafite.

As early as November, immediately after the harvest, I had a first opportunity to taste a few of the wines. They were deep-colored and charged with flavor. Tasting again the following summer, more extensively, I made notes where the same words occur over and over again: "good color," "big," "fleshy." And in the summer of 1972, tasting them once more prior to bottling, I noted that although it was always possible to find an occasional example curiously at odds with the general style of the vintage, the wines were "evenly good," and seemed to be all we had hoped for.

I lost sight of them until early 1974, when most had arrived in New York and were available for tasting there. By then they had lost the forward fruitiness that had been so appealing, and most seemed less massive. Whatever the individual character of the wines, however, they shared the qualities of regular balance and stamina, occasionally a forcefulness, that augured well for their future. There were some striking contrasts among the Saint-Emilions: Château Ausone, neat and finely spun against a full-blown Château Pavie; Château Figeac, an elegantly wrought combination of grace and strength against the solid, mouth-filling scale of its neighbor, Château Cheval-Blanc; Château L'Angelus, light for the year, but as unyielding as a tense drum skin and in strange opposition to the soft, gentle wine of nearby Château Grandes-Murailles. But the expectation of good results from "Merlot" wines had been realized, and that was even plainer in the Pomerol wines: a huge, splendid Château Trotanoy; a Château Pétrus as densely complicated to nose and palate as a medieval illumination is to the eye; Vieux Château Certan showing better than I had known it before, even if the flavor in the sample I had finished rather short; and a Château Nénin, usually a featherbed of a Pomerol, lean and firm, with an enticing, waxy bouquet.

The Médoc classed growths were more austere, and therefore more at odds with their puppy appeal of three years before. This change was less apparent in wines like Cos d'Estournel and Château de Pez, both of which have high proportions of Merlot in the vineyard, than in Château Montrose and Château Meyney, both classically severe Saint-Estèphes. Among the Saint-Juliens three wines stood out: Château Gruaud-Larose, superbly balanced; Château Ducru-Beaucaillou, a powerful wine, for me easily the most distinguished; and Château Léoville-Las-Cases, its intense flavor supported by fleeting hints of bouquet like the never-quite-identifiable tangle of scents in a garden after rain.

The Margaux wines in the group showed no sign of the floweriness we associate with that *appellation*, but Château Palmer had charm, Château La Lagune, though revealing little, was softly balanced and Château Giscours plumply substantial. Château Brane Cantenac, soft almost to the point of sweetness, had an odd berry-like fruitiness reminiscent of certain California red wines that have been aged in redwood.

But it was the group of Pauillacs that came across best of all, and seemed to display the essential qualities of the 1970 vintage. Château Pichon-Lalande, thanks to its generous proportion of Merlot, was supple in contrast with Château Pichon-Baron—very fine but hard-edged and masculine, though both were perfectly balanced; Château Lynch-Bages and Château Grand-Puy-Lacoste were richly generous; Château Latour was elegant despite its scale; and the fresh and delicate Château Lafite-Rothschild was also impeccably in balance. Above all, Château Mouton-Rothschild summed up the vintage with the fortunate choice of Chagall for the 1970 label. No one could have better captured the year's bright, warm quality.

Over the past few years I have dipped into my 1970s sooner and more often than I should, but at least I have had occasional opportunity to observe their development. In the Saint-Emilions and Pomerols the fruitiness of youth has been tempered, and the smoky quality of gravel origin is already showing clearly in Château Trotanoy and Château Figeac. Trotanoy was still quite splendid when last tasted in 1978, and Figeac, though more mellow, has lost none of that early grace. Château Léoville-Las-Cases, when tasted in 1978, had lost none of its intensity, though its bouquet, no less enchanting, has changed as one would have expected. Unforgivably, I had preceded it with a 1974 Caymus Cabernet Sauvignon, then a vigorous wine though since faded somewhat. But the Léoville seemed not in any way diminished by it. More recently, in 1981, I shared a bottle over a perfectly ripe Brie and it was all that a first-class Bordeaux should be—and just at that point when there is still a measure of liveliness and yet, too, that melancholic richness that hints at decline to come. At about that same time I had a similarly fine experience with a bottle of Château Lascombes that I enjoyed with friends in Ann Arbor. Its deep color, rich claret nose, and delicious harmony of flavor were further proof that the 1970s were all we had hoped. Perhaps, now that there are none available to buy, we are beginning to know enough to judge them?

Bordeaux First Growths: A Diversion

THERE IS something tongue-in-cheek about San Francisco's First Growth Club, an echo, perhaps, of those improbably named dining clubs spawned in the coffeehouses of eighteenth-century London. The Sublime Society of Beefsteaks, the Sçavoir Vivre, the Lying Club (the chairman of which was always to be the member uttering the most "stupendous improbability"), and the Dilettanti Society gave rise to some of London's most distinguished men's clubs. Others—the names of which are all too descriptive—provided unusually diverting entertainment for their members after dinner. But the essence of them all was the pleasure that like-minded men found in each other's company over a few shared bottles of wine.

Such is true of the First Growth Club, a group of men who had long known each other and who found that since they were sharing the contents of each other's cellars anyway, they might as well share in the choice of what should be in them. Whenever the reputation of the year seems to warrant it, they subscribe together to buy a case or two of each of the eight First Growths of Bordeaux; and every few weeks, at a moveable feast that settles on each member's house in turn, they dine together to fulfill the self-imposed obligation of keeping check on the development of their wines. On each occasion they draw from the communal stock a bottle of each of the eight growths of the year chosen for review.

Eight? Yes, eight. In a stylish gesture, and long before the French government followed their lead, they elevated Château Mouton-Rothschild from its erstwhile secondary status to join the four Firsts of the 1855 Classification (Lafite, Latour, Margaux, and Haut-Brion). Then they included two Firsts of the 1955 Classification of Saint-Emilion (Ausone and Cheval-Blanc), and, with unself-conscious grandeur, they also confirmed Pétrus as First of the Pomerols, a status that had been merely honorary before.

A member unable to attend has the option of sending a guest in his place, and that is why I found myself strolling down Russian Hill on a Thursday in 1977 in pleasant anticipation of a fine evening. Dinner was to be provided by a member who is both a neighbor and an old friend, a bachelor of some gastronomic distinction in San Francisco. His apartment is typical of a certain period in the city: stairways and loggias give the feeling of entering the Casbah at very least; round oriel windows spring airily (and against all engineering logic) from the corners of rooms to provide unexpected, even mysterious, glimpses of town and bay; and the high-ceilinged kitchen and dining room are given significantly more space and prominence than his sitting room. He is a man who delights in the detail of his life; on every side there are empty bottles to recall past pleasures, letters stacked to be relished again, books and papers to be enjoyed in lazy hours ahead (if he has any). And in the midst of this magnificent eighteenth-century disorder his table is always set with the finest linen, brilliant glass, mellow silver, and the rich magnificence of old Crown Derby.

Awaiting the eight of us, and already decanted, were eight bottles of the 1966 vintage. But first, with a tray of dry sausage from the Italian grocers of North Beach, we drank a magnum of Krug 1962, a Champagne of which I am particularly fond. The house style of Krug combines steely dryness with considerable body, not always a happy association; but 1962 was a year of great finesse in Champagne, and in this vintage the styles of year and house combine to give a wine of rare elegance. In magnum it had held its freshness very well.

As we turned our attention to the red wines, conversation

dropped. They were poured blind so that we could taste and discuss them without the influence of preconceived notions and prejudices.

At its first assessment by the trade, in the spring of 1967, the 1966 vintage was pronounced, cautiously, "satisfactory." It was a large crop in Bordeaux (though not as big as the record-breaking one of 1962) that had somehow overcome unhelpful weather. July and part of August were too cool, and wet besides. September was fine and warm, but at that point, when the vines at last *needed* water to complete the ripening process, there was none, and sugar levels were sometimes disappointing as a result. Too late to be of help, rain came at the end of September, when picking had already started. The effect was not as serious as heavy rain had been during the 1964 harvest, but it tended to weaken some wines without strengthening others. In Pomerol and Saint-Emilion the rain had no effect because picking is always earlier there and most growers had finished. And our group choice eleven years later, perhaps not coincidentally, placed Pétrus of Pomerol and Cheval-Blanc of Saint-Emilion ahead of all the Médoc wines.

I first tasted the 1966 wines of the Médoc early in 1967. My notes refer to "high tannin without much acidity." In my notebook I wondered about their probable outcome, because I thought they would need years to lose their asperity, and at the time I wondered whether there was sufficient acidity for development of bouquet and flavor while this was going on.

In any event, the Médoc wines we tasted that evening were distinctive, in the sense that each had individuality, and they were, for the most part, both graceful and subdued. Some did indeed show austerity, and I attributed that to a lack of those flavors and aromas which give charm and at least an illusion of roundness to a wine.

But by tasting them alongside Pétrus and Cheval-Blanc, I am not sure that we were allowing those Médoc wines to show at their best. The current passion for comparative tastings is taken to extremes, it seems to me, and too often a wine is judged not for what it is, but, in comparison with an unrelated wine, for what it isn't. There are times when that can be instructive but not always is it the way to enjoy the best of a glass of wine. By chance, and very soon after this particular evening, I sampled several of these 1966 wines again in the course of lunches and dinners during a visit to Bordeaux. Tasted in the normal context of preceding wines planned to bring out the quality of each, they seemed silkier and more elegant. In particular, the austerity that had been so marked against the voluptuous styles of Pétrus and Cheval-Blanc was hardly apparent.

My own favorite Médoc of the evening was Lafite, though my opinion was not shared. The others much preferred Latour, which certainly had better weight but which was the sole wine I found to be brutally out of balance. The Lafite had a dry finish, as did they all, but it also had an attractively clear Pauillac-Cabernet nose, so pronounced that when tasting blind I had assumed the wine to be Mouton, usually identifiable from this very characteristic.

With serious consideration of the wines over, we proceeded to empty our eight glasses with broiled lamb chops, followed by a superb Brie, and the club members resumed the conversation they had started in 1962 and that has been running, with interruptions, ever since.

The First Growths of Bordeaux were not selected competitively in the course of a gigantic taste-off. They selected themselves, in a way, by doing the right things at the right time. Until the seventeenth century Bordeaux wines were not sold by name. Wine was a simple agricultural commodity like any other, and quality was rarely attributed to a particular source. In any case, the making and handling of wines was often so primitive that the consumer felt himself blessed if the wine was palatable, let alone distinguished. A wine fleet sailed from Bordeaux each November, with wine barely finished fermenting in the casks, in order to have the current vintage in London taverns for Christmas. The previous year's wine, kept in ullaged casks, open to air and spoilage of every kind in the pre-Pasteur era, was by then distinctly disagreeable. Unlike modern wine, it took a steep drop in price as it got older, especially once the new year's wine was available.

In the 1660s Arnaud de Pontac, a rich and influential wine-grower from Bordeaux, used his position and intelligence to change the marketing pattern of Bordeaux wines and, as a result, the pattern of winegrowing as well. First president of the local Parlement de Guienne in the mid-seventeenth century and later ambassador to London, he decided to use his connections and the prestige of his name to promote the wine from his estate at Haut-

Brion, near Bordeaux. Soon, in 1663, Samuel Pepys was writing in his diary that at the Royall Oake Taverne he drank "a sort of French wine called Ho Bryan, that hath a good and most perticular taste that I never met with." It was the first *named* Bordeau château wine offered for sale anywhere. Later the Pontac family opened a fashionable eating house in London at which, need we say, Haut-Brion was the wine offered.

Pontac's wine sold at prices up to two and three times more than other Bordeaux wine in London. Bordeaux wine, previously considered tavern tipple, became smart and fit for respectable tables. Others followed Pontac's success, and, by the first years of the eighteenth century, the *London Gazette* carried advertisements for three Bordeaux wines in addition to Haut-Brion. When we read their names, we note that these are the very ones that emerged, one hundred and fifty years later, as the four Firsts of the 1855 Classification.

Of course, the connection could be that only the best-managed wine estates on the best sites making the finest wines could afford this early self-distinction and promotion. But if it is true that fine wine commands a high price, it is equally true that a high price can often guarantee fine wine because it allows the rigorous selection of vines, the sharp control of yield, and the strict rejection of below-standard batches that are essential for high quality.

The emergence of named châteaux in the Médoc (in itself a novelty: much of the region was newly planted at that time); the development of the cylindrical bottle with cork closure, without which few Médoc wines could have aged to the point of revealing their charm; new money (brought to Bordeaux by the flourishing trade with the Caribbean) invested in developing the new vineyards and financing the aging of the bottled wines; the new desire in France for delicacy at the table (François Marin's *Délices de la Table*, the first work of its kind, was published only in 1739); and the eighteenth-century passion for classifying everything from wild flowers to vineyards led to many attempts to rationalize the maze of new names in the Médoc. The wine brokers of Bordeaux classified them according to vineyard and year, the latter playing a much stronger role in deciding the price category for a wine than the vineyard of origin. In the early nineteenth century, for example, Lafite, Latour, and Margaux could command 3,000 francs a *tonneau* (equivalent to about a hundred cases) in a good year but only 400 francs in a bad one, less than what the wine of even the meanest vineyard of the Médoc fetched in a good year.

More significant, however, is the modest margin by which the First Growths in those days topped the prices of the wines below them. When the First sold for 3,000 francs, Léoville, Lascombe, Rausan, and others sold for 2,700 and yet others for 2,400. Today, the First Growths tower in price above the other classified Growths, such is their prestige, and the prices they command can be almost as high in a middling to poor year as in a fine one.

But until the 1855 Classification—in fact, nothing more than a public dissemination of the status quo in that particular year as part of the exhibit of French arts and industry at the International Exhibition in Paris—there was still considerable flexibility. In 1851 Cyrus Redding wrote (in his *History and Description of Modern Wines*):

The growers use all their efforts to place their wines in a higher class, and thus emulation is kindled, and they are justified in their efforts by the profits. The prices of their wines . . . is less governed by particular merit, than by the number which they occupy in the scale of classification. It often costs them sacrifices to reach that object. They will keep their wine many years to give it a superior title, instead of selling it the first year according to custom. By this means an individual will get his wine changed from the fourth to the third class, which he had perhaps occupied before for many successive years.

The emergence of the leading châteaux in Saint-Emilion and Pomerol has been more erratic and much more recent. Cheval-Blanc won recognition with its 1921 vintage, one of *the* great wines of Bordeaux, a success later confirmed by its outstanding 1947 wine, still, in 1982, magnificently lively, almost black-red in color and as fruitily rich as Port wine. In the 1850s, Cocks and Féret, the Debrett of Bordeaux, had ranked Cheval-Blanc only among the second-grade Saint-Emilions. What changes, I wonder, might have occurred in the Médoc classification during the course of the last century, had it remained as flexible as that of Saint-Emilion?

Pomerol did not exist as an *appellation* separate from Saint-Emilion until 1923, and although Pétrus first won attention (and a gold medal) at the 1878 Paris Exhibition, it is only in the last twenty years or so that it has been able to command the prices of

Lafite and Mouton. It was without doubt the best of the 1966s we tasted on that occasion.

The evening mellowed, and so did we. Bowls of ripe California strawberries appeared, along with plums and sections of papaya with lime—the last an exquisite accompaniment to a 1959 Eitelsbacher Karthäuserhofberg Beerenauslese, a richly shimmering treat.

And, as befits a gentlemen's dining club, we talked into the new day with Port and nuts—in this case a Sandeman's 1945, rather light for a vintage Port, but ideal for a fogbound summer night by the Pacific.

Trocken-Trocken

T HE MATUSCHKA-GREIFFENCLAU family began the massive pile that is now Schloss Vollrads in the fourteenth century, and in all senses of the word the structure stands at the heart of their vineyard estate. Clang and clatter in the courtyard recently reminded us that ever since its beginnings there have been additions, changes, and restorations. Over a period of two years, Erwein, the newest Graf, restored the medieval roof. Starting with the steep-pitched beam structure and replacing dozens of tiny attic gables, he rehung thousands of the scalloped blue-black slates that cling like scales to a monstrous fish. The new roof of Vollrads is a signal that Graf Erwein is prepared to tackle problems fundamentally at considerable effort (and cost) for what he thinks worth preserving. Less apparent but with wider effect, he has adopted an equally energetic and fundamental attitude in a polemic that presently engulfs the entire *hoch Feinschmeckerei*.

The ferment in France to scrutinize all that had been previously taken for granted in wine and food found an echo in Germany. Already *nouvelle cuisine* seems a wistfully dated expression— whether it really represented anything particularly new is a debate we can leave to others—but there is no doubt it revitalized interest in our own taste buds, reminded us that fresh ingredients tasting of themselves are the basis of all good cooking (*nouvelle, ancienne,* and just plain Grandma's), and reemphasized that lightness and fragrance, in wine as well as food, are desirable qualities.

In Germany, wines were already lighter and more fragrant than the lightest of French wines—that is their essence—so controversy there focused on the question of sweetness. By way of background we should recall that in the late fifties German wine producers financed a study that seemed to indicate that more Germans would drink more wine if it were slightly sweeter than was then the case. At that time the sweetness of a wine (I generalize, of course) depended on its quality. Spätlese and Auslese wines, known for their naturally sweet style, were made from late-picked grapes and inevitably carried both higher production costs and higher prices on the shelf. For a number of reasons cheap sweet wines were rarely as satisfactory. But a technique was then perfected to overcome this. By retaining a proportion of the unfermented grape juice and reintroducing it judiciously into the finished wine, the level of sweetness could be adjusted even in a wine made from grapes with only delicate sugar content. The presence of even a little unfermented grape juice will intensify the grapy quality of a wine's aroma (an obvious advantage in many cases) and the practice enhanced even the most ordinary wine, increasing its charm manyfold.

In the decade from 1963 to 1973, annual consumption of wine per head rose in Germany by roughly 70 percent—and this at a time when consumption in France, the most traditional of all wine-drinking countries, fell by 20 percent. Because of this success, sweetness became the dominating characteristic of German wines. But it was one thing to make everyday wines more palatable, quite another heedlessly to mask the quality and personality of finer products, and reaction was inevitable. A one-way pendulum has yet to be discovered, however, and, to the dismay of Graf Erwein and of those who share his view, the gastronomic new wave is replacing one exaggeration with another. A passion for bone-dry wines has seized the fashionable wine and food establishment in Germany. Increasingly, on labels and on wine lists, one sees the word *trocken* (boldly underlined), not as reference to the dry state of raisinlike grapes, picked late and overripe for luscious dessert wines (as in Trockenbeerenauslese), but to "dry" according to the English usage, describing absence of any perceptible sweetness in a wine.

"Dry" and "sweet" are relative, even subjective, terms. A light, crisply acid Mosel wine with twenty-five grams of residual grape sugar in the bottle, for example, will taste less sweet than a rounder, more alcoholically powerful Rheinhessen wine with only fifteen grams. Finding the right sweet-dry balance for any German wine is difficult (as in so much else, it is a question of deciding how far art might discreetly support nature).

But a German wine of quality depends on a sweet-sharp sensation so finely in balance that neither part dominates. Such a wine provokes and soothes the palate simultaneously, suggesting a universe of tastes and smells but presenting only one. Intense, complex, integrated, it should have what the Germans call "harmony." The higher alcohol levels of most French and Italian wines contribute warmth and fullness sufficient to balance their lower acidities. German wines, the most northerly of Europe, owe their exquisite flavor to the relatively high acidity in the grapes from which they are made, and high alcohol alone could not provide a necessary balance. Even if means were found to "improve" the alcohol to the required level, it would have to be so high that the wine would finish hard and disagreeable, its delicacy of aroma and flavor wrecked. That is why the elegance and style of fine German wines can be preserved only through a carefully judged relationship between acid and grape sugar.

The role of residual sugar in this balance was illuminated recently in a brief comment in the *New York Times*. Frank Prial, then the paper's wine columnist, had tasted a number of new-style *trocken* wines from Germany and found that they reminded him of Alsatian wines (produced from similar grapes in a more southerly and sheltered part of the Rhine and almost always made without residual sugar), except, he complained, for their lack of body. Of course, Alsatian wines have more alcohol, and the high acidity natural to German wines needs either that or sugar if the wine is not to taste thin, or downright scrawny.

To accept the sweet-sharp theory of harmony in German wines is one thing, to make it work in relation to food is another; many are daunted at the prospect of matching German wines to classic dishes. There is a tendency to shrug the question aside, suggesting on the one hand that German wines are best drunk without food (which is true for some but not for all) or that, willy-nilly, they "go with everything" (which is true if one is not overly concerned with subtle combinations of wine and food or if one's preference for German wines is so overwhelming that the more logical choice for certain circumstances would be less pleasurable personally).

To demonstrate the compatibility of German wines with the classic dishes of France and Germany, Matuschka-Greiffenclau invites German restaurateurs and other professionals to Schloss Vollrads for dinners where the finely graded range of his wines is matched to appropriate foods. Schloss Vollrads uses a color code to indicate the quality of the wines, as defined by German law, and supplements the code with a silver or a gold band to indicate the degree of dryness.

For some years Germany has divided wines into three quality categories, based on the degree of ripeness of the grapes at the time of picking. Wines made from grapes with less than a certain level of natural sugar, and which therefore need enriching at the time of the crush prior to fermentation, are described as *Tafelwein* ("table wine"). Few wines of this quality are exported; mostly they are used for everyday drinking in Germany. Wines made from grapes with more sugar than this minimum, but that still need some enriching to be of satisfactory strength, are described as *Qualitätswein* ("quality wine"). Wines made from grapes that need no enrichment at all are described as *Qualitätswein mit Prädikat* ("quality wine with description"). These last always have a descriptive word that can range from Kabinett (a flag word to distinguish "quality wine with description" from an ordinary "quality wine") through Spätlese (made from late-picked grapes, and, though not stated, conforming to more stringent standards than plain Kabinett), Auslese (made from grapes picked bunch by bunch as each becomes ripe), and Beerenauslese (made from grapes picked one at a time to ensure perfect ripeness) to Trockebeeren-auslese (made from grapes picked one at a time, each when over-ripe to a point of dried, raisinlike consistency).

By linking the quality grading to a standard of the grapes at the time of picking and not just to a geographic location (as is the case with *appellations contrôlées* in France), a wine is systematically downgraded in category, no matter where it was grown, if conditions at the time of picking were not propitious for making fine wine. With equal logic, a wine of humble geographic origin is entitled to the appropriate descriptive phrase when unusual vintage conditions create a product of high quality. None of this is automatic. A German wine of "quality" status or above must be submitted to a government tasting panel before it can be sold under the category claimed. The color code used by Schloss Vollrads is green for ordinary "quality wines," blue for Kabinett, pink for Spätlese, white for Auslese, and gold for Beerenauslese. The vineyard adds a distinctive band when the sugar levels are more (or less) than one might reasonably suppose from the quality designation. A silver band denotes a wine drier than one might expect; a gold band, sweeter. But the degree of sweetness (or lack of it) is decided only in accordance with what an individual wine needs to be in harmony because, Graf Erwein will tell you, wines in balance are neither sweet nor dry.

The residual sugar in most balanced German wines is compatible with sauces, whether they are made from reductions or thickened with cream. But German wines do not need the buffer of sauces to marry well with dishes of all kinds. A full-bodied Rhine wine will stand up to most meats and game, though Graf Erwein acknowledges that a red is best with plain roast beef. In Germany the food I eat is usually of the simplest kind, and the wines always seem to be perfect matches. I have enjoyed full-blown Deidesheim wines with roast partridge and cabbage; *Saumagen* (pig's stomach stuffed with chopped pork, carrots, potatoes, and herbs, boiled and roasted, and served sliced thick like a huge sausage) is a superb foil for any Rheinhessen wine; and I remember particularly a Niersteiner, sharp-sweet as any I have had, deliciously in key with pheasant livers and wild mushrooms, served on a bed of creamy mashed potatoes.

One of the finest partnerships of German wines with food that I have ever enjoyed was a pair of 1969 Auslesen from Schloss Rheinhart, one an Ockfener Herrenberg, the other an Ockfener Bockstein, served together at a San Francisco dinner with a plain sauté of cod accompanied by new potatoes rolled in butter and lightly sprinkled with sea salt. The buttery quality of fish and potatoes made an exquisite marriage with the wines, something impossible had they been bone dry. And in a local restaurant just a few months ago, I was served a 1976 Steinberger Kabinett, hardly a dry wine, with a terrine of leeks. A *coulis* of tomato brought out the sweetness of the wine and linked it to the terrine perfectly.

A fine Beerenauslese can be as magnificent on its own as with dessert. The choice of dessert for such a wine, however, must be made with great care; an excessively sweet dish can overpower its delicate sweetness and make the wine seem both dry and characterless. The best accompaniment is a ripe peach; the worst, apart from anything with chocolate, is a creamy, sweet pastry. Matuschka-Greiffenclau claims that upside-down apple cake is best to show off a rich German wine, but the ripe papaya and lime once served to me with a 1959 Eitelsbacher Karthäuserhofberg Beerenauslese was a revelation, and the memory of a 1959 Hallgartner Deutelsberg Beerenauslese served to me with a fresh pear sorbet only last night has been an aid and stimulus as I have been writing.

The most successful conclusion to the *trocken* controversy will be recognition of what German wines are and can be rather than imposition of a style that is fashionable but irrelevant (another wistfully dated word) to German vineyards. Whatever the outcome, however, the battle itself has stimulated fresh and intelligent concern for wine within Germany, and growers always do better for that.

Baden-Württemberg

WITH SALES of basic Rhine and Mosel wines increasing dramatically despite higher prices, it is surprising to discover that roughly one bottle of German wine in four is now made from grapes grown in Baden-Württemberg, a region we hardly ever hear of. In 1981, more than 200 million bottles of wine were produced there, at least twice as much as in the Moselle. But local consumption (Badeners cheerfully drink twice as much wine per capita as other Germans do) and growing demand elsewhere, particularly from northern Germany, is such that there is never enough, despite extensions to the vineyards in recent years. Considering this, I suppose the absence of Baden wines from this side of the Atlantic should not be unexpected.

Tucked into the southwestern corner of Germany, Baden-Württemberg (the two regions are usually thought of together) is a viticultural backwater to most. I have yet to stumble into a discussion of its wines conducted with the fervor usually reserved for the growths of the middle Moselle or the more pronounceable parts of the Rheingau. To be fair, I am not sure that even the best of Baden can equal the best of what we think of as the traditional stretches of the Rhine; but taken as a whole, and particularly in the price range of wines that we meet in the ordinary course of events, I find Baden wines incomparably more charming than other German wines. They are lighter than Alsace wines from across the river (Baden lies between the Rhine and the Black Forest), drier than Rhine wines as they are made today, and, though often as fragrant as most Moselles, they are much softer.

Baden, a long, narrow wine region that stretches from Heidelberg to the Swiss frontier, is divided into a number of areas, each with slightly different characteristics. Württemberg is just to the north and east—in and adjacent to the valley of the Neckar—and extends from Stuttgart to Heilbronn. The vineyards of both regions are among the most romantic in the world: they tumble down precipitous slopes from impenetrable castles in the Ortenau, spread in terraces through Hansel-and-Gretel villages of the once-volcanic Kaiserstuhl, carpet with lush green the sides of the Staufenberg above Heilbronn, and run like leafy ribbons through the pink baroque palaces of Meersburg to the shore of Lake Constance. The Black Forest protects them from the cold east winds, and the Vosges Mountains keep back the Atlantic rains. Baden is Germany's driest and sunniest region. It is also, perhaps, its most beautiful. As if the setting between mountain and river were not already enough, the villages, nestled in vineyard and orchard, are smothered in flowers from spring to fall, with geraniums massed on balconies and windowsills.

Every restaurant and *Weinstube* offers Baden wines in open carafe, and, even when sold without particulars of vineyard or grape, the wines always have a distinctive light, flowery style. The names on the bottles of labeled wines will at first strike a familiar chord. Sylvaner and Riesling, after all, are to be found up and down the Rhine. In Baden-Württemberg they are used together, separately, or in one of the several hybrids that have been crossbred from them. Müller-Thurgau, for example, which takes up fully a third of the vineyard acreage in Baden, brings the zest of Riesling to the good yields and mild flavor of Sylvaner. It shows a sturdier resistance to adverse weather than does the Riesling and a better balance in the finished wine than a Sylvaner.

A closer look at a Baden wine list, however, reveals names of vines quite unfamiliar, or, at least, quite unexpected in Germany. Pinot Gris, for example, known here as Ruländer, is planted extensively in Baden and yields white wine with a style somewhere between that of a plump white Burgundy and a fruity Moselle.

Traminer, labeled locally as Clevner until the new German wine law of 1971 forbade the practice ("What is not approved is forbidden"—bureaucrats will eventually tidy all the magic out of wine), is less heady in Baden than is usually the case in Alsace, but it is no less aromatic. And the Blauer Spätburgunder is none other than the familiar Pinot Noir, used here both for soft, light red wines and for Weissherbst, the rosé of the Kaiserstuhl—created, it is said, solely to assuage the academic rigors of nearby Freiburg. (Freiburg must be a very rigorous place: it is also soothed by the wine of the Glottertal, made from a combination of Spätburgunder and Ruländer and one of the most delicious rosés in the world.) Pinot Blanc, known here as Weissburgunder, is grown in small patches; and in the south of Baden, in the Markgräflerland, most of the white wine is made from Gutedel, a variety said to be unique to Baden but that produces wine with a marked resemblance to that of the simple Chasselas of Alsace.

In different proportions, most of these varieties also grow in Württemberg. There, emphasis is on red and rosé wines, however. Some attractive ones are made from Spätburgunder, even though the growers have adopted the Rhine practice of adding a little of the unfermented grape juice to their Spätburgunder wines. Perhaps enhancing to a thin or characterless white wine, the addition brings an unnecessary—and unwelcome—sweet finish to a red. The Trollinger, a variety that I have never found elsewhere, though great, is more commonly used in the valley of the Neckar. It has little personality and seems most agreeable to me when fermented as a rosé, when it is usually mixed with white grapes anyway. This rosé is a specialty of the Neckar and is known as Schillerwein, not in honor of the poet, but because it is iridescent. It is also the café wine of Stuttgart and the student wine of Heidelberg. Another red wine grape of the Neckar, the Lemberger, is becoming quite rare, perhaps understandably.

I owe my first acquaintance with Baden wines to one of my London colleagues who had returned from a summer visit to cousins in the Ortenau (the heart of the Baden region) glowingly enthusiastic. His description of bucolic simplicity in an old farmhouse surrounded by vines and plum trees was given sharper perspective when he presented me with the notes on the wines he had tasted from the cellars of his cousins and their aristocratic neighbors. "Lords are lordliest in their wine," said Milton, and it seemed as if my friend had indeed caught a glimpse of paradise regained. At that point there was little doubt that I would allow time to see Baden for myself on my next trip to Germany.

That first visit was enchanting. By good fortune I arrived in the Ortenau in early spring, when the orchards were in bloom and young shoots were just appearing in the vineyards. The new wines —the delicious 1964s—were just ready to be sampled, and they were as tender and fresh as everything I saw around me.

I started my tasting tour at the vineyards of Freiherr von Neveu above the pretty village of Durbach. They cover barely thirty acres, most of them surrounding his house and a few at Ortenberg, five miles or so to the south. The vineyards are so steep that they can be plowed only with the aid of a winch. A man sits on the plow and guides it as it is hauled up by motor-driven wire. And after every storm the topsoil must be laboriously carried back up the slopes in baskets.

My host first offered me his Ortenberger Freudental, made from a Riesling-Sylvaner cross, and I could not have had a more delightful introduction to his wines. It was light, fresh, and clear. We tasted from almost every batch in his cellar, including some wines from older vintages. His 1962 Durbacher Grillenhalde (a vineyard name that has been swallowed in the reorganization of German vineyards) made from late-picked Traminer grapes, was one that I bought for our London cellars. The wine was pale gold in color, and the original aroma of the Traminer grape had delicately fused into the more complex bouquet developed in the bottle. Though velvety full, it was not heavy, and the sweetness, perfectly in balance, seemed only to complete—logically, to "close"—the wine.

The vineyard at Schloss Staufenberg, a knightly manor belonging to the Markgraf Max von Baden, sit on the other side of the valley from von Neveu's house. The manor was built in the eleventh century, and the view it commands across the Rhine to the Vosges beyond suggests that the choice of site was not dictated by viticultural needs alone. When I arrived, a checkered cloth had already been spread on a table in the shade of an old linden tree in the courtyard so that we could taste and enjoy the panorama at the same time.

Herr Duhr, the vineyard administrator, began our tasting with a wine from one of the smaller, outlying von Baden vineyards north of Durbach: Schloss Ebersteiner Grafensprung. He intended it as a curtain raiser, nothing more. But delighting in its fragrance and delicacy, I began to realize that the Baden growers take these characteristics so for granted that they no longer perceive them as qualities. They offer graceful wines as a foil for their more complex wines, those with which they wish to please and impress. But the simple wines of Baden are as impressive in their way as the most extraordinary, and therein lies the charm of the region.

We went on to taste each of the other wines produced by Herr Duhr, including the clean, fresh Spätburgunder from Schloss Eberstein; but the wine that pleased me most was again a Traminer, from the Staufenberger Schlossberg. It was a heavy wine, detectably Traminer on the palate, but with a bouquet reminiscent of roses.

I continued my tasting at the third of the great Durbach estates, that of Graf Metternich. I was no longer surprised at my pleasure in the least significant of the wines—this time a Durbacher Hatsbach made from Müller-Thurgau grapes, crisp, clean, and with a bouquet that was almost spicy. Herr Schilli, the manager of the Metternich'sches Weingut, is widely respected in Baden for the skill with which he preserves in each wine the sharp characteristic of its grape variety and the personality of each particular vineyard site. Trained in France and Italy as well as in Germany, Schilli brings an unusual breadth of view to his winemaking. He produced for us a Durbacher Annaberg Spätlese Eiswein, an exceptional wine with a sustained bouquet and the flavor of pears; a Durbacher Herrenberg Sauvignon Blanc, from what are thought to be the only Sauvignon Blanc vines in Germany; an Auslese of incredible richness and fruitier than any Sauternes I have tasted; and what was again my favorite, a Traminer from the Durbacher Schlossberg that was full-flavored, firm, and muscular.

It can hardly be accidental that the three leading wine estates of Baden are all to be found at Durbach, but in terms of commercial activity the center of the Baden wine region is Breisach, an old town on the Rhine close to Freiburg and the Kaiserstuhl. It is the home of the Baden central wine cooperative, the largest and probably the most up-to-date in Europe. At the end of World War II the vineyards of Baden were disorganized, the wines poorly distributed and in chronic surplus. The central cooperative was founded in 1952 as a marketing channel rather than as a means to rationalize production. But gradually the two concepts have become one, and, as I have learned from successive visits, Baden is now by far the best organized viticultural region in the world.

What is especially striking is the care taken in handling even the smallest batches of grapes, despite the scale of the cellar operations. Unlike most other cooperatives that feel compelled to combine all grades of grapes from their members, at Breisach every batch is sorted according to varietal, vineyard origin, time of picking, and quality. Gleaming like a space-age fantasy, Breisach was among the first to practice low-temperature fermentation (one of the reasons why Baden wines are so fragrant) and has been a source of technical know-how to wineries everywhere, including California. The quantities of wine that leave Breisach every day are indeed huge, but the numbers are impressive only because every single bottle is a delight and does credit to the growers.

To make a visit to Breisach even more agreeable, the cooperative has funded a small, elegant hotel in the old part of town, with spectacular Rhine views from the dining room and a kitchen to show off the region's best dishes. Or one can drive into the Black Forest and spend a weekend in Hinterzarten, a chocolate-box village where the Park Hotel Adler gives the visitor the illusion of having stepped back in time—but with the latest, and most delicious, Baden wines to accompany him.

Vineyards of Cyprus

CYPRIOTS LOST the habit of drinking wine during the centuries of Ottoman rule when it was all but prohibited. "In summer we drink beer," a Cypriot friend explained to me. "And in winter, brandy. In tumblers." With thumb and finger spread wide he indicated a daunting measure. "Like this."

His remarks were ironic: though Cyprus produces less than a tenth of an average crush in California, the island has the distinction of being the largest producer of grapes, per capita, in the world. Almost a third of the population is involved, one way or another, in growing grapes and making wine. Grape growing is not only the principal agricultural occupation, but provides, with tourism, an important source of needed foreign currency.

From 1878 until 1960, Cyprus was a British colony, and although heavy wine is not always appropriate for southern climates, it is comforting in January in Manchester. The sugar-rich grapes of the island were turned to good account, producing a sweetish wine of sherry style for export in keeping with popular British taste. The preferential duties formerly applied to Commonwealth wines helped Cyprus sherry, already obligingly inexpensive, capture suburban sideboards, and since almost all of the island's wine production was being exported, it was of some consequence that,

as recently as in 1974, 90 percent of it went to the United Kingdom—a monoculture for a monomarket that would give stomach
cramps to an economic strategist.

And with good cause. Political shifts and Common Market
engagements have since cut Britain's imports of Cyprus wines by
half in just a few years, and the style of wine that so satisfied East
Grinstead has little appeal elsewhere in the world. Buying time
by bartering goods, the government of Cyprus has avoided a
crisis through shipping wine in bulk to the Eastern bloc, and
programs to deal with the problem, already in the offing for some
years, have been accelerated. Basically, they hinge on converting
vineyards to grape varieties better calculated to provide the lighter
table wines that European and American consumers most appreciate. But with scant resources (Cyprus is suffering from the consequences of the Turkish invasion and occupation of a substantial
part of the island) and limited research, it is difficult to know
what those varieties should be, what style of wine would be most
readily acceptable where, and what will be the source of funds
to make it happen.

The traditional wine grapes of Cyprus, growing on terraced
slopes of the Troodos Mountains near Limassol and Paphos in the
southwest of the island, are distinctive. At least three quarters of
them, and perhaps more, are Mavro, a Greek word that means,
simply, "black." Indigenous to Cyprus, Mavro is unlike other
wine grape varieties, not least because of size. Compared with table
grapes, wine grapes are sometimes no larger than peas, but each
Mavro grape can be an inch across, and hangs within massive
bunches ten and twelve inches long.

The second most widely grown grape, the white Xynisteri, is
also indigenous to Cyprus, and even the third, the purple-red
Ophthalmo (the name, of course, means, "eye") seems to have
little connection to standard European varieties. Sultana, a raisin
grape also used for wine, on the other hand, is cousin to our own
Thompson seedless, and Muscat of Alexandria is familiar enough
in the vineyards that stretch along the Mediterranean coast from
Málaga in Spain to Narbonne in France.

Mavro and Xynisteri, resistant to drought, are well adapted to
the parched hillsides of the three villages—Zoopighi, Kalachorion,
and Gerasa—that make up the legally defined area of production
of Commandaria, the ancient dessert wine of Cyprus. Though its

present name is but a few centuries old, Homer mentioned the wine in passing, Hesiod gave detailed instructions for making it that hardly vary from practice today, Solomon sang about it, and in the thirteenth century Philippe August of France, in what must have been the earliest recorded comparative tasting in which French wine ceded place to another, described Commandaria as "the Apostle of Wines." Left for four or five days on mats in the sun, the grapes, their sugar thus concentrated by dehydration, produce a wine with as much as 18 percent natural unfermented sugar. It is easy to see how grapes used to produce such rich wine could have been diverted to the production of sherry; it is also easy to understand why the Cyprus Viticultural Commission was unconvinced that they would be ideal for table wines.

Twenty-five years ago, the then-colonial government had already started to tackle the question by asking a prominent French authority for advice on new varieties of grape that would adapt to the climate of the island and to its rocky terrain while producing, at very least, table wines of sound commercial quality without loss of yield. (Holdings are small, and livings already precarious.) Seventy-five varieties were introduced in 1959, doubtless as a consequence, but, given the different microclimates that each was to be tested in, one has to wonder whether such a huge number was the result of any kind of selection. Be that as it may, by 1964 the range had been reduced to just a dozen or so, and their grapes were brought into a series of winemaking tests at the government Viticultural Research Institute. They included Palomino and Pedro Ximenez grapes from Spain; Carignan, Grenache, and Cinsault, commonly used in the south of France; Merlot, Cabernet Sauvignon, and Sémillon from Bordeaux; and even Riesling and Aligoté from the temperate north. Sixteen years later, the jury is still out, though here and there, usually but not always in experimental lots, a Cabernet Sauvignon, a Carignan-Grenache blend, or a light, dry Palomino will appear unexpectedly and dumbfound those who thought they knew what Cyprus was, and was not, capable of producing.

In Cyprus, vineyards are small, wineries are huge. If there is an estate winery on the island, in the French or Italian sense, I am not aware of it. Perhaps those centuries of official discouragement made it impossible for peasant families to accumulate the basic tools and implements needed to turn grapes into wine. The spanking new wineries, resplendent with shiny steel, that sprout from every Napa knoll allow us to forget that in most wine-producing countries few families can hope to build and equip such a facility in a lifetime, let alone in a year. Vineyards, buildings, presses, vats, and vaults are acquired, enlarged, extended, improved, and replaced over several generations, and in Cyprus the sudden revival of a wine industry was made possible only by the concentrated resources of a few large establishments. There are just five of them. Keo, probably the largest, is "owned by the community"; Sodap (the names are not felicitous, but probably mean something cheerful in Greek) is a growers' cooperative; Loel is a public company; Etko is partly owned by the British brewing company Bass-Charrington. Only Christoforou, the smallest, is a completely private company.

With so few outlets, it comes as no surprise to discover that there is a buyers' market for grapes, and many growers have difficulty disposing of their crop. Grapes are brought to a winery against a prearranged contract, but the companies and the cooperatives give preference to "stockholders." The Viticultural Commission regulates and supervises the sale of grapes; an official once tried to explain to me (unsuccessfully) the procedure by which a grower applies for a government quota certificate that will allow him to dispose of his production to wineries in quantities over and above those contracted for (or not contracted for, as the case might be). The paper chase of multiple applications was too Byzantine for me to follow, but I suppose it is simple enough to those who have to understand it in order to survive.

In an effort to raise quality—and, perhaps, as a first step to uprooting vines in less favored areas—the government is attempting to define "quality zones," grapes from which will command a premium. The program is intended to identify style and quality differences based on geography, and, by bringing Cyprus closer to the European system of controlled appellations, to make Cyprus's entry to the Common Market (a fervent hope) a more practical possibility. As yet, a bottle of Cyprus wine rarely reveals anything of its geographic (or varietal) origin; brand names on labels are either romantically allusive (Aphrodite, Othello, Hermes) or fey (White Lady, Dark Lady, Rose Lady, etc.). But the wineries are experimenting with the new grapes, both alone—Cabernet Sauvignon, for example, and Palomino—and in combination with traditional Cyprus varieties.

Etko gives the impression of being more involved with Cabernet Sauvignon trials than are the other wineries. With pride, the company shows its newly constructed underground cellar in which it holds numerous batches of Cabernet Sauvignon wines made over the past few years for experimental aging. I have not been able to check the results, but other (admittedly young) examples that I have tasted on the island have been agreeably well balanced if underwhelming in distinctive Cabernet character.

Much more has been done in the way of combining new varieties with existing grapes, especially by Loel. For example, under the name Amathus, Loel produces a white wine that combines new Palomino with old, established Muscat. Dry and fresh, there is just enough Muscat to add interest to aroma and taste without distorting the basic delicacy of the Palomino grape. (Loel also makes a wine from Palomino alone. In Cyprus it is sold under the grape name, an important exception to the general rule, and in the United States as Cyprus Chablis. Very pale, very dry, and very neutral, it lacks exactly the lift that Muscat gives Amathus.) Another successful Loel combination brings the bite of Carignan to Mavro, much as Carignan does to Grenache in the south of France. Sold under the name Hermes, the blend sometimes has an aroma of plum or apricot kernels—in no way disagreeable—with the brisk style of a young Claret.

Keo, on the other hand, seems to stay with classic Cyprus varieties, and combines Ophthalmo grown at high altitude with Mavro to produce their red Othello, the first Cyprus table wine that I was familiar with. In the sixties, we used to drink it copiously with *souvlaki* and *stifado* at a Greek restaurant in the shade of London's Post Office Tower, of which I have scruffy but affectionate memories. The wine is agreeably fruity, not too heavy, and ages surprisingly well. A bottle of the 1959 from the cellars of the Forest Park Hotel, high in the Troodos Mountains, was still delicious when I had it there just a year or so ago. (Sodap's Salamis, made from the same two grapes, is similar in style and also develops well in bottle.) Keo has successfully combined traditional local white grapes, too. St. Panteleimon, made from Xynisteri and Sultana, has a crisp citrus bouquet with a slightly sweet finish that I find more to my taste than that firm's Aphrodite (made from Xynisteri alone and aged in wood before bottling) and more substantial than its rather frail Bellepais (made from early-picked Sultana grapes alone). I might be prejudiced about Bellepais. I first had it at a *taverna* in the old section of the port of Limassol as accompaniment to a truly superb *mireni*—some kind of sea bream, I think—which had been split and broiled and served with just a jug of mixed olive oil and lemon juice as sauce. We would have needed wine from Ganymede's cup to have done justice to its splendor. A better example of a single-grape Cyprus white wine is Etko's Graves, sold in the United States as Neferli. It is a clean, pleasantly dry wine from Xynisteri that seems to be fresher and more consistent than Aphrodite.

Though markets in Europe and America are the most important objectives for these table wines, the wineries understand the paradox that healthy overseas trade needs a healthy home market. Despite my Cypriot friend's predilection for beer and brandy, in the last few years his compatriots have already been persuaded to consume a rising 10 percent of the island's wine production. As part of the campaign to make Cypriots themselves more familiar with the island's wines, the public park of Limassol is given over each September to a week-long festival in honor of Dionysus. It is a curiously decorous affair, I have to say, that borrows little from the ancient world. But it allows all who pay the modest entry fee an evening of serious tasting or orderly revel according to taste. In either case, it brings wine closer to those who produce it, and for that, one feels, Homer would nod his approval.

Piedmont: A Changing World

A VISIT TO PIEDMONT a number of years ago rid me of at least one illusion. We had spent a week skiing in Val-d'Isère, and because the Col de l'Iseran was closed for the winter we had to take the long route, backtracking almost as far as Chambéry to reach Modane, the French terminus of the Mont Cenis Tunnel. After the stinging chill of the high Solaise, there was a mild smell of spring in the valley, a foretaste, I thought, of what awaited us once through the mountains. Dazed by bright sunshine, we would emerge into Italy symbolically reborn, to green fields, even wild flowers, perhaps, in the soft drift of Mediterranean air.

Alas, my fantasy was shattered at Bardonecchia, as we swept out and into a blizzard worse than anything we had experienced all winter north of the Alps, and our descent into Turin presented a challenge to downhill courage greater than any slope we had tackled the previous week. Twice we landed in a ditch, and the car, in a final sulk, packed up its windshield wipers so that the last exhausting hour was spent with both side windows down and driver and passenger doing their best with numbed hands to maintain some visibility and avoid total disaster. Dazed, indeed.

Relaxed and restored by a warm bath and a hot rum toddy, we set off for dinner, walking to the Ristorante del Cambio on the

Piazza Carignano. I love the formal arcades of central Turin, and the illuminated snow and recessed shadows gave sharp patterns to the façades of the streets. Our appetites had become pretty sharp, too, in the cold air, and we were glad to arrive in the welcoming atmosphere of the Cambio.

Every time I have been to Turin I have visited this restaurant, but as it is now some years since I was there I can only hope that the changes that have engulfed the city have left undisturbed at least this one distillation of sedate Piedmontese charm. The old-fashioned dining room took its age gracefully, linen stiffly starched and waiters gently courteous. One ignored occasional signs of wear in the red plush, of course, or a random weak spring in the banquettes, with the same respect with which one does not notice the wavering voice of an elderly orator or see the unsteady foot of an older, beautiful woman.

The wine list included the most extensive collection of Piedmont wines I had ever seen, and the selections, I was later to realize, were chosen from among the best growers in the area. Repairs to the car kept me in Turin (not the most miserable of fates), and I was able to sample further the contents of the cellars of the Cambio, as instructive an introduction to the wines of Piedmont as one could have.

The northern romantic sees the vineyards of Piedmont as an extension of the prolific arbors and trellises of the south. But the region is on roughly the same latitude as Bordeaux and the French Massif Central and shares the brusque shifts of weather typical of a sub-Alpine climate. The Piedmont vineyards, small and orderly, are often on steep terraces and produce wines of wide variety. Some of the wines are as big as the imagination allows, though rarely with the intemperate swagger so falsely associated with Italian wines; in Piedmont, alcoholic strength and full body are usually balanced by good acidity and delicacy of flavor. Others, Grignolino, for example, and Freisa—the latter on occasion so perfumed that one might be forgiven for suspecting a fruit essence in the wine—are light, mild, and often slightly sweet.

With wines so varied, the layman (and often the professional) has a hard time making sense of the taste of Piedmont, let alone the names and categories of the wines, despite the introduction of Denominazione di Origine Controllata (the Italian version of *appellation contrôlée*) in the 1960s.

It is confusing that some wines are identified and labeled geographically—Barolo and Barbaresco are both named for the legally defined zones where they are grown—whereas others, such as Dolcetto and Brachetto, are named for the grapes from which they are made, and yet others are named both geographically and varietally: Barbera d'Asti, for example, or Barbera del Monferrato (a wine in which, to complete the confusion, Italian law allows a proportion of grapes other than Barbera).

There are those who will disagree with me, but I find I make sense of Piedmont only if I distinguish between wines made from Nebbiolo and Barbera grapes, wines that I regard as serious, and those made from other grapes, which, charming though they can be, are country wines in the best sense—right for drinking on the spot, and not too critically. Brachetto, Dolcetto, and Freisa grapes make simple wines, often with a light sparkle artfully introduced and sometimes with unfermented grape sugar deliberately retained to give an *amabile* style that may be pleasing but is rarely flattering in the course of a serious dinner.

The best of this "other" group is Grignolino. Drunk young, when its bright ruby color has an unusual orange cast, it is delightfully undemanding. There are good examples in every *trattoria* in Turin, where new Grignolino is held in much the same affectionate regard as young Beaujolais is in Lyon, and for the same reasons. It tastes attractively of the grape and is mild in both alcohol and acidity. Unfortunately, the Grignolino vine is disappearing in Piedmont, unable to resist a virulent vine mold. Even in California, where there was once extensive acreage, there now stand barely a hundred acres of Grignolino (and some maintain darkly that those survive only because they actually contain a hybrid of Grignolino and Brachetto rather than Grignolino itself).

Nebbiolo wines, however, are not to be trifled with. Dark and rich, they are full of tannin when young and sometimes retain a faintly bitter zest even at their peak. Each vineyard gives its own distinct style, and so does the choice of subvarietal (there are several subvarietals of Nebbiolo, of which two are widely used). Barbera wine, without the complexity of flavor and bouquet of Nebbiolo, lacks none of its strength or color. As a varietal it is stable—in the sense that subvarieties are few—and the Barbera vine is recognizably the same wherever it grows, whether in Piedmont or California.

The province of Cuneo, between Turin and Genoa, is the center for Nebbiolo. Production encircles the town of Alba, also distinguished as the commercial source of Piedmont white truffles. To the southwest, Barolo spreads its vines across two valleys of the Langhe hills. To the northeast lies Barbaresco, seemingly larger in area than Barolo but made up of many scattered pockets of vines, which together give an annual yield barely a quarter of that of Barolo. Lastly, to the northwest is the zone where wines called Nebbiolo d'Alba are grown. Barolo has a production of almost half a million cases of wine a year, and roughly the equivalent of 300,000 cases are produced each year with the right to the denomination Nebbiolo d'Alba.

Barbaresco sounds like the name of a character in a minor Mozart opera; Barolo has a full-bellied ring. The wines share something of this simplistic contrast, with Barbaresco less assertive and less robust than its neighbor. Barolo is referred to as the "king of wines and wine of kings," no doubt an allusion and compliment to the House of Savoy, which rose from its Piedmont origins to rule unified Italy until deposed after World War II. All Italians (even those who have never tasted it) will tell you of the excellence of Barolo, as if belief in its superiority were a matter of national pride. Yet despite the hyperbole, enough to drive the most charitable to skepticism, Barolo does indeed stand above all other Italian wines for the consistency with which examples will touch our highest expectations of red wines.

Vineyard holdings in Barolo are small, with few exceptions. Many growers sell their grapes because their acreage hardly justifies the expense of equipping a winery. La Morra, a commune with more than a third of the vineyards entitled to the Barolo denomination, might be a patchwork of tiny farms, but it is more important as a winegrowing center than Barolo itself. Its vineyards face southwest and bear grapes that ripen easily in afternoon sun to yield soft, fat wines. Southeastward, across the valley to the commune of Barolo and then across the watershed to Serralunga d'Alba, the wines get progressively firmer, harder. The subvariety of Nebbiolo most widely used for Barolo is Lampia, a vine of prolific and untidy growth. Michet, less common (and hardly found at all in Barbaresco), is a tight, neat vine giving tight, neat wines. Rosé, a Nebbiolo variety that, as its name suggests, produces light-colored wines, is rarely found now, though it was once

popular. In the chalky soils of the Barolo hills, Lampia and Michet give intensely flavored wines with good color and a capacity for long aging. Barbaresco wines, more perfumed when young, are less forceful and age less well. Nebbiolo d'Alba, grown on the sandier soils across the Tanaro, has the characteristics of wines grown on sand everywhere—fragrance, quick development, and lack of depth.

Other Nebbiolo wines of Piedmont include Spanna, a synonym for Nebbiolo, grown without geographic delimitation; Gattinara from the province of Vercelli; and Ghemme and Sizzano from the hills of Novara. (I once found an amazing wine at Sizzano, made not from Nebbiolo but from Fogarino vines brought back from Sicily by Giuseppe Bianchi. Neighbors mocked, were even scandalized, and his father forbade him to sell the wine he made from these alien grapes. When his father died, Bianchi submitted a sample to the annual wine fair of Piedmont, *the* classic wine event of the year in Italy, just as a lark. He won the top award with his Fogarino wine, to his own and everyone else's astonishment. I tasted his 1958 vintage in his kitchen while we enjoyed a country soup that Signora Bianchi had enriched with a cloud of beaten egg, bread crumbs, and grated Parmesan cheese. I acknowledge that it might have added to both my pleasure and satisfaction in the wine.)

But Gattinara, Ghemme, and Sizzano are made on a small scale and are not found easily outside Italy. Consumed mostly by those who make them, they have changed little over the years.

Barolo, Barbaresco, even the Barberas of Piedmont, on the other hand, have changed quite a lot. When I first went exploring in the region twenty-five years ago, I was more than surprised at some of the things I saw. Young wines were commonly left on the gross lees of their casks long after they had fallen bright, a practice that sometimes gave Piedmont wines a lees-y taste. Even when racked promptly, wines were kept in wood interminably, adding to the harsh, dry qualities of Nebbiolo instead of mellowing them. And wines bottled at the appropriate time, when mature, were often decanted into fresh bottles for shipment to eliminate any deposit that might have formed.

Once, touring the cellars of a distinguished wine company in Piedmont, I entered a room filled with an exquisite aroma. Girls sitting at long tables were decanting hundreds of bottles of old

Barolo so that the wine could be shipped bright to New York. Along with the deposit, the bouquet that had taken twenty years to form was also left behind. (I wonder if those who fuss about the natural deposit that forms in mature wines know what they surrender in order to avoid it?)

Nothing was as strange to me, however, as the technique of a winemaker in Alba. From oval casks I tasted his young red wines: without exception they were extraordinary. But when I tasted his bottled wines, even those newly under cork, I found them miserable—flat, maderized, and uninteresting. I soon learned why. He took me onto the roof and proudly showed me row upon row of five-gallon glass demijohns filled with wine "taking the sun." He gave this treatment to all his red wines for several months between barrel and bottle, a sure method, he explained to me, of guaranteeing stability. Pasteurization by solar energy is the way modern ecologists might describe it.

In order to persuade the grower to sell me in barrel some of the sound, young wines that I coveted, I vowed that once arrived in London, and before bottling, the wine would be transvased into demijohns and given the benefit of a Thames-side sunning above our Tower Hill cellars. The satisfaction of knowing the pleasure I gave our customers by making these wines available in an unadulterated state still barely stifles my twinges of guilt at so deliberately misleading him.

In recent years, there has been a revolution in the making of Piedmont wines. One generation has succeeded another, and new ideas prevail. Prompt racking, early bottling, careful aging are now the general rule, and it is rare that any wine made within the last decade will show the characteristics of old-style Barolo. The grower now aims to produce softer, fresher, fruitier wines. To my taste, these changes, in keeping with current practice everywhere, are improvements.

The difference between old and new was presented to me with unintentional but dramatic clarity at a recent dinner in Berkeley. A sequence of wines was served made by two generations of the Mascarello family of Piedmont, first some wines made by the son, Mauro, winemaker since 1967, and then older wines made by his father, Giuseppe. We started with a 1974 Nebbiolo d'Alba made by Mauro, a suave and elegant wine, followed by a 1971 Barbera d'Alba, which was generous, fruity and easy to enjoy.

The first of the Barolos, a 1970 from the family's Monprivato vineyard, was surprisingly delicate in style, as was the 1968, in which I caught a hint of mirabelle. Then we passed to a 1964 Barolo made by Giuseppe, and the old style was immediately apparent. The wine was woodier, and its complexity was matched by harsher qualities than the younger wines had shown. In a final 1961 we had a perfect example of old-style Barolo, with its strange suggestions of vanilla and old Oloroso.

The dishes that accompanied these wines were both unconventional and splendid. I was the guest of a music historian of some distinction who teaches at Berkeley and moonlights as a wine importer. With the chef of Il Pavone, he had planned a dinner of red snapper, poached in Nebbiolo and served with gnocchi no larger than peas; sorbet of Barbera wine and Barbera grapes; broth enriched with Barolo; and veal with herbs and truffles. My host told me how he had been drawn to Italian wine and food in the 1960s, while living in Bologna and working on his doctoral thesis. It seems he must have spent as much time ferreting out fine wines as he spent researching old manuscripts. When he returned to teach at Harvard, he put Boston wine merchants in touch with his favorite growers so he could continue to enjoy their wines. Soon he was departing for Italy each summer with commissions to find more wine that the world had overlooked, gradually slipping into the role of broker.

A few days later, watching him at work on a risotto milanese in his kitchen, I returned to our earlier talk of Piedmont wines. He produced for me a bottle of the 1970 Barbera d'Alba to compare with the 1971 we had drunk together at Il Pavone. It was lighter, with more bouquet and even a suggestion of bead on the tongue, a far cry from the stolid Barberas of the 1960s. Barbera d'Alba is not the most abundant of the three Barbera denominations (Barbera d'Asti is produced from double the acreage), but it is considered the best and the most fit for aging; Barbera d'Asti is finer and lighter; Barbera del Monferrato, perhaps because of the admixture of other grapes, is more perfumed but has a less robust flavor.

Sadly, many small growers of fine wines in Piedmont are inhibited from exporting their wines by the very procedures set up to help them. The bureaucratic controls imposed on all who wish to export wines from Italy, whether large shipper or small grower, were established to protect the reputation of Italian wines overseas —but they are time-consuming and costly. Growers who have little difficulty in selling their small and highly sought-after crops locally won't bother with the complications inherent in selling to an overseas market, a story that is not restricted to Piedmont, unfortunately. My friend is convinced, nevertheless, that we shall see more good wine arriving from Piedmont in the years ahead. Given the quality and the reasonable prices, I hope he is right.

Chianti:
An Old Wine,
A New Shape

M Y FAVORITE small restaurant in Florence is hardly a guitar strum from the Ponte Vecchio, but, fortunately, its unprepossessing entrance is enough to deter those who would misunderstand its simplicity. It's just a crowded cellar, down six precipitous steps from an already obscure arched alley. But there one eats real Tuscan food—fresh and abundant. With it, naturally, the proprietor serves pitchers of young Chianti—zesty, sprightly, fruity, exuberant, and eminently quaffable Chianti.

When I think of Chianti, I tend to wax nostalgic about my little Florentine *taverna* rather than the fine estates I have visited because, like everyone else, I suppose, I have enjoyed Chianti most often in just such a carefree setting, without ceremony. This popular image of Chianti causes problems for the growers, however, even while winning them friends; because there is more to Chianti than checkered tablecloths. Young Chianti in its romantic straw-covered flask might have been the greatest impediment to our discovering the fine, mature wines of the region, and the winegrowers of Tuscany are now engaged in a careful reassessment of what they want Chianti to mean.

The seven zones that produce Chianti are not extensive, yet they are diverse. Each one, tucked in a valley or fold of the Tuscan hills, claims a style of its own quite apart from the distinction, jealously maintained, between the *classico* zone and the rest. But one division cuts through all of them. On the one hand are Chianti wines made deliberately to be drunk young and traditionally bottled in the straw-covered flask, the very symbol of Chianti. On the other are wines so different in style, let alone quality, that the distance between them and the flask Chiantis is the distance between a *cru* like Moulin-à-Vent and simple Beaujolais, or between a first-rate Hermitage and a no-nonsense Côtes du Rhône. Matured in Yugoslav oak casks, such Chiantis are aged further in bottle— not in flasks, which cannot be binned, but in the shouldered bottle usually associated with Bordeaux wines and used, in fact, wherever red wines are expected to throw a deposit when aged. (The shoulder helps catch the deposit when decanting.) Chianti made for early drinking can be released for sale in March after the vintage, but quality Chianti (known in Italy as *vecchio*) cannot be released, by law, for two years. Wines labeled *riserva* must be held for an additional third year before release. In addition, of course, there are higher minimum quality standards imposed for both *vecchio* and *riserva* wines.

Though some parts of the Chianti region are better endowed than others to produce such wines appropriate for aging, most growers make both kinds in proportions that vary from year to year, depending on the conditions of the vintage. There is a practical reason, too, why growers prefer to make some wine for early consumption as well as some for aging. If the produce of an entire vintage were to be reserved in the cellars, first in wood and then in bottle, with others following in succession, there could easily be a stock of three or four years' production of wine held at any one time. Few growers could find the money to finance such a quantity; and, at the present time, when the finest aged Chianti will fetch a price not much more than the most youthful, there is little incentive for the grower to incur the expense even if he could. With at least part of his crop made into wine that can be released, sold, and enjoyed at once, a grower can pay his bills, and the cost of carrying the balance for aging is easier to bear.

Why would a grower want to age wine at all if it doesn't pay him to do so? Pride, the respect of his peers, personal satisfaction—

all contribute more to winemaking decisions everywhere than do plain economics.

A grower decides for himself which of his wines will be sold young and which aged. Wine for aging is made from more rigorously selected grapes, perhaps from older vines on sections of a vineyard known to produce consistently high quality. But the conditions of each batch at the time of actual picking dictate what the grower will do with it. By varying the proportions of the different varietals used to make Chianti and by adapting his method of fermentation, he can either hasten a wine to early drinkability or reinforce the qualities necessary for long, even development in bottle. For example, all Chianti, no matter from which zone it comes, *classico* or not, must have at least 50 percent of its volume from the Sangiovese grape: it brings body and aroma to the wine. According to the regulations, there must also be at least 10 percent Canaiolo, a red grape that softens the effect of the Sangiovese, and at least 10 percent of a mixture of Malvasia and Trebbiano, white grapes that lighten the wine and give additional flavor. If the grower uses more Sangiovese, the wine will be darker, stouter, and more tannic for aging; more Canaiolo, and the wine will be softer; more Trebbiano or Malvasia, and the wine will be lighter and ready for market sooner.

Then, too, each grower can make up his own mind about the *governo*, a practice traditional to Tuscany whereby the scarcely finished young wine, weeks after the vintage, is provoked into a second fermentation by introducing the juice of grapes held back from the original crush and dried in order to concentrate their sugar. The warmth and activity generated by the renewed fermentation encourage what we call malolactic fermentation as well. Naturally and effectively, malic acid (the acid, present in young wines in large doses, that makes green apples taste green) is transformed into lactic acid (associated with milk). After the *governo* a young wine tastes less harsh, and because the fermentation leaves a slight "bead" in the wine, preserved when bottling as far as possible, it adds that sprightliness, felt on the tongue rather than seen, that is so characteristic of young Chianti.

The differences among the seven zones of Chianti production are easier to recognize, obviously, in wines of the quality that requires aging. Since these are generally the best of the crop of each grower, they are therefore more likely to show individual character and style; furthermore, the aging helps develop these distinctive characteristics.

Foremost among the seven zones, inevitably, is the region officially described as Chianti Classico. It lies between Florence and Siena, on a gravelly, sandy ridge, the ancient heart of Chianti. *Noblesse oblige*: Chianti Classico must conform to minimum standards slightly more stringent than those applied to other Chianti districts. An association of growers had already agreed on regulations to control standards of Chianti Classico long before the Denominazione di Origine Controllata laws were instituted in 1967, using the symbol of a black cockerel to identify the products of their members.

Following Chianti Classico, the zones of most importance are those of the Sienese hills (to the south) and the Florentine hills (to the north), Chianti Colli Senesi and Chianti Colli Fiorentini as they are known in Italian. But neither these names nor the names Chianti Colline Pisane (near Pisa), Chianti Colli Aretini (around Arezzo), or Chianti Montalbano (near Pistoia) are generally found on wine labels. They are generally sold just as "Chianti," even when they are estate-bottled. Chianti Rufina, the seventh zone, has a special reputation for its full-bodied wines, and growers there like to lay claim to their *denominazione*. (Rufina, the zone, should not be confused with Rufino, the brand.)

There is yet another association of growers, who became known as the Consorzio del Chianti Putto after the *putto*, or cherub, that they used as their distinguishing symbol. Founded by growers of the Colli Fiorentini, they too established quality standards for their members before the *denominazione* regulations were written, but they extended membership to *all* Chianti growers of *all* zones who were prepared to accept the criteria of quality that they applied. Today neither *putto* nor black cockerel has the significance it once did as a guarantee of quality because, since 1967, laws impose on all what were once voluntary standards accepted only by a few.

The growers' associations continue now principally to promote Chianti and the wines of their memberships. The use or nonuse of the symbols can be confusing to buyers, who sometimes wonder whether absence of the black cockerel from a Chianti Classico means that the wine is less *classico* than another. In fact, member-

Tuscany

N

Pistoia

CHIANTI
RUFINA

CHIANTI
MONTALBANO

FLORENCE

Rufina

Arno R.

COLLI
FIORENTINI

Pisa

COLLINE
PISANE

CHIANTI
CLASSICO

COLLI
ARETINI

Arezzo

Siena

COLLI SENESI

Montepulciano

Montalcino

Kms.
0   25
0   Miles   25

Area of
map

ITALY

Tyrrhenian
Sea

© 1982 A. Karl / J. Kemp

ship in the associations and use of their symbols is discretionary. It should also be said that wines from producers who belong to neither association can be as good as wine from those who do.

In recent years, the flask has all but disappeared. Countrywomen who were once content to spend their days binding the straw coverings can now find more profitable work. Chianti producers have turned to an alternative, elegantly shaped bottle, restricted to Tuscany. They know that part of the charm is lost, but they hope that if attention is focused on the contents instead of the container, the finer wines of Chianti will at last receive more attention.

But without the captivating flask, sales of young Chianti to export markets have slowed down, whereas sales of the finer mature wines, though growing steadily, have not increased fast enough to take up the slack. Tuscany pulses with fiercely held opinions on the direction growers should take to resolve their difficulties. Some want to see Chianti follow the success of California and of certain northern Italian wine regions by marketing their young wines in liter-and-a-half jugs. Others insist that Chianti has already suffered for too long from the quaffing-wine image of the flask and want to avoid its replacement by a container that would aggravate the situation. They urge less emphasis on the sale of young wine, especially in containers that do nothing to promote the distinctiveness of Chianti, and more concentration on Chianti for aging. They press for revision of the Chianti regulations to reduce the present maximum of 30 percent white grapes in the blends to 15 percent and to lower the minimum requirement of 10 percent white grapes to 5 percent, or even none at all. Without actually saying so, they would obviously prefer to see quaffing Chianti eliminated altogether, an unlikely development both because of the financial strain on growers that would result and because everyone knows there are large quantities of Chianti that are *better* for being drunk young, and there always will be.

Fewer white grapes used in the production of Chianti red wine would, of course, release more for the making of white wine in Tuscany. Currently the *denominazione* Chianti does not provide for other than red wine, and most white wine is without an official appellation. One of the finest white wines of Tuscany, for example, produced on the Pomino estate of the Frescobaldi family, is entitled to no *denominazione* at all, save that of plain "Tuscan white wine."

Surprisingly, the first recorded use of the name Chianti was for
white wine made from Trebbiano and Malvasia grapes; red wine
grown in the area was referred to simply as *vermiglio*. Such was the
case at least until the fourteenth century. How the red grapes in-
filtrated the white and took over the name is not certain. Today so
little white wine is produced in Tuscany, compared with the large
output of red, and so small is the proportion of it entitled to a *denominazione*, that statistics are scant and reveal little. Bianco Vergine
della Valdichiana is the white *denominazione* most frequently seen.
Roughly 7 or 8 million bottles of it are produced each year from
vineyards around Arezzo. With a pale straw color and crisp, not-
too-assertive taste, it is especially good with Tuscan ham and
the local herbed sausage. Vernaccia di San Gimignano, better
known, though of more limited production, is also dry, but more
ample. Sometimes it has the pungent aroma and flavor of certain
Sauvignon Blanc wines, and its fullness makes it an admirable accompaniment to pasta. In the summer of 1977 in Castellina in
Chianti, I drank a 1976 Vernaccia from La Quercia with gnocchi
in a sauce of Gorgonzola and Parmesan cheese and cream. Both
wine and dish seemed to be perfect, but then each brought out
something more in the other.

In an effort to promote white wine, growers of the Chianti
Classico zone have now formed a consortium to establish Bianco
della Lega as the eventual white *denominazione* for the region.
A separate group of growers have formed a consortium to promote
Galestro as the future *denominazione*. For the moment neither
name has the force of law, but both wines are based on the traditional white grapes of Tuscany, Trebbiano, and Malvasia, with
small proportions of Pinot Bianco, Sauvignon Blanc, and even
Chardonnay. The Galestro regulations, self-imposed by the consortium who produce it, include a requirement of fermentation at
low temperature and, most unusually, impose a *maximum* alcoholic
strength of 10.5 percent, to ensure that Galestro is always light and
fruity.

Supporters of the view that Chianti needs fewer white grapes in
the blend are paying an unspoken compliment to the Brunello
wines of Montalcino, within the Chianti region, south of Siena, but
defiantly sold with a *denominazione* of their own. At about the
time, a hundred years ago, that Baron Ricasoli was carrying out his
varietal experiments at Brolio, which led to the classic grape com-

bination of Sangiovese-Canaiolo-Malvasia-Trebbiano for Chianti, Ferruccio Biondi-Santi of Montalcino was experimenting with wine made solely from a clone of Sangiovese, known locally in Montalcino as Brunello. As one might expect, given the characteristics of the Sangiovese, it is heavier and longer-lived than traditional Chianti made from its combination of grapes. Today there are more than seventy growers producing Brunello di Montalcino, including Biondi-Santi's grandson. Their wines have become something of a cult, older vintages fetching prices within Italy that exceed anything paid for comparable vintages of the classed growths of Bordeaux; for as they age, Brunello wines seem to fill out and develop in an extraordinary way. Recently I had the good fortune to taste a series of vintages ranging from 1973 to 1945, all in the course of a leisurely luncheon in the Biondi-Santi's kitchen at Montalcino. We tasted examples of each of the successful vintages during that span of almost thirty years, and it must have been more than the chance style of each year that made them show better as each wine succeeded a younger one. The 1945, with its deep, lively color, was richly full-bodied, its bouquet and flavor giving delicate hints of cherries and vanilla.

The success of the growers of Montalcino has disconcerted the growers of Chianti, for the former have followed not only their own winemaking ideas but their own name, eschewing the *denominazione* Chianti to which they would have been entitled. Nor is Brunello di Montalcino the only wine within Chianti to follow its own course. Vino Nobile di Montepulciano has a history longer than that of Brunello—in fact, it is as old as Chianti itself—yet its reputation has remained largely local. A mixture of red and white grapes is used, as in traditional Chianti, to produce a wine of elegance and velvety softness. I have not tasted Montepulciano wines with more than ten years of aging, so I do not know if they continue to develop beyond that, but I remember a 1969 that accompanied a roast pigeon in a *taverna* of the town a year or two ago that was as near perfect a wine as any I have had. Here, too, the growers emphasize aged rather than young wines.

While the growers of Chianti debate their future, they continue to produce wines of uncommon grace. The *riservas* of the 1975 and 1977 vintages lend weight to arguments in support of more wine of this style and quality. Despite inflation, unpredictable currency exchange rates, and the host of other woes that combine to deprive us of so many classic wines, they are priced modestly and are among the most undervalued fine wines in the world today. If we do not take advantage of our good fortune, how shall we answer our grandchildren when they ask: "Where were you when the best Chiantis were practically given away?"

Chardonnay and Oak

TRISTRAM SHANDY's mother, you will remember, received his father's affections on the first Sunday of the month because that was the day he would wind the large house-clock on the stairs, and with one economical jog to his memory he could then be free from all "other little family concernments . . . at one time, and be no more plagued and pestered with them the rest of the month." It is no wonder that the poor woman developed confused ideas and associations that had no connection in nature.

We can all learn from her difficulty: to confuse ideas that are only circumstantially connected is all too human.

As far as Chardonnay and oak are concerned, in California the two were brought together by the late James D. Zellerbach, one-time Chairman of the Crown Zellerbach Corporation and a United States Ambassador to Italy. For his eventual retirement pleasure he created, in the early 1950s, an exquisite rendering of a small, fine Burgundy *clos*, said to be modeled on the Clos Vougeot. He took his fancy as a simple *vigneron* far more seriously than Marie-Antoinette took her afternoons as a shepherdess, playing with washed and beribboned lambs.

Perched on a hillside in southern Sonoma County, Hanzell Vineyards (a contraction of his wife's first and last names) is just large enough to handle the grapes of the attached twenty acres of terraced vines. Zellerbach sought perfection in Pinot Noir and Chardonnay, the great varietals of Burgundy that he cared so much about, and he had the resources to leave little to chance in his efforts to achieve it.

His winemaking neighbors were amused when he insisted on using small barrels of Limousin oak—imported from the master coopers of Burgundy—for aging his wines. After all, perfectly good barrels of American oak were available. The French barrels, with the rustic splitwood hoops that distinguish fat Burgundian *pièces* from slightly elongated Bordeaux *barriques*, gave an air of sturdy tradition to the aging room of the new winery. The first Chardonnay, produced from the 1956 vintage, was matured in them, and eventually Zellerbach had a few cases shipped to him at the embassy in Rome. To everyone's amazement, including his own, the wine had the elusive but unmistakable quality and flavor that had always been associated exclusively with the fine Chardonnay wines of the Côte d'Or—or, more particularly, the wines of the Côte de Beaune within the Côte d'Or.

Much of the quality, of course, was a direct result of the care with which all vineyard and winery operations had been carried out. Pruning was severe, to limit yield per acre; picking—ripe bunch by ripe bunch only—was selective; fermentation was at controlled low temperatures—Hanzell was one of the first California wineries to adopt this technique, which preserves delicate flavors in white wines; and nitrogen was used to protect the young wines from contact with air during the complex procedures of racking, storage, and bottling.

But it was clear that the key to the characteristic that had eluded California winemakers until then lay in the Limousin oak used to mature Chardonnay wines in parts of Burgundy. The two main oak species grown in Europe for wine casks differ from those found in the United States. Whether it is that difference or the way in which the wood is subsequently dried, treated, and prepared for cooperage that subsequently affects the taste of the wine is still moot; but no one denies that the flavor extracted by Chardonnay wines from European oak, and Limousin oak in particular, is distinct and easily recognized.

At first gradually, and then more rapidly, other wineries in California followed the Hanzell lead. It was a relatively simple change for the smaller wineries for whom the investment required to put modest stocks of wine into French oak was of manageable proportions. The larger wineries, faced with the logistics of acquiring and housing several thousand barrels, in addition to the cost and the magnitude of possible error (who was to say that the different taste introduced by oak would be acceptable to a wide American public, let alone pronounce on whether *different* was also better?), approached the new dogma with caution. For this reason oak-aged Chardonnays first appeared from the small wineries and, in the minds of many, have become associated with the concept of small-scale winemaking.

Unfortunately, the converted in all matters are notorious for their excess, and in twenty years it has become common for California Chardonnays to be judged simply by the degree of oak in the wine. The taste of oak itself, often oppressively exaggerated, has become so confused with what should be the varietal taste of Chardonnay that many assume the taste of oak to be the taste of Chardonnay, and they can sometimes be heard lamenting the lack of varietal character in a wine, when what they really miss is the flavor of oak.

The circumstantial nature of the Chardonnay and oak partnership, not to mention sundry other digressive matters, was brought to mind again a few weeks ago when I dined with one of the partners of the tiny Chalone Vineyard, far off the beaten track on a limestone bench in the Gabilans in the general area of the Pinnacles. To accompany a delicious salmon—cooked in a clay pot and served with a sauce that was adroitly created from some homemade mayonnaise, the pot juices, and tarragon while we sat chatting in the kitchen—he served the vineyard's 1973 Chardonnay together with a 1970 Corton-Charlemagne of Louis Latour. Both wines were superb: the Chalone was huge, robust, heavy; the Corton-Charlemagne, soft, light, and unassertive as many 1970 Burgundies, both white and red, are inclined to be.

At first, I was so overwhelmed by the Chalone with its slap-on-the-palate, well-met, open style that the Corton-Charlemagne seemed prissily withdrawn and its flavor excessively low-key. But as I retasted and reflected I wasn't sure that I didn't prefer the Corton-

Charlemagne. The intrinsic balance of the wine had been scrupu-
lously respected. No one had overlaid its delicate silkiness with a
jot more oak than needed. It gave me aesthetic satisfaction and a
jolt, too, by making me realize how easily we all fall into the trap
of overresponding to heavily oaked wines merely because they
shout louder. And, of course, it is the vociferous praise of oak for
its own sake, rather than for what it can contribute to a wine, that
encourages its insensitive and excessive use, so that it overwhelms
any other characteristic and even, on occasion, produces a disagreeable, barely drinkable result.

The drawbacks to avoiding oak or to handling it with timidity,
however, were well illustrated at lunch another day. Served to
accompany sole stuffed with a purée of sorrel were two Napa
Valley Chardonnays of the 1972 vintage: a Beaulieu Vineyard and
a Chateau Montelena. 1972 was not the most successful year of
the decade in Napa, but it was clear that the Montelena had good
flavor and a moderately generous style that it probably owed entirely to the judicious support of oak aging. In comparison, the
Beaulieu wine seemed light, and, unlike the Montelena and that
earlier Corton-Charlemagne, each with its careful measure of oak,
it showed little sign of oak at all, not even the touch that would
have done so much to add interest now that its early fruit had
faded. But the benefits of at least restrained use of oak have become
obvious to California winemakers, and Chardonnays that do not
rely on oak—and some of them are delicious when young—are
becoming the exceptions rather than the rule.

A perfect example of the elegant balance between fruit and wood
that demonstrates a winemaker's real understanding of the role of
oak was the 1973 Chardonnay of Spring Mountain, which I had the
good fortune to be offered twice when the wine was at its prime.
It reminded me of the same perfect balance that I discovered in the
1971 Mayacamas Chardonnay—today, alas, hardly to be found.

In Burgundy, it is rare to find a wine out of balance in this respect; unlike so many factors of winemaking, it is completely
within the control of the winemaker. Chablis, in northern Burgundy, follows a different practice from the Côte de Beaune. (The
amount of white wine produced on the Côte de Nuits is insignificant and can be ignored.) In the latter region, oak aging is *de
rigueur*: I do not know of a grower there who does not give his
wine a period in oak, varying the length of time with the "weight"

and style of the particular year and *cuvée*. In Chablis, on the other hand, small oak casks are the exception. There wines are both fermented and allowed to fall bright in huge vats, usually of glass-lined concrete. Large wooden *foudres*, holding anywhere from five hundred to a thousand gallons, are sometimes used for short-term storage; but the small cask, the *feuillette* of Chablis, was abandoned long ago and when found serves only to transport wine from cellar to cellar.

At least as much as the Kimmeridgian clay, for which the *grands crus* slope of Chablis above the little Serein river is known, this absence of oak aging establishes the style of Chablis—light and silky, soft yet dry. By their fresh, young flavor, Chablis wines are distinguished from those of the Côte de Beaune. It could be that since Chablis wines are universally crisper and more delicate than the plumper white wines of Meursault and Montrachet, trial and error through the centuries has shown that oak overwhelms these wines and should be avoided.

In the Mâconnais, it is possible to find both practices. Sometimes in the same cellar Pouilly-Fuissé receiving small barrel oak aging will be held apart from another lot stored in an enameled *cuve* until bottling. Generally speaking, it is the better wines, especially those destined for bottling by the grower, that will be matured in oak and the wines intended for sale to the local *négociants* that are kept in bulk. Since all growers believe that certain nuances of flavor are passed on from year to year through contact of their wines with their casks (though no one can be sure if the aromas originate in the wood itself or if it is the organisms harbored in the wood that provoke subtle changes in the composition of the wine as it ages), they become fiercely attached to the wood in their cellars.

Some years ago I found a batch of six hogsheads of Pouilly-Fuissé in the cellar of a grower at Solutré. At that time, following the disastrous 1963 vintage, Pouilly-Fuissé wines were in short supply, and all six casks were exceptionally good. The old man and I went through the ritual of tasting together, and we patiently arrived at a price that was acceptable to both of us. He had never before sold directly to a foreigner, and I sensed, mingled with a certain satisfaction that a wine merchant from London had sought out *his* wine in *his* cellar, the natural suspicion of an old country-man for one whose ways were unfamiliar.

It was the practice at Asher Storey to bottle almost all of our French wines ourselves in the firm's cellars under Tower Hill, and I told him that I would arrange for a local carrier to collect the six hogsheads the following week. When he realized that his casks would not be traveling the expected few miles to the cellars of a *négoçiant* in Mâcon for local bottling but to London and back, he became worried. I assured him that the casks would be well cared for, which was true; and, in what I hoped would be a clinching argument, I pointed out that if I sent other casks for the wine to travel in, as he wished me to do, the change of wood would probably change the style and balance of the wine. And that, I told him with more passion than was really necessary, would be a tragedy.

He was adamant. (For centuries the people of the Mâconnais lived a border life between the kingdom of France and the Holy Roman Empire, and few are as stubborn as they.) I told him I would go in search of the best casks in Mâcon and make arrangements for them to be sent up. The wine could be racked into them without delay for transport to England. To find what I wanted in the coopers' sheds took the better part of the next day. It was already four o'clock, and the February day was drawing to a raw close when I drove back to the house where the old man lived alone. He was not there, and his cellar door was shut and bolted. I drove in the direction of his vineyard, and from the road I caught sight of him, high up on the slope, guiding the plow behind his horse. I stopped the car and hailed him from the grass shoulder, but he didn't seem to hear me.

The freshly turned, muddy earth clung to my shoes as I started up the slope toward him. He *must* have been anxious to finish his plowing before nightfall, because even when I knew he must be able to hear me, he didn't stop. I drew alongside him and talked as we plodded across the field.

"I've found six good casks," I said. "They'll be here on Friday for the wine."

"*Je n'en veux pas,*" he said gruffly, not even looking in my direction.

"But why not?" I asked. "Have you changed your mind about letting your own casks come to London?"

"*Non,*" he said curtly. In two sentences he told me that it was out of the question for his casks to go so far, out of the hands of fellow Burgundians.

But my well-articulated arguments of the risks inherent in trans-ferring the wine to unknown casks, of the importance of balance in wood flavors, had been only too persuasive. No less than James D. Zellerbach, the old man, too, hankered after perfection, and he preferred to lose a sale rather than risk destroying the well-judged balance of his wine.

A Morning Tasting

JOE HEITZ called me one morning early in 1975 to ask me to join him and a few friends at his Napa Valley winery the following Saturday to taste the 1970 Cabernet Sauvignon he was about to release. He was also releasing small quantities of some earlier vintages that he had held back for further maturing, and we were to taste these, too.

It was a good day for tasting. I left the Bay fog behind at Yountville and arrived at the Heitz winery under blue skies. There were six of us, including Joe and his son David, and we set out nine Heitz Cabernet Sauvignon wines, covering five vintages from 1966 to 1970, and three "outside" wines of the 1970 vintage as a comparison base for the latest Heitz wine. All the bottles were carefully masked and identified only by number, and when we each had our twelve glasses ready we set to work.

We were asked to rank the twelve wines according to preference, not an easy thing to do when judging wines of different vintages. Should one prefer a younger wine for obvious potential, if it is there, or a mature wine, less fine, perhaps, but which makes more satisfying drinking now? The passion for introducing an element of competition between wines—other than at official fair judgings—is something I still find difficult to accept, but in a way

I suppose it is what we do every day when we decide to purchase one bottle rather than another. I am bothered by the system of evaluating wine in California, which is much more structured than the practice I am used to. In France, for example, where I have frequently served as a judge, a wine can earn a maximum of 50 points: 10 for color and clarity, 20 for bouquet and aroma, and 20 for flavor and finesse on the palate. These broad divisions give considerable flexibility to the judge, who is even free to ignore a small technical fault if the overall quality, style, and delicacy of a wine are outstanding.

California tends to employ a 20-point system developed for classroom work at the University of California at Davis. The division of points is particularized quite carefully: 1 point each for sugar and body; 2 points maximum each for color, appearance, acescency, flavor, astringency, total acid, and general quality; and 4 points maximum for aroma and bouquet. It is an excellent system for teaching because it trains the taster to pay consistent attention to the individual aspects of the wines he is evaluating, and, provided the wines under consideration are all straightforward, everyday wines, it is as fair a method to rank them as any other. But it was not designed to classify outstanding wines, only to indicate, by award of the maximum extra points for aroma and general quality, that a wine *is* outstanding. If, under this system, a bottle of quite ordinary but fault-free wine were judged against one of the finest bottles to be found, the fine wine might take a point or two more for bouquet, possibly one for flavor, and perhaps another for general quality, but it is likely that both would obtain at least the 17 points necessary to qualify for the "outstanding quality" description that Davis awards to wines in the 17-to-20-point range. Rigid application of the Davis point system in situations for which it was not designed can lead, and has led, to bewildering and misleading consequences.

Fortunately, we were not asked to use any point system, but were left to resolve the cross-vintage comparisons as we thought best. It took about an hour to complete the tasting, and, when the bottles were finally unmasked and the results compared, we were all keen to taste the wines again—this time with knowledge of what was in each glass.

Heitz is one of a band of California winemakers (there are quite a few others, including Bernard Portet, Richard Graff, Warren

Winiarski, Richard Arrowood, Paul Draper, and, especially, André Tchelistcheff) who impose a personal stamp on any wine they make. Regardless of the nuance of the vintage or the characteristics of the particular varietal, there is an individual style recognizable in wines made by these men. Winiarski, for example, often succeeds in achieving the degree of finesse that he seeks above all else. Tchelistcheff's hallmark is a classic, fine-wrought stateliness that has won for his red wines a place among the most respected in California—and in the world. The Heitz style is partly a matter of scale—the wines are as big as the conditions of the vintage will allow—and there is always an echo of the wood in which he matures them. They are large, comfortable wines, with a warm, subtle gleam of flavor. Boldly assured, they rarely lack elegance yet have a certain bravura. When I taste them I am put in mind of richly polished and extravagantly carved Victorian mahogany furniture.

In addition to his regular Cabernet Sauvignon, Heitz bottles a separate vatting made exclusively from the vines in nearby Martha's Vineyard (a confusing name for Easterners). We tasted four vintages of the regular wine and five of the Martha's Vineyard. Of the nine wines, there was little doubt that the 1968 Martha's Vineyard was best if judged on the basis of immediate drinkability. By general consensus, in fact, it was rated the best overall wine of the twelve sampled that day. Perversely, I had preferred the regular Cabernet, Lot C91, of the 1969 vintage. The 1968 was soft, with a delightful aroma of Cabernet. On the palate it seemed to expand, releasing a whole series of flavors with a decided vanilla overtone. The 1969 Lot C91, however, seemed to me to be potentially greater, better even than the Martha's Vineyard of the same year. There was unusual strength in every aspect of the wine: a deep color, a bold blackcurrant fruitiness redolent of certain Pauillacs, an adequate presence of tannin, to underscore the body of the wine, yet all in perfect, graceful balance. I placed the Martha's Vineyard wine of 1969 immediately behind the 1968, third in my overall rating. It had a fine harmony of flavor, tannin, and acids, and I felt that it would match the complexity of the 1968 wine when it had had more time in bottle. When judging wines, all of which are of outstanding quality, the choice is entirely subjective. Lot C91 of the 1969 vintage had a swagger that I found hard to resist—a personal preference, in the final analysis.

Both 1970 wines—the vintage that was at the heart of the whole exercise—were of good quality. It was a difficult year in the Napa Valley. The winter of 1969/70 had been very mild. By April the vines were showing their new growth when a severe frost occurred. Most vineyards lost half their prospective crop. The summer was hot, for once echoing conditions in Western Europe. (It is one of the idiosyncrasies of the wine world that rain in Bordeaux, and its subsequent effect on the quality of the vintage there, can handicap the reputation of wines made in the same year as far away as Australia.) The flowering of the vines was followed by such high temperatures that many of the newly formed grape berries shattered, further reducing the crop. More heat in July and August burned the grapes. These conditions were far from ideal, especially for the white wines, but the reds that survived have shown exceedingly well. With rare exceptions they are big wines with richly complex flavors. Heavier than the 1969s, some of them seemed clumsy at first, for apart from those wines specially brought on for early drinking, it is a year that will need time to develop. Nor is this true only of the traditional long-keeping varietals like Cabernet Sauvignon. Even Zinfandel and Gamay Beaujolais of the 1970 vintage were heavier than usual, and a 1970 Petite Sirah of Robert Mondavi that I had wanted to serve at dinner as recently as 1979 had to be decanted to help it aerate and stretch, or it would have been disagreeably hard to drink.

Of the two 1970 Heitz wines, the Cabernet Sauvignon from Martha's Vineyard was plainly superior to the regular bottling. Its color was deeper and richer; the nose, though seemingly less mature than that of the regular bottling, was stronger and more complex. On the palate it was a solid wine, astringently tannic and harshly unripe, with a good future. Roughly on a par with the 1970 Martha's Vineyard were the 1970 Cabernet Sauvignon Private Reserve of Beaulieu Vineyard and the 1970 Cabernet Sauvignon of Mayacamas, both of which had been included blind. It is of small significance when comparing such peak wines, but I ranked the Beaulieu wine marginally ahead of the Martha's Vineyard and the Mayacamas wine marginally behind it. The other tasters seemed to like the Beaulieu Vineyard wine, too, although the majority placed it after rather than before the Martha's Vineyard.

I found a lack of support from the others for the Mayacamas. It revealed little varietal character and no charm. But, in a way, I was reminded of the closed, hard style of certain Bordeaux classified growths when first bottled. Its perfect structure and balance indicated sound winemaking and gave a good base for development. Since we had not been told what the outside wines were (nor, of course, which they were), I had assumed this one—so clearly not of the Heitz stamp—to be a young red Bordeaux; and although we had not been asked to guess which were the cuckoos in the nest, I had so marked it on my tasting sheet. The others were disturbed by an off-flavor I could not find, and I began to wonder if perhaps they were put off by the wine's strangely withdrawn character. In the context of the other wines, all so positive and assertive, its low profile could easily have seemed a distortion. When the wine was identified, I remembered that I had tasted it a few months earlier. In checking my files later, I found that I had previously noted its good balance, but, in the context of different wines, had then found its hefty scale inelegant.

Of the two older vintages, the 1966 was preferred to the 1967. They were both lighter than the younger wines, and, although the 1966 Martha's Vineyard in particular showed deep color and a finely shaded bouquet of Cabernet with citrus tones, they had not reached—and would not reach—the peak already arrived at by the 1968 Martha's Vineyard. They were destined to be overshadowed by the 1969 and 1970 wines.

When we went into the house to eat one of Alice Heitz's delicious luncheons, we took the bottles with us so we could go on discussing as we tasted (and drank, let it be said) the wine with the food. I made a mental note to watch which bottle became empty soonest, sometimes a more telling evaluation system than any other. But, in the relaxed atmosphere inevitable around such a friendly table, with good food and wine, I must confess that my attention wandered and this valuable evidence is lost forever.

California
Cabernet Sauvignon

I N *The California Wine Book*, Bob Thompson recalls a dinner
in 1968 at which were served the 1951 Cabernet Sauvignons of
Beaulieu Vineyard, Inglenook, Charles Krug, and Louis M.
Martini. Those four wines, he said (I am not quoting his exact
words), represented the only wineries that had maintained a con-
tinuum of making fine wine through the preceding thirty-five lean
years since the end of Prohibition. In the fall of 1979, thanks to
the generosity of a San Francisco friend whose cellar is better provided with old vintages of California Cabernet Sauvignons than
mine (a great deal better than mine, as a matter of fact; newcomers
to the state have little chance of finding such treasures), I drank at
dinner those same 1951s from Beaulieu Vineyard and Louis M.
Martini and, with them, a 1956 Cabernet Sauvignon from Charles
Krug and a 1941 from Inglenook. Those of us at the table knew
what wines were before us, but not which was which, and I confess to having had great difficulty matching two of the same vintage,
deciding which was the youngest and which considerably the
oldest. The wines were distinctive enough but showed no aging
logic that would have helped me place them in chronological order.
All were lively, even robust.

As it turned out, the wines were in receding order of vintage.

First came the Charles Krug, a wine of bright color with fruit so persistent that it seemed almost sweet. Following its soft finish, the 1951 Martini made an austere first impression. The nose, if anything, was tarry. But as we talked, sniffing, sipping, and wondering aloud, the wine changed, its strangeness clearing like morning fog to reveal a youthful berrylike bouquet that contradicted its twenty-eight years. Once the bouquet and flavor came through, flattering the palate, the balance of the wine was restored, the edges softened.

It was perplexingly different, however, from the Beaulieu Vineyard Private Reserve of the same vintage, a wine so rich in those characteristics that we associate with the Private Reserve, including the typical Rutherford whiff of charcoal, that I could hardly distinguish it from the 1970 Beaulieu Private Reserve that I had drunk just a few days previously. Once again I was impressed by the consistency of André Tchelistcheff's style over twenty years.

The 1941 Inglenook, oldest of the four, was also the biggest, an immense, muscular wine. Someone remembered that there had been a dearth of pickers that year, and a day's delay in starting the vintage at Inglenook had increased the already high sugar levels substantially. The color was dark, almost to blackness, yet the bouquet was unexpectedly fresh and elegant. On the palate the balance of the wine was perfect: there was no burn of excessive alcohol despite its size, no hint of clumsiness, no suggestion that the wine might be beginning to dry out.

Such wines restore a sense of perspective to Cabernet Sauvignons made in California today—most of them, after all, in wineries that did not exist in 1970. So much has been achieved in so short a time that we are sometimes guilty of taking for granted or underestimating what went before. The winemakers of the 1940s and 1950s had fewer quality grapes to work with. After the Prohibition years of uprooting and neglect there were barely a few hundred acres of Cabernet Sauvignon standing compared with more than 26,000 in 1980. Nor was there the encouraging support of an appreciative public as there is now. The perseverance and integrity of those pioneers are therefore all the more remarkable. There had been legendary Cabernet Sauvignons even earlier, at the turn of the century, especially that of La Questa, a single-vineyard wine produced down the peninsula, rather in the manner of Heitz Cellars' Martha's Vineyard or Freemark Abbey's Cabernet Bosché from John Bosché's vines at Rutherford. Though we can only guess at their quality and style, there is no doubt that those earlier wines enjoyed considerable prestige. Clearly, California Cabernet Sauvignon was not invented in the 1970s.

The fascination with Cabernet Sauvignon stems from its association with the great classed growths of Bordeaux, though none of the latter, despite what one hears, uses the grape to the exclusion of all other varietals. Some use it in moderation only; and at least one, not at all. In terms of wine history, such high regard for Cabernet Sauvignon is comparatively recent and goes back no further than two or three hundred years. Its early name, Biturica, so obviously deriving from Bituriges Vivisci, the Celtic tribe that lived in what is now the Médoc when Caesar conquered Gaul, suggests that the grape might have been indigenous to the Bordeaux region, or at least established there in antiquity.

But the emergence of Cabernet Sauvignon as the preferred vine of the area does not seem to have occurred before the eighteenth century. Its tough skin has the practical advantage of resisting the onslaughts associated with a maritime climate (an equally practical consideration in the coastal counties of California). Until two hundred years ago, however, almost all wines were drunk within a year of the vintage, and since a tough skin gives a tough constitution, Cabernet Sauvignon wines were unlikely then to have been a source of unmitigated pleasure. Skill in the art of blending, a technique essential in composing an *assemblage* that develops well in bottle, evolved as late as the seventeenth century; the cylindrical bottle necessary for binning away wine followed; and, finally, the extravagant wealth brought to eighteenth-century Bordeaux (the port that with Nantes most prospered from French trade with West Africa and the Caribbean) made the aging of local wines financially feasible. Indeed, just as it was the newly rich who made the wine possible, so it was they who guaranteed a following in their fashionable and influential circles. Cabernet Sauvignon, through the success of these great estate wines of Bordeaux, was thus established as the preeminent black grape variety.

Cabernet Sauvignon grows sturdily and vigorously; its dark green leaves are deeply indented—to me always a sign of a strong-flavored varietal. It yields sparingly: the small bunches of irregular shape are composed of tight, black, spherical berries with a lot of seed in proportion to pulp, a far remove from the juicy opulence of table grapes. Its buds open comparatively late, an advantage in areas like the Médoc and the floor of the Napa Valley that are prone to spring frost. But the qualities of Cabernet Sauvignon most appreciated by winemakers are reliable acidity, even in a hot growing season, and intensity of color and flavor, both inherent in that tough, resistant grape skin.

The characteristic smell and taste of a Cabernet Sauvignon have been variously described as resembling violets, blackcurrants, eucalyptus, and tar, though lately there has developed a whole new school inordinately attached to bell peppers. That we find within Cabernet Sauvignon echoes of other fruits and flowers is not surprising, because all wines share at least traces of most of the acids, alcohols, and esters occurring in everything from bananas to roses. It is this suggestive complexity that makes wine so beguiling and allows each of us a personal odyssey in every glass.

Most who have tasted Cabernet Sauvignon would recognize it again, even when its assertiveness is controlled by the presence of other varieties, but only a novice would judge a Cabernet Sauvignon by the extent to which it projects varietal characteristics. In fact, one of the most puzzling aspects of contemporary wine controversy is the fuss made about the percentage of Cabernet Sauvignon in a wine so labeled when it would be more rational to be concerned with its effect. Some might find "controversy" too strong a word for the shades of opinion and differences of style to be found among the winemakers of California. Opinions are usually most dogmatic, in fact, among nonprofessionals whose passion leads them more often to comparative tastings than to enjoying wine at the dinner table. Those whose interest in wine began in the late 1960s and early 1970s, especially, allowed themselves to be overwhelmed by the scale of experimental Cabernet Sauvignons of that period before they had had an opportunity to develop standards of balance, subtlety, and just plain drinkability.

"It was a time," says Warren Winiarski of Stag's Leap Wine Cellars, "when California winemakers were asking what Cabernet Sauvignon grapes *could* give, as opposed to what they *should* give." Perhaps they had been provoked by a key sentence in the then-current edition of Amerine and Joselyn's *Table Wines*, a standard text at the University of California: "The most common defect of California wines," it ran, "is their lack of distinctive aroma or bouquet rather than the presence of any specific disease or defect." Though winemakers who subsequently explored the extent to which they could push the intensity of their Cabernet Sauvignons were accused of making wines for a remote posterity, of being obsessed with wines that would live, for no specific purpose, forever, few, if any, were aiming to make long-lived wines as such. In fact, their durability is probably irrelevant because it is doubtful if such wines will ever be any more approachable than they are now. They exist, and nothing further can be said.

The point of return from this new extremism to a balance that had already existed was marked by the 1976 Paris tasting organized by Steven Spurrier at which Stag's Leap Wine Cellars' 1973 Cabernet Sauvignon did so well. There are those, I have no doubt, who might resent gauging the success of a California Cabernet Sauvignon on a yardstick made in France, especially as Warren Winiarski was not exactly a prophet unhonored in his own land. But even those who admired his wines were not sure how to take them. After all, the benchmark at the time in California was set by intense, exceedingly tannic wines that overpowered Warren's style. European tasters had no such preconceived notion of what current California Cabernet Sauvignons were supposed to be like.

When asked recently about his 1973 Cabernet Sauvignon, Warren Winiarski told me that he hadn't aimed at any particular style. But, on reflection, he added that, though not consciously done, he could see in retrospect that he had sought moderation in all decisions along the way. The moderation he has sought without articulating it to himself is now a defined goal, just as it has become the goal of most of his California peers. Much oversize Cabernet Sauvignon was a deliberate attempt to test the limit; some was the result of applying extreme experimental techniques. Selection of yeast influences speed of fermentation, and heat generated alters color and flavor. The procedures followed in macerating skins and juice—short duration with frequent pump-assisted turnover, long duration with less frequent pumping over, rigging to hold the mass of skins floating beneath the surface, separation of juice and skins before or after total conversion of grape sugar to alcohol—will modify intensity and scale. The time in wood, the choice of wood, whether or not to clarify the wine—by centrifuge? by fining? by filter?—all are factors in arriving at the balance and final style of the wine.

Of prime importance, of course, is the fruit itself, since balance in wine starts with balanced grapes. Ideally, that balance should be within each grape berry, but vines grow in the same imperfect world as we do. In Bordeaux, winegrowers rely on proportions of secondary varietals to add zest, color, or fullness as required. Malbec, for example, has good color but loses its acidity easily (one reason why it is unpopular in California) and is therefore a useful support to Cabernet Sauvignon in Bordeaux in years when acidity might be high and color weak. Merlot brings a softer, more feminine style; Cabernet Franc matures early and is therefore useful in poor-ripening summers. These qualities are less necessary to balance Cabernet Sauvignon grown in California, though many winemakers use varietal blending. Winiarski has 4 percent of his vineyard planted in Merlot and feels that even a small presence of it in his Cabernet Sauvignon adds a "grace note."

Louis Martini has long used varietal blending to give subtlety and polish to his Cabernet Sauvignon wines. A few years ago he produced for the Berkeley Wine and Food Society six batches of 1968 Cabernet Sauvignon made at his winery, each using a grape mix or aging technique slightly different from every other. The Private Reserve included 25 percent Zinfandel with the Cabernet Sauvignon. Lot 1, an elegant wine, easily my favorite, was 100 percent Cabernet Sauvignon, but half the grapes were grown in Sonoma County and half in the cool Carneros region, which lies between Napa and Sonoma close to San Francisco Bay. Most of this wine had been aged in 1,300-gallon vats made of American oak. Less than a quarter of it had been aged in 50-gallon barrels—also of American oak, then the only kind used at the Martini winery—before blending.

Lots 2 and 3 were experiments with Merlot and Malbec, varying the proportions of these grapes to see what effect they could have: Lot 2 had 20 percent Merlot and 10 percent Malbec, with the balance Cabernet Sauvignon; Lot 3 had 30 percent Merlot and 15 percent Malbec. In each instance the Cabernet character was attenuated, and in Lot 3 the higher proportion of Merlot and Malbec, besides lightening both color and body, introduced a scented strain to the bouquet that was not present in any of the other batches. Lot 4, 100 percent Cabernet, all from Sonoma County, and aged entirely in 50-gallon barrels, was the choice of most of those present. It was preferred to Lot 5, the same wine aged in 1,300-gallon vats, which doubtless tells something about aging in small cooperage. It is possible, of course, that the same combinations grown in a year other than 1968 could have yielded quite different results.

With a range of microclimates in California both more varied and more extreme than in Bordeaux, however, perhaps geographic blending makes more sense here than varietal blending. Ric Forman (formerly winemaker at Sterling), for example, used hill-grown Cabernet Sauvignon to balance the qualities of grapes from the Napa Valley floor. The 1975 Cabernet Sauvignon from Joseph Phelps Vineyards that won such admiration required a blend of grapes from warm vineyards at the Calistoga end of the Valley with others from cool properties south of Yountville, closer to the Bay.

Most winemakers try to ensure that balance and development potential need not be mutually exclusive, others make wines with total emphasis on early drinkability. The latter recognize, after all, that few can plan daily wine consumption years in advance and that most of us, most of the time, need nothing more than a reasonable bottle of wine, at a reasonable price, that we can take home and enjoy that same evening.

Cabernet Sauvignons from what is called the Central Coast, mainly in or near Monterey, San Luis Obispo, and Santa Barbara counties, have suffered from criticism of excessively heightened varietal character. But those who judged so early may have forgotten that the vineyards were composed entirely of young vines grown on their own roots, as opposed to the standard grafted vines of California. In these counties there is no danger from phylloxera, the vine louse that decimated European and California vineyards in the last century, making a graft onto phylloxera-resistant roots obligatory almost everywhere else. At a recent tasting of pre-phylloxera Château Lafite in Texas, André Tchelistcheff was heard to remark that it reminded him of the wines in Monterey County. Perhaps, as they mature, these "pre-phylloxera" vines will astonish us. Already Cabernet Sauvignons from mature vines in Santa Barbara County are showing exceptionally well, as recent releases from Carey Cellars, Firestone Vineyards, and Zaca Mesa Winery attest.

Easiest of all to experiment with are the Cabernet Sauvignons made to be drunk as soon as released. Most of the large producers offer at least one (at dinner recently, where a group of us were half tasting, half drinking a varied collection of recently released

Cabernet Sauvignons, I noticed that the 1978 Almadén from Monterey County was the first empty bottle on the table), and some of the smaller wineries are also seeking to please rather than impress. The point to remember is that no hierarchy of California Cabernet Sauvignons exists to match the categories of Bordeaux's classification. The tasting charts, rosettes, and medals, by and large, are not promises of excellence. They are nothing more than a record of group preferences in tasting, *not drinking*, situations. And when it comes to preferences, there is a lot to be said for following your own.

A Jug of Wine

I N AT LEAST one respect, our present regard for basic red and white wines from California began back in the sixties, when Almadén introduced its now familiar pear-shaped gallon flagons. Until then, ordinary California wines were sold in squat jars with thumb holders at the neck. That container, still around, has the advantage of packing safely and economically, but is hellishly difficult to pour from, merits few compliments on appearance, and did little to project a quality look for California wines.

Unpretentious but graceful, the new shape helped broaden the market it was created to satisfy. Presenting sound, consistent wine in an attractive package at a reasonable price, the Almadén jug probably did more to make California wine acceptable at everyday meals than any number of recent California tasting successes around the world.

At the same time, new plantings were extending the wine-grape acreage, an activity that gathered momentum in the early seventies. Increased availability of Chardonnay, Cabernet Sauvignon, and Johannisberg Riesling is obvious from the proliferating labels of new small wineries. Less obvious is the recent and unprecedented abundance of workaday varietals like Chenin Blanc, French Colombard, and Barbera that has made possible a marked improvement in jug wines. As recently as 1971, the grape crush in California (for some years fairly constant at about 2.2 million tons) contained little more than 0.5 million tons of wine varietals in total. The rest was made up from table and raisin grapes. By 1978 that 0.5 million had swollen to 1.6 million tons, most of it destined for everyday wines. From 60,000 tons in 1971, for example, production of French Colombard had increased to 250,000 tons by 1978; production of Chenin Blanc, a grape that gives intensely fruity aroma to wine when properly handled, rose from 19,000 tons in 1971 to almost 165,000 tons in 1980. There has been similar tonnage growth of other red and white varietals not previously available to makers of everyday wines in quantities adequate for demand. Thompson seedless grapes, better left to raisin production yet once, *faute de mieux*, the most important part of the crush at many Central Valley wineries, are now insignificant in the production of table wine. Most of the Thompson seedless still crushed is used for dessert wines and grape concentrate.

At last producers have grapes available from which they can make balanced wines with attractive aromas and flavors. They have an audience eager for every improvement, so that, above all, they have the incentive to invest in the equipment and storage needed to take full advantage of their new situation. For instance, mechanical harvesters, now increasingly in use in California, permit grapes from a vast acreage to be gathered in hours instead of days. An entire vineyard can be picked quickly at peak maturity. What is more, and surprising to many, nature cooperates to make mechanical harvesters more selective than the traditional hand-gathering of bunches. When a vine is shaken by the harvester's rods, only fully ripe berries fall; unripe berries remain attached to the vine. Stems are not detached either, and leaves shaken free are blown from the grapes as they are carried on a short belt to a crusher that moves through the vineyard alongside the harvester. Within seconds of leaving the vine, free of stem and leaf, mechanically picked grapes are crushed and protected from oxidation. Another advantage: a harvester works as easily in the dark as by day, so that grapes can be picked at cool, night temperatures—an aid to cold fermentation and a boost to flavor.

There has been a revolution in the making of white wines in the last few years. Crushed white grapes are freed of all extraneous matter as quickly as possible, then some winemakers chill the juice or otherwise restrain fermentation for a day or two so that organic matter from the grapes can settle out. Most then pass the juice through a centrifuge for a natural clarification that removes all risk of off-flavors developing during fermentation. Almost universally in California, transformation into white wine takes place in stainless-steel vats, each with a jacket through which flowing cold water maintains an even low temperature to protract the fermentation process and thus preserve fruit flavor that would be lost in the heat of tumultuous yeast action. When fermentation is finished, the wine is again passed through the centrifuge to rid it of yeast cells and matter in suspension, a process that otherwise requires months of standing and racking to allow slow precipitation, during which time risks of spoilage increase and freshness is lost. In weeks rather than months, ordinary white wines can be ready for drinking while they are still lively and youthfully aromatic. As a result, California white jug wines have better flavor and balance and are cleaner and fresher than ever.

To release color and flavor from the skins, red wines, on the other hand, are fermented at higher temperatures; then, to develop properly, they usually spend at least part of their early months in wood, sometimes in American or European oak, but, in the case of jugs, more often in large redwood tanks. Experiment in methods and duration of maturing everyday red wines still preoccupies California winemakers. Their aim is to make soft, quaffable wine with enough fruit in aroma and flavor to be attractive, but not to the point of distracting from the food it accompanies. Months in small oak cooperage, followed by a year or two in bottle, is an ideal but expensive process. Relying on a little residual sweetness, as in the past, to mask or balance the tannins and acids of inadequately matured wines distorts the subtleties that winemakers now strive to extract from the superior grapes available to them. Some are moving toward a style long associated with Bardolino, Beaujolais, and red Valdepeñas, wines that are fermented so as to be soft when young and are intended to be drunk cool. Hence the recent spate of rosé reds and the like.

Demand for everyday California wines has grown with these improvements. One indication is the fact that, though total output of glass bottles in the United States was roughly even from 1979 to 1980, production of the 1.5-liter size most used for jug wines expanded by more than 40 percent. Fortunately, that higher demand means more rapid turnover in the stores, and the winemaker can allow freshness to be a part of his style. Most of these wines are ready to be consumed when sold and rarely gain from further aging.

The carefree occasions on which we enjoy jug wines are not usually conducive to reflective, let alone comparative, tasting. To be sure of indicating some of the more interesting ones available, those that illustrate current trends in varied styles, I bought an assortment of a hundred or so (to the delight of my many neighbors, who generously shared the responsibility of finishing them up). I let price rather than nomenclature be my guide and didn't bother too much whether or not the wineries concerned would consider the particular product as "jug." Obviously, I couldn't taste everything on the market, and if a wine isn't mentioned it is probably because my hands were full when I passed that shelf, not because of excessive tact.

The most satisfying white wines among those I tasted fell into one of two broad categories. Some, usually slightly (or not so slightly) sweet and moderately fruity, seemed ideal for cool drinking in warm weather or for parties. Others, completely dry and with restrained aroma in the European style, would go well with food and not overwhelm subtle dishes.

Of the sipping wines, easily my favorite was Colombard Blanc from Souverain. The name was chosen, William Bonetti, the former Souverain winemaker, told me, because the wine is made mainly from French Colombard and Chenin Blanc. But the French sound of the name gives no indication of the wine's German-like delicacy. Restrained in alcohol, with low residual sugar carefully adjusted to balance the zest of acidity, the wine has a delightful, fresh grapy aroma. Another wine to impress me in this category, though a little heavier and fuller, was Colony Chenin Blanc. For a moderate price, this clean and well-made product offers fruit and acidity in agreeable balance and is sure to please those who can accept a little sweetness.

I liked several French Colombards. Gallo retains a piquant aroma in its wine, made almost entirely from grapes grown in Sonoma County. When this blend was first put on sale a few years ago, it was quite dry, but now, depending on the acidity of the wine, residual sugar varies from 1.5 to 2.0 percent. The wine is light, easy to drink, and particularly pleasing to those who like French Colombard character.

The same varietal sold under the Inglenook Navalle label is fuller than Gallo's, with a decidedly sweet finish and less assertive character. If French Colombard is to be completely dry, it is more successful when the varietal character is muted or at least restrained. Foppiano French Colombard, for example, is given a short time in oak before bottling. It is light, fairly neutral, not unlike a pleasant Muscadet.

Most offerings labeled Chablis show heavier style with little flavor, though all are clean and usually innocuous. Two that pleased me particularly by their lighter, more graceful style and delicate fruitiness were Paul Masson Chablis and Foppiano Chablis. Both have a Chenin Blanc base; the Foppiano is drier.

To find acceptable, inexpensive *dry* white wine is not easy anywhere in the world. Too often, absence of sugar leaves acidity unbalanced or harshness undisguised, and the very plainness of a simple white wine leaves no cover for off-tastes arising from sloppy handling in vineyard or winery. Five bone-dry California whites that few will quarrel with are J. Pedroncelli's rather austere Sonoma White Wine, made from French Colombard and Sauvignon Vert; Foppiano's clean Sonoma White Burgundy, made from mostly French Colombard but with a nose that hints at the generous proportion of Sonoma Chardonnay in the blend (and I do mean *Chardonnay*, not *oak*); Fetzer's Mendocino Blanc de Blancs, a light, "spritzy" wine with a typical French Colombard nose and a fresh, citrus undertone that might originate in the Grey Riesling that winemaker Paul Dolan uses; and Robert Mondavi's White Table Wine, with its pleasing fullness and subtle flavor that could mislead one into questioning what is in fact the absolute dryness of this blend of Chenin Blanc, Sauvignon Blanc, and French Colombard.

Light wines have added a further dimension to quaffing since my original tasting. Calories saved drinking a whole bottle of light wine, as opposed to normal table wine, would be fewer than those found in an eight-ounce serving of low-fat yogurt, so I am not sure what the fuss is about. On the other hand, at least one of them, Masson Light, seems to have all one would most want in a fresh, young wine for summer drinking. If you feel it doing you good at the same time, so much the better.

Faced with thirty-six assorted red wines, I hoped at last to discover the characteristics intended to distinguish California Burgundy from California Claret from California Chianti, because there must be some rationale in the use of those borrowed terms. Alas, I am no wiser. It is easier to distinguish among the styles of the different wineries than among different types of generics. Each winery appears to have its own idea of what a "Burgundy" or a "Chianti" should be within the overall house style it chooses to follow. I can now generalize, however, that within each winery's range Burgundy usually has more heft and seems to finish sweeter on the palate, whether or not residual sugar is present, and a Chianti label, at least in the examples I had chosen, indicates a brisk style that verges on coarseness.

I had included in my selection a few inexpensive Zinfandels and Cabernet Sauvignons. Compared with certain prestigious wines made from these same varietals, they would hardly attract attention, and most of us would ignore them as unimportant examples of their kind. But seen just as inexpensive red wines, more or less on a price par with generic reds, they offer good value. The Cabernet Sauvignon of Guasti, for example, was far from the scale and complexity we expect of a north-coast Cabernet, but it was at least the equal of a well-made Bordeaux Rouge, with the same dry finish, and at half the price. Similarly, both C. K. Mondavi and Foppiano Zinfandels (the latter somewhat the drier of the two) have more zest and style than most generic reds at similar prices.

Whether labeled Burgundy, Claret, or, as is increasingly the case, Red Wine, the generics I liked fell into two categories, as the whites had done. On talking later to some of the winemakers, I was interested to discover that all of the group that I classified as "traditional California" had been aged at least partially in redwood. Redwood seems to impart a berry strain to the bouquet of a red wine and softens it by suggesting a sweetness on the palate that isn't necessarily there. Falling into this group were Christian Brothers California Burgundy, a soft, very pleasing wine with a clean finish; Cresta Blanca North Coast Burgundy, a blend based on Petite Sirah; Emile's California Burgundy, from the Santa Clara winery of E. Guglielmo, a wine with a curiously smoky flavor; and Louis Martini's California Mountain Red Wine. The newly released Maison Rouge of Almadén's Charles Lefranc line costs more than most of us would pay for quaffing, but it has an agreeable balance of redwood and oak character, suitably dominated by the Pinot Noir from which it is made.

And what of nontraditional wines? Two of those tasted had had some redwood aging, too, according to the winemakers, but otherwise break away from traditional California styles. J. Pedroncelli's Sonoma Red Wine has a lightly fruity bouquet but an agreeable dry finish; Fetzer's Mendocino Premium Red, on the other hand, has so much fruit that the dry finish—though by no means abnormally astringent—comes as a surprise to the palate. Robert Mondavi's Red Table Wine, a blend based on Zinfandel, Cabernet, and Petite Sirah, is pleasing on nose and palate and finishes so softly that it hints of sweetness though there is no residual sugar. A Guasti Burgundy was one of two wines tasted that resembled young Beaujolais. The other was San Martin Burgundy, a soft, zesty wine made from a negligible proportion of Napa Gamay and most Carignan, Zinfandel, and Cabernet. Both are good examples of new-style California winemaking applied to traditional grapes. I also liked very much Sonoma Vineyards' California Red Table Wine. It is a little fruity and reasonably soft, with a clean, dry finish.

California Pinot Noir: The New Frontier

CALIFORNIA PINOT NOIRS have been criticized for lack of color, lack of varietal character, lack of body, and lack of staying power. We are told that we have the wrong clone, the wrong climate, the wrong soil, the wrong yields, the wrong yeasts, and the wrong ideas. We probably use the wrong gum on the labels, too. Such is the prevailing conviction that Pinot Noir and California are at odds with each other, that every example that demonstrates the contrary is dismissed as a fluke, and every winemaker who devotes time and energy to Pinot Noir is regarded as quixotic. But since 1969 the acreage of Pinot Noir planted and bearing grapes in California has quadrupled from some 2,500 to well over 10,000, and that excludes the acreage of Gamay Beaujolais, now accepted as yet another clone of Pinot Noir. Compared with the 24,000 tons crushed in 1978, the 1979 vintage brought in close to 33,000 tons of Pinot Noir grapes, enough to provide for 24 million bottles—a rather large number to be wrong about.

Though it is unfair, and perhaps illogical, to compare California Pinot Noirs only with the full-blown wines of the Côte d'Or in Burgundy (there are, after all, light, fragrant Pinot Noir wines made in Switzerland and in the Baden area of southern Germany), most regard the wines of Burgundy as the best that Pinot Noir can produce, so it is inevitable that they provide the standard against which California is measured. Burgundian Pinot Noir—even allowing for differences from Côte de Nuits to Côte de Beaune, from grower to grower, and for lapses in standards in recent years—has a combination of strength and grace that is difficult to match. There are California Pinot Noirs that have the color, scale, and depth but miss the shimmering aroma, simultaneously insistent and delicate. Others that promise well on the nose disappear on the palate.

The most impressive Pinot Noirs I have tasted during my years in California seem to have had some common roots. Most often the winery grew the grapes as opposed to purchasing them; the vineyard was usually young, with the low yields expected from immature plants; there was always a degree of heresy in the winemaking (I have yet to taste a California Pinot Noir worthy of more than a pat on the barrel that has been made by the book); and the wines were aged, and sometimes partially fermented, in French oak barrels. Some of the Pinot Noirs I have enjoyed have come from wineries as geographically diverse and varied in size and style as Pedroncelli and Robert Mondavi, Caymus and Chalone. Consistency with the grape is elusive, however, and, because there is constant experiment, few winemakers are satisfied and even fewer dogmatic.

Early in 1980, a few samples of Pinot Noir arrived in my office unannounced from a small winery south of Hollister. (Hollister is not what we think of as a wine town in California. It is a serious farming community of the kind where shopkeepers would be puzzled rather than amused by the current big-city fad for "merchandising" jeans and work shirts.) The wines, all of the 1978 vintage, were raw and unusually vigorous, with something of the closed, dark style of young wines from the Côte de Nuits. I had been planning a trip south to Santa Barbara County and was sufficiently impressed to start out a day earlier, allowing time for a detour to meet the man who had made these wines.

Josh Jensen worked in Burgundy in the early 1970s, following two vintages from vineyard to cellar. Convinced he could make similar wines in California, he searched to find a chalky terrain similar to that of the Côte d'Or, set in a corresponding climate. In the Cienega Valley, remote in the Gavilan Mountains of California's central coast, he found outcroppings of the limestone

bench that, some twenty-five miles south, supports the vineyards of Chalone. On two separate knolls he planted about twenty-four acres of Pinot Noir.

The day I drove down there was brilliantly sunny. We had just come to the end of a period of devastating rainstorms, and the hills were a bright, washed green. Jensen's Calera Winery is set into the face of a steep slope, using the multilevel foundations of what had been intended as the crushing plant of a limestone quarry. The plan to use gravity in pulverizing rocks has been cleverly adapted to winemaking. From grapes to must to wine, the flow from one level to another needs no mechanical aid. I felt I was inside a rather busy Aztec temple. We came to a scantling of French oak on which both Jensen's 1978 Pinot Noirs and his 1979s were stowed side by side. The first crop in 1978 had yielded little more than a ton, not quite enough for three full barrels. In 1979 his twenty-four acres had given him seven tons, still less than a third of a ton to the acre. His 1978s in wood were not quite as I had tasted them in San Francisco, though recognizably the same wines. The wine of none of the three barrels resembled that of the other two: all had good color; a Burgundian nose and flavor, but each its own degree of hardness. It was not a good time to be tasting the 1979s (they had just been racked and were tired), but they seemed to promise even more than the 1978s.

Jensen told me he made his wines by putting half the grapes through a conventional de-stalker, where rollers crushed them on their way to the fermenting vat. The rest of the grapes went straight to the tank in whole bunches, stalks and all, with no attempt to crush or even break the individual grape-berries. He introduced no yeast culture but allowed the fermentation to start spontaneously from the wild yeasts in the bloom of the grapes and encouraged the fermentation temperature to rise to a warm 92 °F. He didn't pump the fermenting juice over the cap of skins and stalks that soon floats thick on the surface but, like a Burgundian, punched it down into the wine, keeping the juice and skins working together until all the grape sugar had been converted to alcohol.

His reference to whole bunches at first confused me into thinking that he was using a modified version of whole-berry fermentation, usually referred to as "carbonic maceration," the standard method for producing soft, fruity, early-maturing wines. But his was an open vat, not the kind that traps carbon dioxide as it forms, holding the grapes in anaerobic suspense; and the style of his wines was neither soft nor early maturing. Jensen explained that adding bunches was a way of retaining a proportion of the stalks, a practice that enriches the wine with tannin and toughens it for aging. Most other winemakers who add a proportion of stalks first remove them from the bunches and sometimes chop them before putting them into the fermenting vat. It is a matter of convenience: whole bunches, even whole stalks, would jam the must pipe taking crushed grapes to the fermenting vat. But Jensen felt that stalks added "in the bunch" were less harsh and, more important, that whole bunches in the must released sugar to the yeast more slowly, extending the fermentation and giving a more complex result.

Jensen was trying to follow as closely as possible what he had seen done in Burgundy, but in allowing spontaneous fermentation in California he was taking a risk. Through centuries of making wine and spreading the residue back on the vineyards, Burgundian growers have encouraged certain dominant strains of yeast to develop. Though any number of others might find their way into the fermenting vat, each contributing a thread to the complex pattern of flavor that eventually emerges, the dominant strains take over quite early and bring the fermentation to a predictable conclusion. The University of California at Davis has taken a stand against spontaneous fermentation in favor of introducing known, selected yeast strains because California wine regions are too young to rely on local yeast populations. This policy of meticulous control has been a principle of California winemaking. The consistency and reliability of most California wines spring from this basic, orthodox attention to detail. But, at risk of being labeled a mystic (or worse), I must ask whether there isn't a point beyond which to know more is to understand less. Aristotle advised us to look for precision in all things only so far as the nature of the subject permits. Are not the subtle shades of flavor in Burgundian Pinot Noir attractive to us because they are fleeting, indefinable, and immeasurable? And, if so, how can meticulous control reproduce such mysterious qualities?

The main purpose of my trip had been to visit the Santa Ynez Valley. Since my previous visit four years before, wineries had been opened, vineyards extended, changes made. My first day of visits was illuminated by the enthusiasm of the winemakers. There were richly complex, barrel-fermented Chardonnays, oak-aged Sauvignon Blancs, Sémillons (at Santa Ynez Valley Winery) of a delicacy and crispness I would not have thought possible from this grape, and Cabernet Sauvignons from mature vines that, once released, will end once and for all the prejudiced denigration of this varietal from the central coast. The elegance and balance of the wines were remarkable.

Late in the afternoon, tasting with Tony Austin, then wine-maker at Firestone Vineyard, I was shown a 1977 vintage reserve Pinot Noir, to be released the following year, that took me back to my conversation with Josh Jensen. In every way the wine was splendid. It had been made from a second crop of Pinot Noir grapes picked at the end of October in 1977, a gathering of small bunches that had been still green when the main picking had taken place, weeks previously. They gave a ton and a quarter to the acre, with better sugar and acidity than the first crop. About 25 percent of the stalks had been added to the fermenting juice, which had been allowed to reach temperatures in excess of 92°F. Tony Austin told me all this and then added, in a very matter-of-fact way, that the fermentation had been spontaneous. I was delighted (I enjoy piecing together hypotheses) and amazed (Firestone is a substantial and well-controlled winery). Small yield; some stalk; spontaneous, wild-yeast fermentation; warm temperature—and, of course, a year in previously used French oak barrels. It seemed a familiar story. But I had been struck by a new factor: the date of picking.

Pinot Noir matures early, and, in California, where it is usually picked in the first week or two of September, it ripens in the high temperatures of late summer. But experiments a few years ago examined the result of Pinot Noir ripened more slowly at cool temperatures with little variation between day and night. The grapes were enriched with color and tannin, properties inherent in the anthocyanins that were thus intensified in the skins.

I mulled over the significance of cool climate ripening to the late picking at Firestone as I drove to the winery and vineyard of J. Richard Sanford and Michael Benedict. Lying several miles closer to the ocean than do the rest of Santa Ynez's vineyards, Sanford and Benedict enjoys summer temperatures rarely past the mid-seventies

and always at least ten degrees cooler than at the vineyards farther
up the valley.

The winery, a modest wooden building, stands above the vineyard close to a crest of trees and was guarded, like the Capitol of
ancient Rome, by a flock of highly vocal geese. Michael Benedict
introduced his wines by explaining that his winemaking began in
the vineyard. A third of their 110 acres is planted with Pinot Noir.
At present he prunes to control the crop to a maximum ton and
a quarter to the acre, as opposed to the three tons to the acre that
conventional wisdom allows, but thinks he might eventually extend that to as much as two tons as his vines mature. Restrained
yields are essential in a temperate climate to allow the grapes to
ripen fully and to give the combination of sugars and acidity that
he needs. (Three tons to the acre is not much beyond the limita-
tions imposed for today's *appellations contrôlées* of Burgundy,
but it is double the yields common there in the nineteenth century,
when Burgundies were richer and more full-bodied than they are
today.) After crushing his grapes into open vats of American oak,
he adds stalks in proportions that vary from year to year. An
evolutionary biologist and botanist who once taught at the University of California at Santa Barbara, Benedict is not overawed
by bugs. He introduces selected yeast strains at the start and at a
later phase of the fermentation, but makes no effort to incapacitate
or restrain the wild yeasts that might be present in the must. The
subtleties they introduce, he says, cannot be obtained in any other
way. He, too, ferments at warm temperatures, in excess of 92°F,
punching down the skins and stalks at regular intervals, but otherwise working to no special theory. "I read a lot, research a lot,
and then use the seat-of-the-pants method," he says cheerfully.
"You can call me an organic winemaker."

The combination of stalk, wooden fermenting vats, and longer
than usual barrel-aging gives Sanford and Benedict Pinot Noirs
more tannic astringency when ready for bottling than most other
California Pinot Noirs. The winemaker tempers this by fining with
egg whites, in line with European practice, using four or five per
barrel.

Michael Benedict and I met again very soon after my visit to his
winery. His Pinot Noir was one of three presented at the 1980
California Vintners' Barrel Tasting at The Four Seasons in New
York City, along with wines from Beaulieu Vineyard and Ken-

wood Vineyards. Each presented a barrel sample of new-made 1979 and an example of an older vintage from the same vines. The comparison of wines and ideas was instructive.

Beaulieu grows its grapes in the Carneros region, a cool area close to San Francisco Bay between the Napa and Sonoma valleys. For their 1976 wine—one of those shown—they had taken a small yield, barely a ton to the acre. They fermented without stalks, at moderate temperatures, allowing no wild yeast activity. Kenwood's wines, on the other hand, were both made from the same patch of Pinot Noir vines on the steep Jack London Vineyard in the Valley of the Moon in Sonoma County. Again, yield was small—less than one and a half tons to the acre—but the vineyard, with a full-sun exposure, is hot. Robert Kozlowski, the winemaker, is emphatically against wild yeast. He ferments in water-cooled stainless steel at temperatures kept well below 80°F. Afterward, the wine falls bright in redwood tanks and is aged in French oak barrels.

The only factor that *all* these wines had in common was small-yield grapes. The Beaulieu Vineyard 1976 was elegant and mild-mannered; Kenwood's 1977 was big, with a rather voluptuous soft, fruity style; and Sanford and Benedict's 1977, predictably, was harder, with a complex, less direct flavor. The differences of style made sense in terms of what was known about the way in which each wine had been made. The uniformly high quality of the wines seemed to make sense only in terms of sparsely cropped vines. One thing for sure, though: there was nothing wrong with any of them.

Amador County, California

To NOTICE on a wine list that five of the twelve Zinfandels
come from Amador County, better known for sleepy gold-
rush towns and Saturday night fiddling than for wine, was
a signal not to be ignored. Dining at Chez Panisse one recent eve-
ing, after a postcard Pacific sunset when the whole sky glowed
and for just a few minutes the waters of the bay glittered purple,
I ordered a bottle of a 1974 Amador County Zinfandel made at
the Mount Veeder Winery. I didn't quite see the connection
between the Sierra foothills and the higher reaches of Napa, but
the wine was a revelation to me and could not have been more
appropriate to the evening: darkly glowing with a rich bouquet and
ripe flavor that seemed both to symbolize and to contain the heady
cornucopia of California.

Amador County lies east of Sacramento. After twenty-five
miles or so of flat valley the foothills rise abruptly at the county
border, then Amador climbs in a long narrow wedge to the Sierra
heights. It is said that the odd shape, rather like an elephant's
trunk, was caused by the county founders' determination to wrest
the Carson Pass road from neighboring Calaveras County. It was
a lucrative toll, especially in the mother lode country, and any fan
of Bret Harte's can imagine how they might have schemed to do it.

At the lower, western end of the county, Route 49, an appropriately numbered highway, meanders through spruced-up mining towns that have forsaken the streams and workings to make fortunes anew from macramé, herb sachets, relics of the forties (the nineteen-forties, that is), and cheerfully preserved inns and saloons. There is reassurance in the neat conical hills, looking for all the world as if Botticelli in a moment of whimsical generosity had scattered another Tuscany in the West, and it is easy to understand why the miners planted their vineyards and orchards here with the confidence of permanent settlers. By 1860 there were already five hundred acres of vines in the county, and the number continued to grow until Prohibition. Many of the miners retired to vineyards and cottages; even the notorious Madame Pantaloons, who mined at Jackson's Gate in men's clothes and boots (with delicate concern for detail), sold her claim in the 1880s and planted a small vineyard nearby. By 1890 there were more than a hundred small wineries flourishing in the hills.

The frost of Prohibition closed down the wineries. One of the few old ones to survive is the D'Agostini Winery near Plymouth. The old building, set back a little from the road, is made from locally hewn oak and stone quarried from a nearby hill. The vats and casks, huge ovals in the German manner with deeply concave fronts, were coopered by the Uhlinger sons, members of the Swiss family that founded the winery in 1856, and by John Davis, one of those men of the West whose origins are always described as mysterious but were probably no more difficult to explain than those of many another new Californian who just cut loose from whatever domestic ties held him east of the Mississippi to seek riches and adventure on the new frontier.

The D'Agostini family bought the winery in 1911 from the Uhlingers and started up again as soon as Prohibition ended. They began with barely twelve acres of vines, but they have gradually purchased and planted more as sales have grown and now have about a hundred. They use only their own grapes and sell most of their wine from the winery door. Twenty years ago, a prospective buyer would taste down the line of barrels until he found exactly the wine he wanted. "That one," he'd say, and they would run off the wine for him.

Those days are long since past, but the winery remains a simple operation with the charm of age and good housekeeping. It has the unusual distinction in California of being one of the few wineries to allow natural yeast fermentation. Normally, the strains of yeast attached to the "bloom" of the grapes that arrive at the crushers in California are so varied that they are unpredictable. A more vigorous, cultured strain is introduced to take over, and in this way the winemaker can be sure of the outcome of his fermentation, secure from off-flavors. But at D'Agostini's, as in Europe, a small quantity of grapes is picked early to make a starter—what in Europe is called a *fond de cuve*—and some of the briskly fermenting juice is then introduced into each new vat as it is filled.

Perhaps it is the almost continuous use of the winery (there was some activity there even during Prohibition), or the fact that the grapes are consistently from the same vineyards, or the isolation of Amador from other vineyard areas, or a combination of all three that makes this possible. D'Agostini tells of the day three or four years ago when the University of California descended on him. "They were in here tasting the wines, and they wanted to know what sort of yeast I was using. I told them none, and they wouldn't believe it. 'It's impossible,' they said. 'The wines taste clean.' You know, they expect natural yeasts to give a strange flavor. They asked if they could come back at crushing time and take away some of the must, and they studied it for about a year. They have a fellow over at Davis who's worked all over Europe on yeasts, and he traced our yeast back to Germany." He shook his head. "Can't think how it got here."

When the wineries shut down during Prohibition, there was a corresponding decline in vineyard acreage. Some demand for Amador grapes continued from home winemakers, permitted by the law, and considerable quantities were shipped to the Basque shepherd communities in Nevada, even as far as Montana. The home winemakers liked the rich style and sturdy sugars of Amador grapes. And it was through this home-winemaking connection that the renaissance of Amador came about.

The catalyst was Charles Myers, a professor of English at Sacramento City College, a keen amateur winemaker now turned professional on a modest scale. Myers had found his way to Amador in the early sixties and was buying grapes from Ken Deaver, the step-grandson of the mysterious John Davis. Darrell Corti, a Sacramento wine merchant, tasted some of the huge Zinfandel wines that Myers produced. By that time, in the late 1960s, the small Sutter Home Winery in Napa was making wines for Corti's own label but was being hard pressed by the rising price of Napa grapes. Corti suggested to Sutter Home's Bob Trinchero that he try Amador County, and together they went to see Ken Deaver, who still cultivated the vines planted by his step-grandfather. The first batch of Zinfandel from the Deaver ranch was fermented by Sutter Home in the fall of 1968, and, when the wine was eventually released, its success was such that Bob Trinchero virtually stopped making any other kind of wine and now specializes in Amador County Zinfandels. Because good news travels fast, other wineries followed. Ken Deaver, a tall, spare man with a wry country humor, is amused at the commotion. Not so many years before, he'd taken grapes on the back of his truck to the wineries in the Napa Valley, and no one would even look at them because they weren't Napa-grown.

I sat in the Deaver kitchen recently, talking with Ken and his son. "We always knew our grapes were good," he said, "but no one seemed interested. We liked to sell to the home winemakers because they would pay a little more for the ton. Otherwise we just hauled them down to the big Central Valley wineries and they paid us Central Valley prices, even though our yield per acre is half what they get down there and the quality is twice as high. The fruit of our Zinfandel even looks different," he went on, "with darker grapes and looser bunches."

In those days there was no question of a grower making a return on the value of his land; no one could think of replanting. All the work was done by the rancher, and he just hoped to have a few more dollars in hand at the end of the year than he had started with. But since then prices for Amador County grapes have risen steeply and now run pretty close to Napa prices. The quality of Amador grapes springs from the soil of the hills: a decayed granite, red with cinnabar and iron. And the style is determined by hot days and cool, breezy nights. The grapes have an unusual combination of high sugar and high acidity, and the wines they give are both robust and zesty. To discuss them in terms of alcohol, acid, and tannin, however, is like describing Nureyev's leaps in terms of muscle dynamics. Amador County wines have a vigor, a strength, and a warmth that is as much the essence of the California foothills as a finely etched red Graves is the essence of the drawing rooms of Bordeaux.

Ken Deaver was trying to remember the age of his vines for me. His acre of Mission was the oldest. These had been the first vines planted in the county and must have been there for "about a hundred twenty years." The Zinfandel went in later, "perhaps in the 1880s," he said.

Mrs. Deaver looked up from the pie she was making to correct him. "Grandpa was eighty-seven when he died in 1961, and he planted those vines when he was sixteen," she said.

Ken Deaver has seventy acres of vines, mostly Zinfandel, but within the last four or five years he has put in some Cabernet Sauvignon. While we sat in the kitchen, we drank a wine from his first Cabernet crop, 1974, made my Charles Myers at his Harbor Winery in Sacramento. It was a big, firm wine with the distinctive varietal taste of Cabernet subtly woven into the Amador style.

There are now about fifty acres of Cabernet Sauvignon planted in the county, all of it since 1969. But Zinfandel still dominates, with nearly nine hundred acres planted, more than half of which were bearing fruit long before the recent revival and probably even long before Prohibition. There are now scatterings of other varieties, too, particularly in the Shenandoah Valley. Shenandoah isn't really a valley at all, just a depression between two ridges; but it was given the name by settlers from Virginia, and it is there, at some 1,800 feet, that the best vineyards are concentrated. Along with Deaver and D'Agostini there must be twenty or thirty growers, some working just an acre or two, and others, like the Monteviña Winery, with almost two hundred.

Cary Gott, the driving force at Monteviña, was one of the first to try his hand at other varietals. He put in Cabernet Sauvignon seven years ago, and he was the first to plant Merlot, Barbera, Sauvignon Blanc, Ruby Cabernet, and even a little Nebbiolo, the grape used to make Barolo in Italy. He is exuberantly enthusiastic about Amador County and likes to experiment. He has tried sun-drying Mission grapes before crushing (like a French *vin de paille*) for a dessert wine; he has made "Zinfandel Neuvo" (Amador's riposte to Beaujolais *primeur*); currently he is experimenting with a sweet Sauvignon Blanc in the style of Sauternes. In his new winery, wines age in small casks, mostly of American oak. His 1977 Special Selection Zinfandel was as fine an example of Amador as you could get. Even his Ruby Cabernet, a hybrid developed by the University of California for the Central Valley and planted in Amador County by Gott, is a full, rich wine that would put some Cabernet Sauvignons of distinguished origin to shame.

With a small vineyard acreage—less than a twentieth of that of Napa—and a total production that can't exceed 150,000 cases a year on present plantings, Amador County wines are unlikely to hit supermarket shelves. But along with the wines of Sutter Home, Harbor Winery, Monteviña, D'Agostini, Ridge, and Carneros Creek, there are Amador County grapes in the blends of Zinfandel of several large California wineries. They are prized for the intense flavor they bring.

I asked Ken Deaver how he felt about Amador's being rediscovered. He looked at me for a moment before replying, "We didn't know we were lost."

California Johannisberg Riesling

T HOUGH A CYNICAL observer might suppose that the sudden
extension of vineyards in California in the early seventies
was less a demonstration of confidence than a glimpse of the
ingenuity we apply to protect taxable income, none could deny
the faith of those who chose to plant Johannisberg Riesling. At
the time, few examples of California wine made from this variety
had created much of a stir, even though Frank Schoonmaker and
Tom Marvel in the 1941 classic *American Wines* had predicted that
the grape would produce one of the best American white wines
when "given the legal protection it deserves." Perhaps they confused two issues. Whether the description "Riesling" should be
restricted by law to wines made solely from the vine variety using
that simple, unqualified name in Europe is a matter for debate;
whether that same, true Riesling grape, whatever it be called and
however much its name be borrowed and abused by varieties at
best distant cousins, is able to produce wine of outstanding quality
in California's climate is a matter for speculation.

Of course, if we were to believe Frona Eunice Wait, writing
back in 1889, the question had already been settled. The quality of
California Riesling, she said in an omnibus statement, was recognized "not only in California but [was] conceded by connoisseurs

east of the Missouri River and in Europe." Her regard for eastern connoisseurship was no doubt appropriate, but her bounding enthusiasm for all California wines and for everything and everyone remotely connected with their production does give pause to doubt her critical judgment. Her book, *Wines and Vines of California*, praises so broadly and so lavishly the wines, vines, vineyards, hills, and dales of California, with long lists of the winemakers, grape growers, businessmen, and state officials, that I am reminded of the instruction I had from the editor of a small-town paper where I worked as a junior reporter one high school summer. "Put in all the competitors' names," he said tersely, returning my draft account of event winners at the local annual horse show and gymkhana. "We shall sell more papers if they all send copies to their friends and families." I expect that Frona Eunice Wait's book sold pretty well.

Riesling is one of those few grape varieties that have come to impose style on an entire region, or at least define it. And, by establishing criteria, it continues to impose itself even when combined with, or replaced by, similar grapes. Despite the variations of soil, climate, and grapes used, it is Riesling that brings recognizable unity to the cluster of wine districts that border the Rhine and its tributaries in Germany and France, just as Cabernet Sauvignon, present in the wine or not, makes coherent the many facets of Bordeaux, and Chenin Blanc, the confusing abundance of sweet and dry wine of the middle Loire Valley. Though the name Riesling is sometimes qualified—as in Franken Riesling (a synonym for the Sylvaner grape) and in Riesling Italico, grown in the border areas of Italy and Yugoslavia—when used alone in Europe it has only one meaning and refers to only one grape.

In California, that same grape is known in the vineyards as White Riesling, a name occasionally seen on wine labels, too. More commonly, however, wine made from the true Riesling in California (and elsewhere in the United States) is labeled Johannisberg Riesling to distinguish it from wine labeled simply Riesling, the latter sometimes made from Sylvaner grapes, with an obvious allusion to the Franken Riesling synonym, but more often from a blend of various grapes of greater or lesser Riesling association. There is even a California variety grown and sold as Grey Riesling, a local name for what the French call Chauché Gris. It is a respectable wine, but it is not a Riesling. Inevitably, there are many

who feel, and with justification, that the qualifying word Johannisberg, obviously connoting the village and *Schloss* of that name
on the Rhine, has no place on a California wine label. But the
practice of using the word Riesling on blends has now such wide
acceptance that it would be quixotic to hope to restrict it to the
true Riesling. Attempts to revert to the name White Riesling, and
thus avoid use of Johannisberg, have been less than successful. "So
how does that make it different from other Rieslings?" is the usual
consumer response. "Surely they're all white?" Fortunately, the
style of label used in California and the obligation to include some
kind of geographic appellation are enough to make the origin clear,
and the continued use of the word Johannisberg on California
wines is probably a source of greater irritation to purists and to
growers of Johannisberg village in Germany than it is of confusion
to the American wine drinker.

There are two reasons in particular why the European Riesling
has been so successful in the northerly vineyards of the Rhine and
Moselle. The breaking of the first tender leaf buds occurs later
with Riesling than with many other vine varieties, a protection in
regions where dawn frosts are possible and indeed common until
May. And the clarity of the Riesling varietal flavor and aroma is
emphasized by the effects of long, evenly temperate, northern
summer days. Rocky soils and extensive surfaces of river water
keep night and day temperatures close together within a range
that ripens grapes only moderately rich in sugar, hence with alcohol
that does not overwhelm either flavor or charm. At the same time,
an absence of heat stress ensures a natural fruit acidity to perk
the palate and contribute to the development of bouquet.

California winemakers have always recognized that similar conditions would be necessary if they sought to duplicate a German
style of Riesling. But, although growers here look to European
wines for style guidance and quality criteria, they know that California wines do not have to be identical to be equal, whether in
quality (however we define it) or in pleasure-giving properties
(on whatever scale we use). So, most recent efforts in California
have been directed toward finding growing conditions for Johannisberg Riesling that will provide sugar and acid in appropriate balance to make a wine that is good in Californian, rather than in
European, terms.

Recently I talked about the search for "best" climatic condi-

tions for Johannisberg Riesling with Walter Schug, the winemaker at Joseph Phelps Vineyards, a man born and raised on the
Rhine. We had been discussing how the unusually cool summer
in California in 1980 had given the state's Johannisberg Riesling
growers their best opportunity for many years. Schug reminded
me of the narrow temperature range within which Riesling grapes
ripen best. "On hot Napa afternoons," he said, "the vines just shut
down. The stomata of the leaves close up to prevent moisture loss
as soon as the temperature gets into the mid-nineties; transpiration
stops; and the sugar-making function of the leaves ceases as well.
In those conditions the vine is stressed and loses its acidity." He
thinks the best Johannisberg Riesling grapes will come from high,
east-facing slopes where morning sun will get the temperature up
to 55°F quickly, allowing the plant to function early in the day,
and where, with luck, the vineyard will be protected from the
western sun, missing the worst of the afternoon heat.

Idwal Jones, in his delightful book *Vines in the Sun* (1949),
recommended "altitude, remoteness and a thin, rocky soil" for
Johannisberg Riesling vines in California. He referred specifically
to the eastern slopes of the Santa Cruz mountains down the peninsula from San Francisco, where the "white Riesling of Johannisberg
is being grown under the green pennons of the redwoods." The
very few Johannisberg Rieslings made from Santa Cruz grapes
that I have tasted have not been sufficiently impressive to convince
me of the area's superiority, though I have heard good things about
a striking 1966 and a lighter 1967 produced by Ridge Vineyards
in a German Spätlese style, both long since disappeared.

Better evidence of the beneficial effect of high east-facing vineyards was to be found in Johannisberg Riesling produced in that
same late 1960s period by Fred McCrae of Stony Hill and Lee
Stewart at his old Souverain Cellars winery above Napa Valley.
It could have been a coincidence that Stewart's grapes also came
from McCrae's vineyard, but I doubt it. At a time when, to use the
word of Walter Schug, California Johannisberg Rieslings were
"klutsy," theirs were outstandingly delicate. In those days, according to Schug, most winemakers handled all white grapes iden-
tically, so that Riesling, Chardonnay, and Sauvignon, processed
with little regard for the subtleties of each variety, inevitably lost
whatever distinction they might have had. Today, despite degrees
of competence and variations in individual practice, faultless wine-

making, at very least, is universal in California. Thus, the measure of a Riesling's quality is more likely to come from the origin of individual batches of grapes and the trouble that a winemaker will have taken in his own vineyard or imposed on his growers. In short, whether the grower and vineyard are now named on the label or not, their importance is unquestionably recognized.

Joseph Phelps owns two Johannisberg Riesling vineyards, one close by the winery, about halfway up the valley and therefore moderately warm, and the other at Yountville, where temperatures are cooler. The winery vineyard often suffers from intense summer afternoon heat that will shut down the vines and wear out the acid. "If I waited for those grapes to reach a sugar level appropriate to Napa, the acidity would by then be so low that the wine would be flat," Schug told me. "But I can let my Yountville grapes hang longer, let them go to higher sugar, and they will still retain better acids than the grapes grown at the winery. They are not so stressed." He handles separately the grapes from these two vineyards, paradoxically making the lighter, crisper wine of the two from the grapes grown in the hotter vineyard because those are the vines he deliberately harvests early.

Robert Gorman, in his *California Premium Wines* (an intelligent and perceptive book that deserved much wider notice than it received when published in 1975), summed up the making of Johannisberg Riesling:

The first [way] is to make a very basic white wine without any elaborate cellar treatment and put it in large (preferably German) oak barrels of 100 gallons or more for anywhere from six months to two years. Most of the older California and German Rieslings were made in this manner. The method still survives in some of the more southerly German wine districts. They are rich, perhaps heavy wines (they have been described as Wagnerian), medium dry and soft, with big earthy and woody flavors. These are good wines for accompanying, say, duckling or rabbit.

The second approach is relatively new in Germany, the result of both a very sophisticated wine technology and some extraordinary vineyard conditions. The objective of this method is to produce Riesling which on the one hand is very crisp and delicate and on the other hand has great intensity of flavor and finesse. Very little, if any, oak is used in this method. The wine is intended to be very fresh and very clean. To this end, the Germans developed temperature controlled fermentation and special centrifuges to render the wine clean and brilliant without the need for excessive filtering. Most of the great Rieslings of the Rheingau and the Moselle regions are made in this manner.

Walter Schug believes these two methods should be complementary rather than mutually exclusive. The control allowed by the use of stainless steel is undeniable, but time in wood—not in French oak, which would introduce a flavor and style at odds with Johannisberg Riesling, but in more neutral German oak—allows the young wine a degree of oxidation necessary for complexity. It also gives the wine a chance to lose its rough edges, and the combination of this acquired complexity and softness contributes to the balance, so that residual sugar to offset the wine's natural acidity is only minimally necessary. Tony Austin, when winemaker at the Firestone Vineyard in the Santa Ynez Valley, agreed. Rieslings that have spent time in wood, he said, gain an extra dimension. He couldn't say why or how, but he believed some mark of the individual cellar or winery was then more likely to be present. His own Johannisberg Rieslings spent a short period in wooden vats specifically to develop a soft blur of fragrance rather than the single, rather floral, note of Riesling character. His 1980 Johannisberg Riesling, with its attractive hint of peach, was a good example of his style in a year when the elements were already in his favor.

In recent years, there has been a move to soften Johannisberg Riesling by holding down the level of alcohol through early harvesting. Alcohol plays a strange role in wine. At moderate levels it warms the mouth and therefore increases the perception of roundness and fullness, its presence helping to balance acidity. But at slightly higher levels the warmth sometimes becomes burn, and then the alcohol might harden rather than soften the wine, reinforcing rather than diminishing the effect of acidity. In California, low-alcohol "soft" wines are made by picking grapes when sugar concentration is still low but acid reasonably high. The presence of that natural acid allows the winemaker to stop fermentation by chilling or by removing the yeast in a centrifuge, leaving a wine at an alcohol level of about 10 percent with about 1 to 2 percent residual sugar to balance the acid.

Richard Arrowood, whose success with both Johannisberg Riesling and Chardonnay at Chateau St. Jean in Sonoma County has earned him wide respect as a winemaker, believes it possible to pick Johannisberg Riesling early and yet attain the varietal character normally present only in fully ripe fruit. There is a point, he says, at which the greenness of immaturity fades, and success depends on recognizing that exact moment to pick before sugar climbs and acid falls. His crisp 1980 Early Harvest Johannisberg Riesling from the Robert Young Vineyards, with slightly less than 10 percent alcohol, was a good example of his theory in practice; but I have to confess that I was more impressed by his two 1980 Johannisberg Rieslings made from normally harvested grapes. The 1980 Kabinett from Robert Young Vineyards, though higher in alcohol, was no less balanced, with superb firmness of style and flavor. Arrowood's 1980 Belle Terre Johannisberg Riesling is decidedly fuller, heavier, richer. It has less elegance than the Robert Young wines, but I prefer it to his 1979 Belle Terre. In the latter, a wonderful bouquet of tropical fruits led to a bony finish that I found inappropriate.

Though not presented specifically as "soft," other Johannisberg Rieslings that I have noticed in this style have included the delightful 1980 of Santa Ynez Valley Winery (labeled, no doubt to the satisfaction of many, White Riesling rather than Johannisberg Riesling), a pale, fresh wine with unmistakable Riesling fragrance; the 1979 Zaca Mesa, which was a little flabby for my taste but full and pleasing; and the 1979 Franciscan Vineyards' Johannisberg Riesling, with a bouquet so perfumed that it was more redolent of Muscat than Riesling.

In 1980, however, growing conditions for Johannisberg Riesling were such that balance came to the wine naturally and early picking was hardly necessary. Low afternoon temperatures left grape acidity intact, and, even when a dramatic heat wave struck northern California at the end of September, its initial effect was to dehydrate the grapes, concentrating everything there—sugar and acid—without changing the equilibrium. Those 1980 Johannisberg Rieslings, with 11 and 12 percent alcohol, were as graceful as any Moselle. Among many that I enjoyed (in addition to those already mentioned) were the 1980 from Raymond Vineyards, with its unexpected suggestion of honey in the aroma, probably a result of some botrytis in the grapes; the Alexander Valley Vineyards' wine, with its tingling, fresh, almost Sauvignon Blanc flavor; Hacienda, a more subdued but equally fragrant wine; Trefethen, with its strikingly intense fruit and slightly hard finish that augured well for keeping; Joseph Phelps, both the aromatic early harvest (bottled, appropriately, in the green glass of the Moselle) and the fuller-flavored regular harvest; Chappellet, with its sprightly, apricot nose, the first of these remarkable 1980s that I tasted; and my favorite (though I apologize for mentioning it because I understand that the couple of hundred cases produced were all sold within California), Flora Springs, a small new Napa Valley winery.

If it was a remarkable year for Johannisberg Rieslings in California, 1980 was not a remarkable year for *Botrytis cinerea*, the fungus that attacks the skin of ripe Riesling grapes and causes them to shrivel rapidly, concentrating both sugar and acid in a way that gives an extraordinary, luscious dessert wine with intense bouquet and flavor. Doubtless there will be late-harvest wines of similar sweetness, but, when the juice is concentrated only through the slow dehydration of grapes left late on the vine, the resulting wines do not capture the honey aroma of botrytis and frequently lose freshness. Too often they have raisin rather than grape fragrance, and, without the glycerine that botrytis brings, they lack the rich viscosity that turns sweet to luscious. For those who had foresight and stout purses (the best of these wines now sell at $25 and $35 a *half* bottle) the 1978s of Joseph Phelps and Chateau St. Jean will provide consolation while we await more propitious conditions. Just a few months ago friends shared with me their last half bottle of Phelps 1975 botrytized Johannisberg Riesling. It was an exquisite, golden wine, in both the literal and metaphorical sense, and we sipped it with a soufflé of ripe persimmons served with whipped almond cream. My diary records only that it was "a successful combination," but I suppose there are times when even I am at a loss for words.

Jerez de la Frontera

ONE OF THE THINGS about breakfast in England that compensates for cold toast (whoever invented the toast rack?) is a chance to prop *Times* or *Telegraph* against the marmalade jar and digest, along with kedgeree or kidneys, or kippers, or sausages, those solemn accounts of human foible that the Home News pages of both papers provide in abundance. Enjoying a second cup of coffee and regaling myself with more than I deserved to know about my fellow men during a recent trip to London, my eye fell on the headline "Sherry is Top People's Drink." An opinion poll had uncovered the fact that though wine (presumably table wine) had now overtaken sherry by 1 percent as the most popular drink in Britain, sherry still appealed most to mature, "top" people, especially those who lived in the shires of the south and west of England and on the wide flat farms of East Anglia, a region where I spent my entire childhood without ever once feeling warm. (Copenhagen, the only windbreak between the Russian steppes and eastern England, is not very effective for the purpose.)

It was reassuring, in a way, to read that in 1979 England imported more than 20 million imperial gallons of sherry from Spain, compared with less than 4 million gallons consumed by the Spanish themselves and little more than a million gallons imported by the

United States. Of course, some of those British gallons, bottled in Bristol, found their way to American shores, but the figures alone show to what extent Jerez de la Frontera, the center of sherry production in Spain, looks to Britain as its prime market and explain the sherry shippers' optimism for eventual growth of consumption in the States.

But in England sherry is not just something that one consumes. At one level, I suppose, it carries an aura of petty gentility, but, to balance that, sherry has associations of urbanity, of donnish civility, and above all of the well-ordered, albeit old-fashioned, domestic life. In England, sherry is the symbol of hospitality at home. It is as right to offer a guest a glass of sherry as it is wrong, somehow, to order one in a pub. "Will you have some sherry?" is still a common, polite way to propose a casual drink, though it is understood that a guest is equally welcome to a gin and tonic or a glass of beer.

Asked for "cocktails" in England, no matter how deceptively low-key the invitation, one knows to wear polished shoes, collect the family jewels from the vault, and complete a few limbering-up exercises in smart chitchat. But an invitation to "come over for a glass of sherry" promises a relaxed communion of friends, comfortable shoes, and old sweater, an occasion that no one will be using as part of life's strategic game plan. It's a matter of familiarity: the English have been drinking sherry for centuries, and, even if Falstaff's sack differed from the sherry we drink today, there is no doubt we would recognize it.

The name of the wine is a corruption of "Jerez," and was first recorded in English late in the seventeenth century. But as words, particularly then, often circulated for some time before they found their way into print, it is likely to have been in colloquial use long before. Sherry started, and starts, life as a white wine produced in an austere region of Andalusia in southwestern Spain close to the sea and confined between the Guadalquivir and Guadalete rivers. The three sherry towns of Jerez de la Frontera, Puerto de Santa Maria, and Sanlúcar de Barrameda, about twelve miles from each other, form a triangle that encloses much of the best vineyard land.

I said *starts* as a white wine because sherry is as much a result of the art of man as it is a consequence of nature. It is nearly thirty years since I was first sent to Jerez to learn about both. I had a small scholarship from the London Wine Trade Club and a modest inheritance from my grandmother to sustain me. Today's jets swoop down to the south of Spain in a couple of hours, but in the early 1950s propeller planes had to stop for refueling in Bordeaux and Madrid. From Seville there was a long drive, and I eventually arrived after midnight to discover, to my northern amazement, groups of men still drinking and talking at tables in front of the bars and cafés of the Calle Larga as if they intended to remain all night, while streams of people, young and old, crowded the narrow sidewalk. Needless to say, I joined them, and six o'clock seemed to arrive as soon as my head touched the pillow.

When do the Spanish sleep? Not in the afternoon, whatever the popular mythology. In Jerez they drank sherry and nibbled on *tapas* until lunch at three. From five to eight there was often work to do, and from nine until eleven there was more sherry and *tapas* before dinner. Theater and movies started at midnight.

The bitter coffee and sweet rolls of a Spanish breakfast revived and consoled me, and I reported for work at Mackenzie & Co., a small independent sherry shipper now absorbed by Harvey's. Ramiro Fernandez-Gao, the managing director, was waiting for me in the tasting room, in front of him a line of tulip-shaped *copitas*, each with an ounce or two of liquid that ranged from almost color-less to a dark chocolate brown. Before we started to taste together, he explained that when the juice of the Palomino grapes finished fermenting, each butt of wine—in Jerez referred to as *mosto* (grape juice) until a year old—began to acquire a character of its own. Identifying that character, encouraging its development, and successfully blending it to a constant style that could be shipped under a recognized label from year to year without variation was the role of the sherry shipper.

The process starts when the foreman of the *bodega* checks every butt of new wine, drawing a sample with the aid of his *venencia*, a narrow silver cup at the end of a flexible wand of whalebone. Wines that are light, balanced, and clean are distinguished by a short stroke of chalk, a *raya*. Two *rayas* indicate a wine with less promise (between one and two there is a demigrade, *raya y punto*), and three *rayas* a wine that is harsh or inelegant, most often distilled for brandy.

The foreman looks for *flor*, the most important and distinctive influence in the making of sherry. *Flor* is a yeast that grows on the surface of the wine in spring and autumn. Butts are left with gen-erous air space above the wine to encourage it, but the spores are selective and develop most readily on wines with a light, elegant style. In those a veil spreads quickly and soon looks like a layer of lumpy cream. Pliny, almost two thousand years ago, recognized that this velvety growth was not to be confused with the vinegar microbe. On the contrary, *flor* protects the wine from any vinegar attack, diminishes volatile acidity, and greatly increases the nut-like esters and aldehydes that we recognize as the typical sherry fragrance.

Once racked off their heavy lees into other casks, wines classified with one *raya* are again checked for their *flor* growth, essential to the satisfactory development of Fino-type sherry. If the *flor* is strong and the wine delicate, the alcohol is marginally adjusted to the optimum level, between 14.5 and 15.5 percent by volume, the ideal strength to encourage further growth. If the *flor* is weak or the wine less delicate, the alcohol is adjusted beyond 15.5 percent to discourage further growth of *flor*, a move that will direct the wine toward Oloroso type. The *raya* with *flor* is now further distinguished by a small stroke sprouting from the top of the larger one like a primitive palm tree, and the wine becomes known, in fact, as *palma*. Here, then, is the first parting of the ways: *palma* and *raya*, one with *flor*, the other without; the first destined for light Finos, the second, for more full-bodied Olorosos.

As Finos age, they darken from straw to gold and take on a pungent, complex aroma. Olorosos acquire a deep amber color and aromatic flavor. Each, in its natural, unblended state, is quite dry. Sweetness, when required, is added to a blend at the last moment through judicious use of *vinos dulces*, special wines made from Moscatel or Pedro Ximenez grapes. Color, too, is adjusted through the use of minute quantities of wine made from grape juice concentrated in huge copper cauldrons, dark and spicy.

With this basic framework Ramiro Fernandez-Gao introduced me to the twenty or more samples on the tasting bench. They started with a young wine that had barely finished fermentation and could still develop in any direction: perhaps as a young *palma*, eventually becoming a mature Fino; or perhaps a *raya*, with the possibility of becoming an Oloroso of great age. Then came a series of Finos, ending with those that had rounded out with age and acquired the style known as Amontillado. (Amontillado, unfortunately, is a name too often abused. It should describe those Finos that have acquired, with age, something of the round, earthy style

of the Montilla wines produced a hundred miles or so northeast
of Jerez. But they can acquire that quality along with a depth of
flavor and a rich viscosity only in maturity. By its very nature a
genuine Amontillado is costly to produce. Inexpensive "commercial" Amontillado blends, with color carefully adjusted and flavor
judiciously balanced, might be satisfactory enough, but they can
give no idea of what a true, aged Amontillado can be. To those
who have never tasted one, it is a revelation.)

As a bridge to the *rayas* and Olorosos, Ramiro had included a
palo cortado, a rare changeling sherry that combines the aroma of
an Amontillado and the body and flavor of an Oloroso. As we tasted
Olorosos of increasing age, I could see how their flavor deepened
with the years to a level that the palate could not accept, eventually reaching an intensity that seemed to burn. Such wines need the
soothing presence of *vino dulce*, or must be used only in small
amounts to give complexity to a blend. For the most part we
worked with the nose alone, but, as the session was intended to
teach, every wine was also tasted, often two or three times to get
the differences clearly fixed in my mind. We finished by tasting unblended examples of *vinos dulces* and aged *vino de color*. It was an
exhausting morning.

There was to be a reward for my effort. The last big fight of
the season was to take place that afternoon in the Seville bull ring.
Swept off along the dusty highway without discussion, I had no
time to ask myself whether or not a bullfight was something to
relish. We ate lunch in Seville at the Hotel Madrid. I have never
been back, and I fantasize against all probability that it is still there,
unchanged. Built like a Moorish palace, its façade glittering with
multicolored tiles on a narrow side street and its cloistered interior
a lush, tropical garden, the Madrid at that time was popular with
the Spanish movie world. We sipped our sherry under the shady
arcade of the patio while actors with somber Byronic faces gestured
melodramatically and actresses, softly rustling silk dresses in clouds
of perfume, arched their heads gracefully, a posture necessary, perhaps, to support the weight of their extravagant eyelashes. I was
young and impressionable, and they seemed to me to be infinitely
exotic.

The *corrida* was an exhilarating spectacle, despite its uglier
passages. Ramiro kindly explained the language and tradition of
the ring, the sequence of moves, the ritual. As the matador played

the bull to show his complete control, the band struck up a *paso doble*, and the crowd threw an *olé* of encouragement and admiration at each turn of the cape. For a moment I felt myself part of an audience that had been sitting in that ring (or another) for several thousand years watching bulls, acrobats, and bravura.

We returned to Jerez to dine late at the Fernandez-Gao home, where I made the acquaintance of a typical Jerez *crema*, richer in color and taste than the usual *crème caramel* because the egg whites used for fining the wines leave huge quantities of yolks for cooking, and in Jerez they find their way into just about everything. I suppose cholesterol hadn't been invented.

At seven the next morning I was in the *bodega* and ready to learn about the *solera* system of blending sherry. "The basis of the system," Ramiro explained, "is that a small quantity of suitable young wine, blended with a larger quantity of older wine, will in a short time be absorbed into the style of the older wine. It will be easier to understand," he said, "if you imagine ten butts of sherry blended and aged to a certain required style. It would be very difficult, if not impossible, to replace those butts with wine from later vintages and expect that there would be no appreciable difference."

The problem is avoided by not selling off the ten butts, one at a time, but by selling a butt drawn in small quantities from each of the ten and filling the ullages with quantities drawn from a second rank of ten butts, slightly younger, ready for this very purpose. The second rank in turn is filled from ten other butts, and so on back to selected one-year-old wines chosen for their style to enter the "scales" of this particular system, *palma* or *raya*, as appropriate for Fino or Oloroso. The series of preparatory scales in the system is known collectively as a *criadera*, best translated as "nursery." The final scale, "the row of butts" from which the wine is actually drawn for blending or bottling, is known as the *solera*, or "foundation." On a blackboard Ramiro drew a diagram with scales of butts stacked one upon another, pointing to them as he explained again how sherry would be transferred, a little at a time, from one scale to another as the sherry aged and as the *solera* of the system needed replenishment.

When I seemed to understand the theory, he explained that in practice the different scales of a *criadera* might be widely separated in different sections of the *bodega*; that a *solera* providing the basis for a popular brand of sherry might have several hundred butts in each scale of its *criadera*; and that the final stage, the *solera* itself of a particular system, might be both a source of wine for a blend and the initiating source for the *criadera* of yet another *solera* system, aging some of the wine to an even higher level.

Finos, he told me, present special problems. By law no sherry can be sold before it is three years old, but Finos, to retain their freshness during that period, must be moved constantly and rapidly through a *solera* system to keep the *flor* refreshed. Because the moves are frequent, the quantities each time need to be small so as not to change the style of wine in each butt. And, because the process must continue over such a long time for the wine to conform truly to the required style of the *solera*, a Fino *criadera* needs many scales with many butts in each. There is much labor in producing a mature Fino.

The relationship between sales volume and its demands on the *solera* systems in any *bodega* is crucial. Sudden, large shipments would deplete the *soleras* and *criaderas* too quickly, and, even if quality didn't decline, the styles of each *solera* could suddenly change. Recognizing that, the Spanish appellation law for sherry, unlike any other, restricts a *bodega* to selling no more than 40 percent of its stock in any one year.

Wines drawn from a single *solera*, however, are rarely bottled and shipped without further blending. A *solera* might provide the basis of a particular blend, but added to it will be a proportion of wine from a second *solera*, perhaps, or some young wine not yet part of a *solera*. The formula for making each standard blend for shipment might require the addition of Pedro Ximenez wine to adjust sweetness or *vino de color* to reach a standard hue. My morning ended with some practical work in the tasting room, learning how to use the various *soleras* and other wines to match samples sent from England and Holland for price quotations.

Gradually my days took on a Spanish measure. In free time I explored the narrow streets between the Calle Larga and Alcazar, the old Moorish citadel of Jerez. I roamed the undulating vineyards planted in the improbably white *albariza* soil of Jerez Superior. I walked in blazing sun to visit the town's remote Carthusian monastery. For a short time I was sent to work with another shipper in Puerto de Santa Maria in a *bodega* that specialized in Finos. (While there I lodged in an old hotel, where at three every morning a servant arrived to light a small wood-burning stove in my bath-

The Sherry Region

SEVILLE

ANDALUSIA

Guadalquivir R.

N

Sanlúcar de
Barrameda

JEREZ DE LA
FRONTERA

Guadalete R.

© 1982 A. Karl/J. Kemp

CADIZ

Puerto de
Santa Maria

Atlantic
Ocean

Miles
0 ———————— 10
0 ———————— 10
Kms.

SPAIN

Area of
map

room so that I could have hot water at six. I offered to bathe at
night to make life simpler for them, but they wouldn't hear of it.)
Closer to the ocean, with cooler temperatures, Puerto de Santa
Maria shippers emphasize their Fino and Amontillado sherries,
which do well there. But the difference from the Finos of Jerez is
barely perceptible when both are compared to the Finos of Sanlúcar
de Barrameda, the third of the sherry towns, on the estuary of the
Guadalquivir. There the wines have a light, brisk pungency that
sets them apart. Manzanillas (as they are called) of Sanlúcar are
made from Palomino grapes picked at least two weeks before the
general harvest. Partly because of this premature picking and partly
the result of cool sea air over the estuary, Manzanilla has unusual
zest and fragrance. And then the alcohol of Manzanilla is slightly
lower than that of other Fino sherries, an aid, perhaps, to preserving its delicacy and its penetrating bouquet.

Manzanilla was at its best on Juan's jetty at Sanlúcar. Juan is now
dead, alas, and the fishing boats unload a mile away. But in those
days the fishermen landed their catch on the beach below, and it
was understood that the best was reserved for him. While waiting
at rickety wooden tables in the salty air, his customers could watch
the fish, still palpitating, on their way to the kitchen in his small
house across the street. With a bowl of small green olives or a
dish of prawns, a platter of fried octopus rings or morsels of sword-
fish to stave off hunger and a bottle of Manzanilla on ice to generate
patience, time passed quickly.

And so it had. My coffee was cold and I had lost half the morning in reverie. It was time to check my host's cellar to see what he
had in the way of a decent sherry for lunch. I hoped he would
qualify as a top person.

Wine and Wok

LONDONERS KNOW, and most visitors do too, that the best Chinese food in that city is to be found in and around Gerrard Street, near Cambridge Circus. But I seem to have done most of my sampling in London in one or another of the Cantonese-style restaurants clustered about East India Dock Road, establishments hardly distinguishable from the "caffs" surrounding them. At some time, I suppose, there really must have been the Limehouse China-town of popular fiction; and these humble restaurants today, with their strange kinship of names, "Old Friends," "New Friends," "Young Friends," "Good Friends" (never, curiously, "Just Friends"), are the vestiges. Dinner at one of the "Friends" was usually a prelude to taking visitors for a jolly evening around the dockland pubs, so it is hardly surprising, under the circumstances, that I remained ignorant of the subtlety of Chinese cooking despite the frequency with which I ate it.

I moved from London to New York, and as chance would have it, my very first lunch in Manhattan was Chinese. A wine-trade colleague I wanted to meet was on jury duty, so we ate close to the Federal Courthouse. Fortunately, he had lived for many years in Hong Kong, and, when he ordered for me in a nearby China-town restaurant of his choice, it was as if I had never eaten Chinese food before. The lunch was a good start, and I often went back to Chinatown in the years that I lived in New York, learning to appreciate the different regional as well as personal styles of cooking of its restaurants.

My favorite spot was a noisy, basically Szechwan restaurant near Chatham Square where the tables were usually crowded with large family groups. Trips to Chatham Square always seemed to come at the end of good cocktail parties, and those evenings have associations for me of earnest discussions with taxi drivers on the legal limit to the passenger capacity of Checker cabs, of New Yorkers' optimistic assumption that even a popular restaurant can always "squeeze in" a party of eleven, and of the rather awful white wines that were generally accepted without question as an appropriate accompaniment to Chinese meals. It would have been difficult for any wine to be appropriate, really, because although the food tasted as delicious as it looked, there was always a jumble of dishes on the table at one time—a bit like an eighteenth-century European dinner—and, as everyone sampled everything in whatever order pleased him, there was no basis for a rational selection of wine.

By happy chance, one of the first people I met when I moved to San Francisco was the late Helen Kan, owner of Kan's restaurant on Grant Avenue in Chinatown. I was a guest at several dinners in her restaurant, and the planned sequence of dishes served there showed me that my earlier experience had been no more revealing of Chinese culinary art than a meal of assorted *quenelles, choucroûte, daube d'agneau, coq au vin, écrevisses à la nage*, and *ris de veau financière*, all served together and sampled in no particular sequence, would have been a measure of French gastronomic genius. I found, too, that in private houses in San Francisco, where some families employ Chinese cooks, I was just as likely to be served an exquisite series of Chinese dishes for dinner as a series of Western ones. As I gained a deeper respect for the cuisine, I became even more conscious of the careless choice of wine that usually went with it. There was often an apology for drinking wine at all, and never a planned sequence of wines to match the well-ordered dishes.

I tried to experiment in various Chinese restaurants, looking for interesting contrasts and harmonies of wines and foods, but I found few had a wine list to match the range and quality of the cooking. It was difficult to experiment at length when most had little more than two or three whites, a red or two, and a rosé—sometimes sound, well-chosen wines, but always very limited.

I asked Mrs. Kan to help, and, with her chef Pui Wong, she prepared for me and some friends seven of the restaurant's most popular dishes, each presenting a different facet of Chinese cookery, so that I could select a wine for each. The dishes were served as a suite of courses, but there was no intention to have them represent a properly balanced meal.

By way of an apéritif, we drank a cool Ockfener Bockstein Kabinett 1971 of Dr. Fischer. A light white wine is always a good apéritif, if it has personality and flavor. Discreet, unassertive wines have their place; but presented at the beginning of a meal to an unstimulated palate, they are as exciting as a gray morning. The Ockfener was a good choice: it was elegant, light, and had a shimmer of sweet and sharp that pre-echoed what we were expecting to follow.

The first dish presented was Peking duck. "It is normally served at the close of a banquet, a climax to a series of dishes," our hostess told us, "but then no one can appreciate it because they have usually eaten too well already." Peking duck is a breed of duckling raised specifically for this dish. The preparation is long and includes many applications of a syrup glaze while the duck is suspended in a cool, airy place. The skin of the roasted bird is crisp; the meat, delicately aromatic. At Kan's Peking duck is served with steamed buns, a plum sauce, and slivers of scallion. I had selected two red wines to accompany it: a Ridge California Zinfandel 1972 and a Château Roc-Saint-Michel 1970, a Saint-Emilion. The Zinfandel was light and very fruity. In California, 1972 was an unusual year; the autumn rains started quite early, coinciding with a late crop, and many of the red wines, particularly from Napa and Sonoma where these Zinfandel grapes were grown, are lighter than one would normally expect. The Saint-Emilion, with more color, more body, and a firmer edge of tannin, seemed to withstand the plum sauce better than the Zinfandel, although we all agreed that as a wine the Zinfandel was more pleasing.

One of the guests wondered whether the reds would overwhelm the delicacy of the duck if it were not for the sauce. So we brought forward a 1971 Meursault that I had earmarked for a chicken-with-almond dish to come and tried it with the duck. Many purists maintain that Peking duck, with its very subtle flavors, should be enjoyed without further accompaniment, and in this instance that theory proved to be correct. The Meursault was soft, with an almost sweet overtone; and the duck, which had been overshadowed by the red wines, was thrown into delicate relief by the white. With the sauce, however, the Meursault seemed to disappear; the rich sweet-sharp quality of the sauce was too tough to compete with. A bold, weighty red was needed: the Saint-Emilion—young and vigorous—went well with it, but so would a Côtes du Rhône or a heavy Barbera.

The chicken with almonds that followed was chosen as a bland dish, one in which the contrasting textures are as important as the flavors. I had thought that the Meursault would accompany it well, and I had also brought along an Orvieto Classico 1972 of Barberani. Both, it turned out, were too unassertive. For blandness in a dish to be positive—in Chinese cooking, *tom* is not an absence of taste, but a quality that contributes to the overall balance of tastes and flavors—the wine needs to have an edge to it. A dry white Sauvignon, perhaps a dry Graves, would have been much better than either of the wines I had chosen; and even a Riesling, provided it was quite dry and not too fruity, would have matched the dish well. Later, when we came to taste a Chenin Blanc, we thought that it combined fullness with just enough flavor to give relief, and it, too, would have made a better marriage with the dish. (Chicken with almonds, I might add, in which all ingredients are cut to the size of the almonds in accordance with a basic principle of Chinese cooking, is devilishly hard to eat with chopsticks, especially when concentrating on wine.)

Pui has a chicken specialty that is cooked with a sharp lemon sauce and a hint of the musky scent of coriander. When it was described to me, I decided we would need a strongly scented wine to go with it and chose an Eltviller Sonnenberg Spätlese 1971 from the Langwerth von Simmern estate. I was quite wrong. It was immediately clear that the dominant lemon flavor should not be interfered with: the grapiness of the Eltviller was simply an irritant. The dish needed a big wine, as soft as the Eltviller but unassertive. The lemon of the dish was supported by other strands of flavor so that a chord was produced rather than a single note, but so subtly was it set together that one more flavor destroyed the balance. The Meursault, of which we still had a little, was much better. A number of us agreed that any Chardonnay-based wine would go well with the dish, but finding the right wine to serve with a citrus-based sauce is always a problem. I remember some years ago the *Revue du Vin de France* ran a forum on selecting a wine that could accompany a duck à l'orange. The final choice was the very pungent, almost sherry-like *vin jaune* from the Jura hills of eastern France.

We moved on to a marinated lamb preparation in which the sweet-spicy note of hoisin predominates. Braised and stir-fried, the small pieces of lamb are brown on the outside and delicately pink inside; the sauce is rich but low-key. For this specialty I had planned a Château Thivin 1973, a fresh young Beaujolais from the Côte de Brouilly. The wine was delicious but no match for the lamb. The dish was far more stately than I had expected, and the Brouilly seemed frivolous beside it. We tried some of the Beaune Theurons 1969 that was ready for a later course and found that its greater fullness (1969, a light year in Bordeaux, gave particularly big, tannic wines in Burgundy) provided a much better foil. At this point our hostess told us that the wines were bringing out flavors and nuances that were new to her in dishes that she had eaten all her life.

The wine and food combination that followed seemed to satisfy all of us. The dish was prawns in a black-bean sauce, very delicate but unctuous; and the moderately dry, full-bodied Chenin Blanc 1972 of Chappellet was perfect with it. We felt that the Meursault or any soft, full-bodied white wine with an unassertive flavor would have done equally well. As with Peking duck, the sauce had to be considered rather than the fish or meat itself.

We paused for a few minutes before tasting the sweet-and-sour pork. The wine choices were a Beaulieu Vineyard Riesling-Sylvaner 1972 and a fine Gewürztraminer 1970 from Alsace. More than any other, I think, Gewürztraminer has always been suggested as the one most suitable wine for Chinese sweet-sour dishes; but we found that the strong, aromatic style typical of a good Gewürztraminer was irrelevant, an unnecessary baroque flourish totally unrelated to the food. One guest felt it might have gone better with the Peking duck, but I am not sure that the same objection would not have applied there equally. The Riesling-Sylvaner, unfortunately, was too inconsequential, lacking body particularly; and the Chenin Blanc, still on the table, went better than either.

We concluded the meal with Peking beef, a fairly spicy combination, served with crispy cooked snow peas. With it we tried a Ravello Rosso of Gran Caruso and, at the same time, the Beaune Theurons 1969. The Beaune made the better match: it blended more easily into the established harmony. And that, I concluded, was the secret. We look for a wine to *accompany* a food, or we think of a food that will show off a wine to advantage. But any Chinese dish is so carefully balanced that the wine must either bring its own harmony, or must complete an overall equilibrium. I suppose it's another aspect of Yin and Yang.

Dessert Wines

BROWSING THE secondhand bookshops of the Fulham Road one summer, I came across an old copy of T. Earle Welby's *The Cellar Key*, a little book published in the thirties, full of forthright good sense on wine (by which I mean, as we all do when we use such a phrase, that his opinions coincide by and large with my own).

The book was a delight to read; but I was uncomfortable with Welby's assertion that a good dinner, with great red wines, should end with the best of them. It was not that he was prejudiced against dessert wines as such; he felt, rather, that since no dessert wine could rise to a higher plane than the best red wine, to serve one after a suite of fine reds could never be more than an anticlimax. Even so, there is a passage in the book that confirms him to have been capable of appreciating a fine Sauternes. He once served a very old Château d'Yquem to a Scottish visitor of even greater age, a man quite unfamiliar with sweet white wines (which I find hard to believe) but "nobly fanatical about claret." "As the wine took him," said Welby with a questionable excess of lyricism, "he passed into rapture." "I have never cared for sweet wine, but you are right," said the Scot. "This *is* wine." And then, careful of his words in rapture or not, he added, "I will never drink it again. I will keep it as a memory of our evening together." At which T. Earle Welby was both charmed and gratified.

Not that ending dinner with a magnificent red wine was, or is, uncommon. In nineteenth-century England all red wines, more often than not, were kept until *after* dinner, when the ladies had withdrawn and there could be serious drinking. (That is why there still exists in England the curious habit of eating cheese after the sweet course of dinner: a *lady* would no more think of eating cheese than she would of drinking red wine, so the cheese, too, was kept until the men were alone.)

William Younger, in *Gods, Men, and Wines*, gives the menu of a dinner offered sometime in the 1850s by Sir William Hardman to George Meredith and Dante Gabriel Rossetti, among others, at which the *filet de boeuf* and lamb cutlets were accompanied by Amontillado sherry, the chicken Marengo and a strawberry omelet were alike washed down with sparkling hock, and only *after* dinner were those who survived this bizarre presentation rewarded with some decent, mature Chambertin.

The tradition of sitting round the table after dinner with a few bottles of fine red wine can, of course, be quite jolly in a blowsy, Rowlandson sort of way, even though, in Hesketh Pearson's words, "It is many years since the nodding and lolling and snoring of a company of gentlemen at the dinner table was considered an appropriate conclusion of a hearty meal."

As the nineteenth century moved from the plain trencherman fare and plainer drinking of its beginning to the elaborate fantasies of Edwardian gastronomic enterprise of its end, old ideas and new became hopelessly confused by the overriding need to be fashionable rather than sensible. Iced Champagne was served with game; and Claret, making its arrival at the table earlier than before, but obviously not early enough, was drunk with the sweets and dessert. (In 1899, "dessert Claret" was among the wines listed at the then Trocadero restaurant in Shaftesbury Avenue.) Sauternes at that time had other uses: Professor Saintsbury (he of the *Notes on a Cellar-Book*), for example, chose Château d'Yquem 1870 to accompany grilled red mullet.

At Oxford colleges, the practice of drinking red wine after dinner continues: I am sure that a good red Bordeaux is still served, with the nuts and fruit, to the dons of St. Edmund Hall, along with Sauternes, Port, and Madeira, whatever has happened to the pound. To offer a continuation of red wine with dessert to those who prefer it is civilized; to impose it, however, or, worse, to deprive those who might enjoy a small glass of sweet wine at the close of a good dinner is hardly considerate.

Even in Bordeaux, a superb luncheon often rests on the lingering memory of the last of the red wines. I have been surprised to notice how few are the occasions when a fine Sauternes is served (except in the Sauternais itself, of course). Sometimes I have been bewildered by a concluding dry Champagne, served just when the palate needs no further stimulation.

When I have shared with friends and eaten well, those few hauntingly sweet, golden sips of dessert wine are particularly fitting as the evening mellows to post-dinner talk. But in our calorie-conscious age, all sweetness is suspect. Or perhaps it is not our present flight from sweet dishes but the sweet dishes themselves that turn us away from rich, old Vouvray and honeyed Beerenauslesen. "Sweet dishes," thunders Mr. Welby, "are destructive of all wines except the most luscious of Sauternes." The Germans, sensing this, drink their finest sweet wines unaccompanied after the meal; and I have to admit that in many instances carefully plotted combinations of sweet dishes and sweet wines have fallen far short of the memorable experiences they were intended to be.

Just this spring, when the delightful new Muscat wine of the Angelo Papagni winery first appeared in San Francisco, it was served at the end of a dinner party with a feathery confection that seemed to be made of air, cream, and ground hazelnuts in about equal proportions. Most of us were already familiar with the wine and were surprised that it seemed curiously thin and lackluster, despite the minimal sweetening in the hazelnut cream. But the cream itself, coating the mouth, masked both the weight of the wine and its zest.

On the other hand, I remember drinking a glorious Château Filhot 1953 with a summer pudding (an English nursery dish of fresh raspberries and currants, both red and black, pressed firmly into a pudding basin lined with plain bread and left to chill overnight) smothered in the rich, yellow cream of the Loseley herd.

Once back home, I looked through my own old dinner menus and saw that I had been instinctively restrained when serving old Sauternes: orange salad with brown crystal sugar; compote of fresh peaches; ripe figs in raspberry purée; nothing very rich or creamy. But in my notebook there were numerous entries of sweet wines I had enjoyed elsewhere with dishes of much greater variety: a Château d'Yquem 1954 with strawberries Romanoff in New York; the exciting 1973 Edelwein of Freemark Abbey with a freshly made ice of orange and chestnuts at a friend's house in Napa; a delectable Château Suduiraut 1947 with a rich strawberry tart; and, just recently, a young Château Rieussec with a *soufflé au Grand Marnier* at San Francisco's French Club.

Harry Yoxall, in his book *The Enjoyment of Wine*, cautions against serving any fine wine with egg dishes but excepts a sweet white wine with a sweet soufflé, because, he says, "well, because you can." In an old issue of the Wine and Food Society's quarterly I found, over his initials, an account of a dinner at the Dorchester Hotel in London in 1963. The evening concluded with a *soufflé Marie Brizard*, accompanied by a Niersteiner Rohr-Rehbach Riesling und Sylvaner Trockenbeerenauslese, Original Abfullung Dr. Jur. A. Senfter 1953 (when the Germans catch up with California and start to mention on their labels the sugar level of the grapes, the pH of the must, and the fermentation temperature as well, we shall get a really good read for our money). Neither the diners nor the wine were ruffled by the eggs. "Against the mild and well-risen soufflé," wrote Mr. Yoxall, the wine "offered a glorious sweetness, but without any cloying." Obviously the occasion itself —happy, as one deduces from the rest of the account—would have heightened the appreciation of the wine, and one can hardly criticize a wine with a pedigree that long.

The more I read and thought about combinations of sweet wines and sweet dishes, the more I realized that I had paid less attention than I should to the effect of one on the other, inexcusable in one who can spend hours wondering whether a rack of lamb or a simple beef daube would be best for a particular red wine. Only idiots, I reminded myself, take their pleasures frivolously.

So, on my first idle Sunday afternoon, in a spirit of inquiry, I assembled ripe peaches and raspberries, a slightly sweetened but otherwise plain apple mousse, and an apple fool (the mousse stirred with whipped cream). I made a *crème caramel* and bought the best vanilla ice cream I could find, a strawberry tart with thick *crème pâtissière*, a cake smothered in rich dark chocolate, and a rum and chocolate truffle. To match the sweets I brought out one of my last bottles of Château Suduiraut 1967; a Schloss Vollrads Auslese '59; a sweet California wine, a light Muscat of Alexandria bottled by Corti Brothers; and a heavier Moscato di Canelli as well as a Malvasia, both from Cresta Blanca. Fortified dessert wines— Port, Madeira, and cream sherry—are impossible to taste at the same time as table wine–strength wines: they obliterate the lighter wines.

A friend who called unexpectedly froze at the sight of my dining table and declined my invitation to stay and assist. I was somewhat daunted myself, I have to confess, but I remembered Bertie of the Guards, the hero of Ouida's novel *Under Two Flags*, and took heart. Bertie drank Curaçao liberally with his breakfast, and the love of his life, Zuzu (a young lady, evidently French, but of uncertain antecedents, whom he had "translated from a sphere of garret, bread and cheese to a sphere of villa, Champagne and chicken"), prescribed for his three-o'clock-in-the-morning depressions Crème de Bouzy with crushed pineapple, and Parfait Amour, a sticky, purple liqueur that hopefully restored him to that equilibrium necessary to assure a good night's sleep for both of them. Compared with that, mine was hardly a test of fortitude.

I started with Château La Salle of the Christian Brothers. Against the peach and the plain apple mousse it was fresh and clean, lightly fruity, and with an agreeably balanced sweetness. The raspberries subdued its flavor, but the addition of a little cream to the raspberries toned *them* down and restored the flavor of the wine. The ice cream deadened the palate, and I had no taste impression of the wine at all; the eggs in the *crème caramel* robbed the wine of flavor and made it taste thin. The fruit tart with *crème pâtissière* also detracted from the fullness and flavor of the wine, and the sweetness of pastry and glaze made the wine seem dry. The chocolate cake and the rum and chocolate truffle both distorted the wine completely.

I drew breath and a glass of Château Suduiraut 1967. It was exquisite against the peach but, to my surprise, even better against the raspberries. Their sharp flavor made the Sauternes seem more luscious, even though its flavor was toned down. It seemed to finish dry against the apple mousse, on the other hand, and against the apple fool it tasted quite dry and hard. Ice cream stunned the wine, leaving just a thin, dry taste. The *crème caramel* and the fruit tart again made the wine lighter and less flavored. The chocolate in both the cake and the truffle distorted the wine as before.

Schloss Vollrads is a rich, golden wine with a perfume and flavor of ripe fruits and honey. Against the peach it was superb, but the raspberries robbed it of flavor. It was drier against the apple mousse and even more so—with less body and less flavor—against the apple fool. I went back to the peach to make sure there was no taste carry-over from the deadening fool to the *crème caramel*; but again the *crème caramel* and *crème pâtissière* of the strawberry tart subdued this huge wine and made it thin and insignificant. Amazingly, the wine was more powerful than the ice cream, and, though the frozen palate had no reaction at all, a diminished fruity aroma came through. The wine was distorted by the chocolate.

By now I was beginning to feel rather shaky, but I drank a glass of water, walked twice round the apartment, and was ready to continue.

Corti Brothers' Muscat of Alexandria is a delicate wine with only slight sweetness. None of the foods enhanced it in any way: it was best drunk alone. The natural sharpness of the raspberries brought out the slender sweetness of the wine but diminished its flavor, and everything else gave poor exchange for what it took from the wine.

The Moscato di Canelli was more powerful and, in fact, more agreeable with its strong flavor toned down by the raspberries, than it was with the more delicately balanced peach. For the first time the *crème caramel* and fruit tart improved a wine by taming the overbearing flavor. The wine even dominated the chocolate, though tasting rather thin and acid against it.

The even more pungent Malvasia, with a marked Muscatel flavor, also was better with the raspberries than the peach. It was more palatable against the apple fool and considerably toned down against the *crème caramel* and fruit tart. But at this stage, unfortunately, my courage failed, and I cannot say how Malvasia stands up to rum and chocolate truffle, chocolate cake, or vanilla ice cream.

Hot and Cold

SOMEWHERE IN a pantry drawer reserved for broken decanter stoppers, useless corkscrews, candle ends and old corks (they might come in handy), I have a special thermometer with which I could regularly check the temperature of wine in my glass before I drink. I say *could* because I have been uncomfortable with the idea of using it ever since a distinguished French *chroniqueur gastronomique*, now departed, used hers with such startling effect at a Paris luncheon at least twenty years ago. Those assembled were on the point of bringing to their lips glasses of freshly poured young Beaujolais, served at cool cellar temperature, when she leapt to her feet. "Stop!" she cried. Wondering what horror I was being protected from, I put down my glass. She held her own aloft, a thermometer sticking from it, in a pose not unlike Liberty with her torch, and came straight to the point. "The temperature of this wine is only nine degrees centigrade," she said. "We must wait until it reaches ten."

And wait we did, watching in silence while she watched the mercury. Fortunately the room was warm, and it seemed barely a minute or two before she relaxed, smiled and nodded. "Now," she breathed. We smelled and we savored—but the spontaneity of our pleasure was gone, though no one was ill-mannered enough to ask even himself how such pedantry could stop the wine continuing to creep up to eleven degrees, to twelve and to thirteen. It is inevitable that wine will warm in the glass: That is why the *Académie Internationale du Vin*, in their published notes on wine service, advise starting to pour wine slightly below the optimum temperature.

Which brings us to the question: What *is* optimum temperature? Though neither glass nor bottle will stay obligingly on the button, what, at least, should we aim for? There never has been total agreement on the temperature at which wine is best served. In one of Robert Browning's poems, a bishop coos with satisfaction at the chill of his claret, urging a companion to put the decanter back in the ice—to the outrage of Professor Saintsbury. ("Icing good claret at all is barbarous," he said in *Notes on a Cellar Book*, "but the idea of freezing, thawing and freezing again is simply Bolshevik.") Politics aside, keeping wine cool seems to have been an obsession in the nineteenth century. Cyrus Redding, in *Everyman His Own Butler*, published in London in 1852, advised no one to "pour out more wine with his dinner than he intends to take at one sip, and then immediately to reverse his glass." Wineglass coolers filled with the coldest water were set by each place and glasses without a base were sometimes used so that it was impossible to omit reversing them in the water. Apart from the awkwardness of reaching for decanter or bottle for every swallow of wine (it was presumably pulled from and plunged back into the ice repeatedly), I am not sure that I would care to have every "sip" of wine diluted by the drops of cold water clinging to my baseless glass.

Conventionally, there are three "temperatures" at which we serve wine: "room temperature," a misleading term we use to suggest something in the range of 60° to 65° Fahrenheit; "cool" or "cellar temperature," from 50° to 55°; and "cold" or "iced," from 40° to 45°. Instinctively one feels that wine would be at its most refreshing served cool. Rabelais thought it best that way ("drink it fresh if you can" is a rough translation of something he said somewhere), and Keats, of course, preferred his "cool'd a long age." Instead of finding it necessary to justify drinking wine cool, perhaps we should have good reason when we choose to drink it any other way. Instead of asking, "Why do we drink Beaujolais, a red wine, at 'cellar temperature'?" perhaps we should ask, "Why do we drink red Bordeaux at 'room temperature'?"

If we accept a cool 55° as a norm, at least hypothetically, we can ask ourselves why we would serve any wine warmer or colder and establish for ourselves a guide more practical than the printed tables that link temperatures to wine names as if all Cabernet Sauvignons were the same, all Sauternes indistinguishable, one from another, and all red Burgundy of equal maturity. Food eaten directly from the refrigerator lacks flavor, as we all know. Similarly, when we serve a wine at a temperature below the norm we neutralize taste and smell increasingly the colder we go. Wine served below 45° releases almost nothing of its aroma and bouquet, and, in fact, anesthetizes rather than stimulates the taste buds. As a wine's temperature mounts from the norm toward 65°, on the other hand, so aroma and bouquet are increasingly released until, at about 68°, evaporating alcohol begins to dominate, and some of the other volatile compounds present, agreeable when barely perceptible, become more intense and make the bouquet less attractive. Hence the need to keep even red wines cooler than the average American dining room.

Aroma and *bouquet* have precise meaning in relation to wine, and differ from each other. Young wine has *aroma*, uncomplicated odor of the grape and of fermentation—fruity, sometimes floral, universally appealing. *Bouquet* (associations with a mixed bouquet of flowers or of herbs are deliberate) is a result of changes and combinations that take place in the sealed bottle. It is a legacy of time, and was thought, for many years, to be the result of oxidation. Though there is still little agreement on the nature of wine's bouquet, generally it is now accepted that, in table wines anyway, it is a result of reduction, the opposite of what was thought before. During fermentation, usually presented to us with a simplified formula showing only the transformation of sugar into familiar ethyl alcohol and carbon dioxide, there are formed traces of many other alcohols. Since they are in the presence of organic acids of equal diversity, interaction, along with the aromatic mutation of substances otherwise without odor, leads in time to an immeasurable complexity of evanescent compounds that volatilize when wine is poured.

When all the talking is done, capacity to develop bouquet is the real measure of wine's quality: that is the point of aging it at least. Not all wines are suitable, and we say of them that "they do not age well." In time, the grape and fermentation aroma present in such wines fades, and there is nothing to take its place. The capacity to form bouquet is relative to balance and to depth (as opposed to superficiality) in the wine. It does not appear to depend on scale, nor, in particular, does it depend on heavy tannin or on alcoholic strength, though a well-composed wine, one that will lend itself appropriately to aging, will have due proportion of each. Contemporary methods of winemaking, particularly in California, ensure that elements of grape and fermentation aroma persist to a certain extent, even in mature wines, so we need not be surprised to detect varietal characteristics, for example, in red wines ten and fifteen years old. The important issue is that if bouquet is the objective of fine winemaking, then when it exists it should be appreciated fully. That means drinking the wine as close as possible to 65° as other factors allow.

What other factors are there to consider? Don't we just trade the fresh, cool feeling of 55° for the increased satisfaction of taste and smell at 65°, or vice versa? Often that is exactly the exchange we make. Young white wines without bouquet are drunk at cool temperatures that suppress slightly their aroma because the refreshingly cool pleasure we gain seems fair compensation. In the case of a fine, mature white Burgundy, a complex Chardonnay, or an old white Graves we are less willing to sacrifice taste and smell, so we find instead a compromise temperature.

But the direct effect of temperature on the wine is only half the question. We ourselves react physiologically to the temperature of what we drink. For example, we are most sensitive to sweetness in wine when the wine is warmer, and become less so the more it is chilled. An undistinguished white jug wine with coarse aroma and unattractively sweet finish can be rendered at least acceptable if served very cold. A fine old Sauternes, on the other hand, probably much sweeter, but matured in bottle long enough to have acquired a richly complex flavor, should never be served cold, whatever is said about icing sweet wines. One finds a degree of coolness that will balance the desired restraint of sweetness against appropriate opportunity to appreciate fully the wine's bouquet.

White wines that seem either too high or too low in acidity are typically wines that can be served with advantage at temperatures below the norm. If the problem is lack of acidity, flabbiness will be less apparent; and a low temperature, numbing slightly the taste buds, will mask excessive acidity. White wines with good acid balance do not need such assistance, and serving them at temperatures below the norm suppresses taste and smell for no balancing gain, and therefore serves no pleasurable purpose.

Although, at low temperatures, sensitivity to acids and sugar is reduced, it is increased to bitterness and astringency. A red wine that slips down easily at 65° can become hard and astringent to us at 50°. It is this amplification of bitter and astringent elements of red wine at low temperatures that lies behind the conventional wisdom of serving red wines warmer than white. Red Bordeaux, tannic when young, *bouqueté* when mature, has always something to gain from being served at "room temperature." Others, like Beaujolais, low in tannin and drunk for their aroma rather than for bouquet, lose little by being served cool, and thereby gain in their quality as refreshment. Red Burgundy, rarely as tannic as Bordeaux, can be served on the cool side when young, but not when mature bouquet has formed.

Electing to serve a wine at 65°, 55°, or 45° is one thing; getting it there, just right and just when you want it, is another. If the cellar, closet, kitchen corner or boot-box where wine is kept is no cooler than the rest of the house or apartment, some adjustment will always have to be made, even for red wine. In my experience, wine needs to be placed in the refrigerator for at least two hours if it is to be cold, but an hour or an hour and a half is usually enough to make a bottle quite cool, depending on the setting of the refrigerator and the original temperature of the bottle. Red wines to be brought down to 60° from a normal apartment temperature need forty-five minutes in the refrigerator: the "twenty minutes" sometimes recommended does little more than cool the glass.

The quickest way to cool a bottle of wine is to plunge it into a bucket of ice and water, but if the bottle stays too long in the mixture the wine will continue to get colder. Depending on how quickly the bottle will be used and on the temperature of the room there is sometimes more satisfaction to be had if the wine is first allowed to become a little cooler than ideal, and then left out of the bucket while consumed. Since wine is always best within the parameters of 45° to 65°, temperature adjustment need never be a major problem. Twenty minutes of cold air in the freezer is hardly more severe than twenty minutes in an ice-and-water bucket, and unless one lives in an igloo, only limited patience is needed to raise the temperature of a bottle of red wine from "cellar temperature" to "room temperature." The counsel often given that a red wine needs to be placed in the dining room three days before required implies that such a bottle will somehow adjust to the ambient temperature more gradually than a bottle placed in the same room three hours before required. The idea that a bottle of wine might control its own rate of temperature change is from a metaphysical realm beyond my experience.

Whatever applies to still white wines applies to sparkling white wines except that, generally speaking, sparkling wines should remain quite cold if bubbles are to be released gradually. A bottle is therefore best left in its bucket of ice and water. But an older champagne, especially one that is late-disgorged, is approached as any other older, fine wine: bouquet and flavor will be stunned if the wine is too cold. The trade-off is not too difficult to make because older champagnes release their less forceful *mousse* more slowly anyway, and they have less need to be thoroughly chilled. In this, as in everything else connected with wine, common sense and personal preference will prove to be better guides than simplistic rules.

INDEX

CL.74

The Making of Britain
1066–1939

General Editor: Andrew Wheatcroft

The Norman Heritage Trevor Rowley
The High Middle Ages Trevor Rowley
The Age of Exuberance Michael Reed
The Georgian Triumph Michael Reed
The Transformation of Britain Gordon Mingay